PORSCHE
RACING CARS
A HISTORY OF FACTORY COMPETITION

Bill Oursler

MBI Publishing Company

First published in 2000 by MBI Publishing Company,
729 Prospect Avenue, PO Box 1, Osceola, WI
54020-0001 USA

The information in this book is true and complete to the
best of our knowledge. All recommendations are made
without any guarantee on the part of the author or
Publisher, who also disclaim any liability incurred in
connection with the use of this data or specific details.

We recognize that some words, model names and
designations, for example, mentioned herein are the
property of the trademark holder. We use them for
identification purposes only. This is not an
official publication.

MBI Publishing Company books are also available at
discounts in bulk quantity for industrial or
sales-promotional use. For details write to Special Sales
Manager at Motorbooks International Wholesalers &
Distributors, 729 Prospect Avenue, PO Box 1, Osceola,
WI 54020-0001 USA.

Library of Congress Cataloging-in-Publication Data

Oursler, Bill.
    Porsche racing cars : a history of factory
    competition / Bill Oursler.
        p. cm.
    Includes index.
    ISBN 0-7603-0727-X (hc. : alk. paper)
       1. Porsche automobiles—History. 2. Automobiles,
    Racing—History. 3. Automobile racing—Europe—
    History. I. Title.

TL236.0936   2000
629.228—dc21   00-056851

On the front cover: During the early 1970s, nothing
dominated the sport or captured the public's attention like
the sleek Porsche 917. Racking up victories in Europe
and the United States, the 917's, whether driven by
privateers or by factory-supported entrants (like that of
John Wyer's Gulf team pictured here), was the brainchild
of Ferdinand Piëch. *Bill Oursler*

On the frontispiece: As conceived by the FIA, the Group
5 "silhouette" production-based prototype formula
instituted for 1976 would infuse new life into sports car
racing by creating stronger identification ties between the
car and the fans. By the time the Group 5 silhouette era
ended in the early 1980s, the cars, particularly the 935,
barely resembled their assembly-line counterparts

On the title page: The brightest star in the Porsche
heaven—the venerable 917 comes together with a
challenging Ferrari at the start of the 1970 endurance race
at Watkins Glen. Despite the apparent tension at the race's
start, teammates Jo Siffert and Brian Redman, Pedro
Rodriguez and Leo Kinnunen posted an easy victory in
the 1970 Watkins Glen six-hour enduro. *Bill Oursler*

On the back cover: (top) The Porsche 904 demonstrated
potential even before its approval as a production car by
winning its class as a prototype at both Daytona and
Sebring. After being approved by the FIA as a full-
fledged production automobile, it won the Targo Florio
outright. The 904 would garner victory laurels in rallies,
hillclimbs, and endurance races before being replaced as
a factory racer by the 906. *Porsche Werk*
(bottom) After McLaren won the 1995 Le Mans race,
Zuffenhausen sent Norbert Singer back to his drawing
board to create a car that could beat the supercar. The
result was the Porsche 911 GT1 Turbo, half production
911 and half prototype 962. Although fastest at the Sarthe
for the three years from 1996 to 1998, the Singer-
conceived turbo didn't achieve its ultimate goal of an
overall victory until June 1998. *Porsche Werk*

On the endpapers: This air-born 911SC performed
amazingly during the 22-day Paris-Dakar rally that
covered some 9,000 miles of rock-strewn wasteland and
trackless dunes in the early 1980s. The 911SC was
superceded as Porsche's rally car by the 911SC RS and
finally, by the 959, an amazing Class B car that joined the
ranks of brutally powerful rally machines that are
referred to simply as the "Killer Bees."

Edited by John Adams-Graf
Designed by Dan Perry

Printed in Hong Kong

contents

introduction

Perhaps the hardest part in telling the story of Porsche's factory racing efforts is to define them in the first place. Unlike other manufacturers, Porsche used surrogates almost from the start. Whereas Ferrari and Jaguar built and fielded their own cars, the Porsche factory at Zuffenhausen would often be represented by so-called "privateers," who just happened to be using the latest in factory equipment, supported by factory personnel, and on occasion, factory drivers.

In large measure this was due to the limited funding available, which forced the factory to seek creative alternatives in terms of resources. This, in turn, blurred the lines between what was an official foray and what was not. Further complicating the issue was the fact that on many occasions, the factory stepped back completely, and in actuality let its customers, with some back door help, run the show themselves.

Men such as Reinhold Joest have crossed and recrossed this line many times. Joest's last two victories at Le Mans came in cars that were either owned by the factory or at least in some measure part of Zuffenhausen's motorsport plans. And, if Joest isn't enough, consider also the cars of Peter Gregg and Al Holbert, sometimes listed as "customers," sometimes considered "friends," and, in certain circumstances, deemed actual arms of factory policy. All of them have played a role in the history of Porsche factory motorsport, as have the likes of John Wyer and Roger Penske, men contracted to carry out Zuffenhausen's bidding on the competition scene.

Still if Porsche has been a master at fashioning "special" relationships throughout its motorsport history, it has been equally willing to step to the plate under its own banner. Indeed, from the start, Ferry Porsche, his sister Louise Piëch and their father, Dr. Ferdinand Porsche, employed racing as a means of cost-effective self-promotion. Unlike Enzo Ferrari, for whom motorsport was a passion supported by sales of street vehicles to wealthy customers, Porsche has always viewed competition as a means to an end. It was this view that has shaped and continues to shape Porsche's involvement in the sport.

Whereas Ferrari immediately played on the grand stage, Porsche was content to take a more restrained approach, eschewing the center court spotlight until the arrival of Ferdinand Piëch (now chairman of Volkswagen) as head of the factory's racing fortunes in the mid-1960s. It was the ambitious and often controversial grandson of Ferdinand Porsche who took Porsche from the role of a class leader to an overall leader in the sport, changing forever the character of the company in the process.

This book traces the sometimes convoluted history of Porsche factory racing from the immediate post–World War II era through the latter half of the twentieth century to its 1998 triumph at Le Mans. From the Gmünd Coupes to the Spyders and their open-wheel counterparts of the 1950s and early 1960s, on to the plastic Porsches of the Piëch era, and finally to the production and later prototype turbos of the years since, the author has tried to put them all into perspective.

Even so, the reader should understand that while this work is confined to what is roughly a 55-year span, the history of Porsche racing extends far beyond this time limitation. The elder Dr. Porsche played a major role in motorsports at Mercedes as far back as the early 1920s, before helping to create the famed mid-engined Auto Union Grand Prix racers of the 1930s. In 1939,

the Porsche design bureau developed the Type 60K 10, a sleek aerodynamic coupe based on Porsche's Volkswagen project, in which the passenger essentially sat behind the driver. This vehicle was intended to be run in the 1939 Berlin-to-Rome long-distance race that was canceled by the outbreak of the war. Many believe that this competition-oriented car was the spiritual father to what a decade later would become the 356 Porsche, also based on the VW platform.

While the Porsche family may have used motorsport for the most practical of reasons, it is equally clear that racing has long been intertwined in the fabric of the company. It is likewise clear that competition will continue to play a major role in the future of Porsche through achievements as yet unimagined. Perhaps it will be a Porsche that first captures a motorsports contest on another world. And, if that should happen, it will provide material for others to chronicle in the ever-continuing history of Porsche factory racing.

—*Bill Oursler*

The First Racing Porsches

1

If Porsche's Type 360, the Cisitalia Formula 1 car, had been designed under normal circumstances, it still would have been one of the landmarks in the sport. The fact that it was brought into being in an Austrian sawmill by those trying to ransom the head management of their firm simply makes the Cisitalia even more remarkable.

Like companies throughout Europe in 1945 and 1946, Porsche was attempting to carry on as a functioning business amidst the ruins of a civilization that would eventually be rebuilt only with hundreds of millions of dollars from the United States. It was difficult, particularly after the French decided to hold Dr. Ferdinand Porsche, his son-in-law Dr. Anton Piëch, and his son Ferry hostage for their own purposes. Still, Porsche was in better shape than many of its contemporaries.

The Porsche Type K64, better known as the Berlin-to-Rome Coupe, was the very first Porsche produced for the firm, as opposed to design projects for other customers. Like Ferrari's Type 815, intended for the 1940 Mille Miglia, the K64 bore only a number, rather than the moniker of the company responsible for its design and construction. Three were built; this one is the only survivor. *Porsche Werk*

The lines of the Type K64 reflected those that would later define Porsche's first post–World War II sports car, the Type 356. The narrow cabin of the K64 forced the occupants to be seated in tandem, rather than side-by-side. Although the Berlin-to-Rome did not take place, the K64s were used throughout the war as personal transport for Dr. Ferdinand Porsche and other ranking members of the company's management. *Leonard Turner*

When the company moved to rural Gmünd, Austria, in 1944 because of the allied bombing of Stuttgart, it brought with it its most valuable asset, the heart of its engineering staff, most of whom were also skilled hands-on craftsmen. In addition, the firm also had its drawings and the determination of Dr. Porsche's daughter, Louise Piëch. Together, these elements combined to create a formidable basis for the survival of the struggling design studio.

Initially, after the war, Porsche existed at Gmünd by repairing the various Volkswagens and pieces of farm equipment that had managed to survive the conflict. Even as the dust settled into the bomb craters, the future of Porsche was being charted. The first step came in the form of a letter from Carlo Abarth, an Austrian expatriate now living in Merano, Italy, whose wife was Anton Piëch's former secretary. That correspondence increased after Ferry Porsche was released from custody in July 1946. The younger Porsche

realized Abarth's location was a means toward the expansion of the company. Abarth could travel freely in Italy, where conditions were returning to something approaching normality, while Porsche's men in Gmünd were severely restricted.

In addition to Abarth, former Porsche employee Rudolf Hruska, who had served on the prewar Auto Union Grand Prix team and as a coordinator for the Volkswagen project, had also moved to Merano at the end of the conflict and was likewise in contact with Gmünd. Within a short period of time, Ferry Porsche asked Abarth and Hruska if they would be agents for the company—a question to which the two responded affirmatively.

It is at this point that Tazio Nuvolari, considered to be one of the greatest drivers of all time, entered the picture. Nuvolari was a small but colorful man who raced flat out all the time, and who had become the Babe Ruth of motorsport. Indeed, in 1935 Nuvolari, in one of the most famous drives ever seen, urged his obsolete Alfa Romeo

past the supposedly invincible Mercedes team to win the German Grand Prix before the unhappy faces of Third Reich officials.

Eventually the disadvantages of the aging Alfas forced Nuvolari to seek other employment, and he joined the Auto Union team in 1938. After the war, Nuvolari maintained his ties with his old Alfa team manager, Enzo Ferrari. However, since the latter's car-building business was still in the drawing board stage during 1946, Nuvolari faced the choice of using either an old Maserati or one of the Fiat-based Cisitalia single-seaters, both of which were quick, but not head-lining contenders.

Nuvolari and the man behind Cisitalia, Turin industrialist Piero Dusio, had dreams of moving up to the forefront of Formula 1. Dusio, whose company was also in the process of making a

Fiat-based sports car, had grand ideas of becoming an automotive power on and off the track. To this end, he had brought in another Italian star, Piero Taruffi, and designer Giovanni Savonuzzi to help him with those Fiat-Cisitalia programs. In addition, he had ties to Count Giovanni Lurani, a well-known driver and one of the prime movers in postwar Italian motorsport.

The problem Dusio faced was finding a design team capable of giving him the kind of single-seater he so desperately sought to propel him to the publicity-rich front ranks of the Grand Prix scene, a difficulty solved when he discovered Gmünd. The initial step toward the union between himself and Porsche came through a visit by Nuvolari to Abarth. With Italian journalist Corrado Millanta as an intermediary, they met with Lurani in the fall of 1946, a

The Type 360 Cisitalia was the first post–World War II design project for the beleaguered Porsche firm. The car shown here in the center with the later Type 804 Formula One single seater of 1962 was a masterpiece. The Type 360 featured four-wheel drive and a supercharged flat 12-cylinder engine. Unfortunately, because of financial problems, the car was never properly developed by the man who ordered it, Italian industrialist Piero Dusio. *Leonard Turner*

While only one complete example of the Cisitalia was ever made, enough parts existed for the Donington Collection to partially assemble a second example. Under the agreement with Porsche, the car will never be fully completed, although the state is such that the basics of the advanced design are clearly evident. The car can be seen today in the British facility next to the restored Donington Racetrack. *Bill Oursler*

session that led to a series of further meetings between Dusio, Ferry Porsche, his sister Louise, Porsche's chief engineer Karl Rabe, and Hans Kern. Those gatherings, in turn, finally brought about a contract-signing ceremony in February 1947 that committed Porsche to design four projects for Dusio: the Type 323 small tractor, the Type 370 five-passenger GT/sports tourer, the Type 285 water turbine, and the Type 360 Grand Prix open wheeler.

The importance of the contract could not be overestimated from Porsche's point of view. Dusio arranged for the payment of one million francs to the French, which resulted in the release during the summer of 1947 of the 72-year-old elder Porsche and his son-in-law, Piëch. What the Italian got in return was an elegant single-seat design so far ahead in its thinking that some features remain advanced even to this day.

Under the watchful eyes of Rabe, and with help from former Auto Union engineer Eberan von Eberhorst, a chrome-moly steel tube-frame chassis (one of the first of its kind) was created with pannier fuel tanks running alongside the chassis on both sides of the driver's seat. The drivetrain,

including the clutch and the gearbox, were located in front of the rear axle, the layout requiring a rather long wheelbase and an overall length of about thirteen feet. Dry weight of the car was 1,583 pounds

The powerplant itself was a 1,493-cc, twin supercharged, water-cooled flat 12-cylinder, with four overhead camshafts. In its final configuration, the engine was theoretically capable of pumping out 450 horsepower. (In actuality, the only time the engine was ever tested, it only produced 383 horsepower at 10,600 rpm, still remarkable in 1947 for a 1.5-liter unit.) The superchargers were mounted on top of the rather compact motor to create a very neat package.

Still, the real engineering lay in the design of the transmission. Using torsion-bar suspension front and rear, the 12-cylinder's torque was taken up through a five-speed Porsche synchromesh gearbox that was hooked into a differential system, allowing the driver to choose either four-wheel or two-wheel drive. Ironically, the idea was to use the four-wheel configuration for acceleration only, relying on the two rear wheels to push the car through the corners.

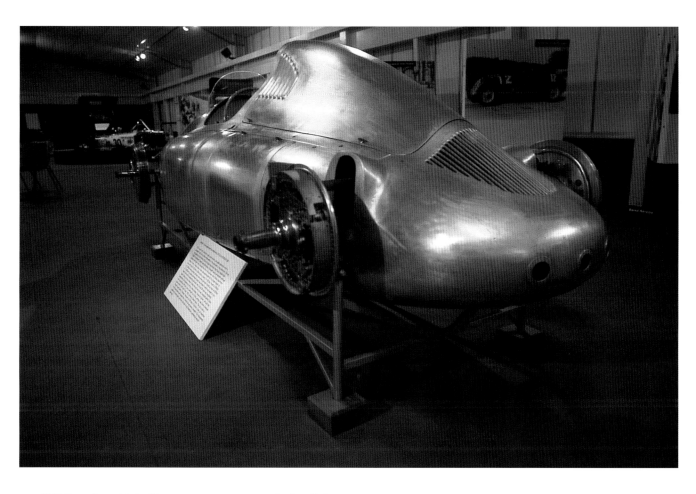

The lines of the Donington Museum's Type 360 clearly show the influence of the prewar Auto-Unions penned by Dr. Ferdinand Porsche. The midengined configuration remained unique until the late 1950s, when it was introduced into Formula One by Britain's John Cooper. Had the Type 360 been properly developed, there is no doubt that it would have been a dominant factor in Grand Prix racing. The Cisitalia's only potential flaws were its inadequate drum brakes. Not until Jaguar introduced the much more efficient disc brakes in the early 1950s would braking be improved. Even so, with its all-wheel-drive feature, the handling of the Cisitalia would have been far superior to its rivals. *Bill Oursler*

While the Cisitalia never was raced, it did receive praise from an important source. In August 1947, when old Professor Porsche saw what had been accomplished during his absence, he concluded, "I would not have made any screw different." These words were high praise to Ferry Porsche, Karl Rabe, and the design team that had worked on the Cisitalia.

The talents of Nuvolari (not to mention those of Taruffi) and the engineering specifications of the Type 360 ought to have ensured the transformation of Dusio's dream into reality. Unfortunately, like so many other promising aspirations, that is not what happened. The first difficulty was that Dusio's grandiose ideas were costing him a great deal of money, so much that he was going bankrupt. The second problem came following a visit by Ferry Porsche and Rabe to his factory in 1947. There they were introduced to the idea that a successful sports car could be built using inexpensive mass production parts, which in their case meant Volkswagen and which also meant that their interest in Dusio lessened considerably. By the following year, the Italian was struggling just to keep his financial ship from sinking.

Porsche's first factory racer was the Type 356 SL. This was merely a relabeling of the first aluminum-bodied Gmünd Coupes, made obsolete with the introduction of the steel-bodied 356s after Porsche moved back to Stuttgart in 1950. The 356 SL was first entered for the 1951 Le Mans 24-Hour Classic, although this particular example was crashed prior to the race. *Porsche Werk*

In spite of all this, the first Type 360 was completed and shown to the public during 1949. By the time Dusio was ready to race it, however, he had run out of funds and was forced to accept the offer of Argentinian dictator Juan Peron to move to that South American nation. Dusio did that in 1950, taking himself, his company, and the only Type 360 in existence with him.

While Ferry Porsche and Rabe discovered enough parts to assemble a second Type 360 Cisitalia during a March 1950 inventory of Dusio's assets, the one Type 360 in Argentina remained the sole completed example. Only briefly was it to see the environment for which it was created. This came when, after sitting in Argentina for nearly three years, it was poorly prepared, hurriedly tested, and unsuccessfully practiced by Felice Bonetto and Clemar Bucci for the 1953 Argentine Grand Prix. Later, despite a distinct lack of performance, Bucci broke the flying South American 1-kilometer record in it with a mark of 144.7 miles per hour.

Shown here during practice for the 1951 Le Mans 24-Hour endurance event were the factory's two 356 SL Gmünd Coupes. Only minor modifications were made to the cars, including replacing the rear quarter windows with vented metal substitutes and enclosing the wheel wells with removable spats. Number 46, nearest the camera, gave Porsche its first class victory, while Number 47 was destroyed in a practice accident. *Porsche Werk*

The lines of the Gmünd Coupe were visibly different from those of its steel bodied 356 successors. It featured a much higher green house as well as curved front vent windows. In addition, the fender lines and the shape of the front hood were slightly different. For Le Mans, the car was improved through the use of wheel spats, which gave it a nearly 100 mile an hour top speed on the Mulsanne straight, despite a less than 50 horsepower output from its 1,100-cc engine. *Porsche Werk*

Porsche's first Le Mans triumph came at the hands of Auguste Veuillet, the company's French importer, and Edmonde Mouche. They took their aluminum-bodied Gmünd Coupe to an uneventful yet dominant class triumph in the 1,100-cc category against rag-tag opposition that included small French production sedans. The Type 356 SL would repeat its performance again the following year, as Porsche began a tradition of excellence that to this day has not been equaled at the Sarthe. *Porsche Werk*

After logging that record, the Type 360 was placed in storage in a warehouse. Ferry Porsche, though, didn't forget the project and retrieved the rotting car in 1959, bringing it back to Stuttgart, where it was restored and placed in the Porsche museum. Meanwhile, the famed Donington Formula I Collection in England purchased the spare parts from Porsche for the second Type 360 in 1971, partially assembling them for display purposes when its own museum opened in 1973.

If the Cisitalia formed the foundation for Porsche's involvement in post–World War II motorsport, it would be a very different car with which the factory would actually begin its racing career. This would be the famed 356 coupe, first produced in Gmünd in 1948. In part inspired by what Porsche and Rabe had seen Dusio do, the aluminum-bodied, Austrian-built 356s were a mixture of innovative thinking applied to mundane VW-based mechanicals.

There are many who believe the 356 was a hastily thought-out project, one that came into being as Dusio's financial picture started to

crumble. In truth, the Porsches and their engineers, including body designer Erwin Komenda, had been considering such a project ever since they built the 1939 Type 60K10 Rome-to-Berlin competition coupe.

With the collapse of the Dusio relationship, the plans so carefully harbored during the intervening years were again taken up. In all, Porsche would build approximately 50 cars at Gmünd before moving back to Stuttgart in 1949. With Porsche's arrival in Germany came the decision not only to change the material for the 356's body from aluminum to steel, but to revamp its shape as well, thus in effect making orphans out of the Gmünd Coupes the company had brought back with it.

When Ferry Porsche was approached by his firm's French importer, Auguste Veuillet, and his fellow countryman, journalist Charles Faroux, about racing at Le Mans in 1951 with the 356 in the 1,100-cc class, he saw an opportunity. While the Gmünd Coupes may have been obsolete in terms of potential sales for street usage, they were

The venerable Gmünd Coupes were used for many years by the factory before being retired. This included rallies, other racing events, and even speed record runs. During the twilight of their careers, to keep the cars competitive, Porsche borrowed a page from the book of the California customizers, chopping several inches from the cars' A-pillars to lower the front roof lines and improve the cars' drag figures. The change is clearly evident in this photo. *Porsche Werk*

anything but obsolete for the track. The "unsellable" aluminum Gmünd models were obviously lighter than their steel counterparts, and they had a narrower greenhouse, which reduced their frontal area and their drag. Thus was born the Type 356 SL. To increase its performance potential, Porsche added underbody fairings front and rear; enclosed all four wheels, which were ventilated with aluminum spats to increase cooling; and replaced the rear quarter windows with louvered steel panels to help evacuate hot air from the cockpit. Additionally, the front-mounted gas tank was extended around the spare tire and its filler neck raised through the hood, where it was topped with a quick release cap. Meanwhile, the 1,086-cc (73.5-millimeter bore X 64-millimeter stroke) Volkswagen-based pushrod four-cylinder had its output increased to 46 horsepower. The

final gear ratios were also raised. These changes, combined with improved aerodynamics, allowed the 356SL to achieve a top speed of 100 miles per hour on the 3.5-mile-long Mulsanne straight.

Over the course of its career, the Gmünd Coupe served Porsche well. In addition to Le Mans, the lightweight coupes were used in a number of other events. Among these were the Liege-Rome-Liege rally, in which the little Porsche was particularly successful, and at the high-banked Monthelery circuit outside Paris, where it set a number of international speed records.

It was Le Mans, though, for which the 356 SL is best remembered. Ironically, it was a program almost ended by unforeseen circumstances before it began. In the spring of 1951, two of the 1,400-pound 356s were prepared by Zuffenhausen. Then came the trouble. While veteran driver Paul von

Guilleaume was testing one over the public roads, which constitute the bulk of the Le Mans course, he swerved to avoid a bicyclist, seriously damaging the car.

A third Gmünd 356 was quickly modified as a replacement. But during official night practice that June leading up to the race, Porsche found itself down to one car again when Rudolph Sauerwein lost control of his 356 SL at Maison Blanche, destroying it and injuring himself in the process. That left Veuillet and his partner, Edmond Mouche, to carry Porsche's banner with the last available SL. The two met the challenge. Running without any serious problems, they brought the coupe home 20th overall and first in the 1,100-cc category, covering a total of 1,765.09 miles at an average speed of 73.54 miles per hour. Additionally, they were 5th in the coveted Index of Performance.

The following year there were no less than three Gmünd 356 SLs present at the Sarthe. Again the 1,100-cc class win went to Veuillet and Mouche, who were 11th overall and 8th in the Index of Performance, having covered 1,836.407 miles at an average of 76.51 miles per hour. Of the remaining two cars, one was disqualified and the other, which had future Porsche team manager Huschke von Hanstein as one of its drivers, retired. Still, as in 1951, the lightweight Gmünd-built Porsche had succeeded in beating the best-placed 1.5-liter class machine to the finish, adding to the moment for the still infant car manufacturer.

Times, however, were changing. Having seen the benefits to be gained from the motorsport scene, Porsche was about to become far more serious about its participation, as it started work on the first of its famed 550 Spyders.

Although this restored 356 Gmünd Coupe is seen as a private entry, in point of fact very few escaped the factory's control. For the most part they served Zuffenhausen well until the introduction of the first of Porsche's purpose-built Spyders in 1953. While best known in their "skirted" configuration, the cars were occasionally raced with open wheel wells. *Leonard Turner*

17

The Spyders

2

The year was 1952, and the Italian OSCA company, headed by the Maserati brothers, was beginning to discover the 1,100-cc and 1,500-cc categories in sports car competition. Although Porsche, as a factory, had been involved in racing for little more than a year, running its modified aluminum-bodied Gmünd coupes, the company realized that something else would be needed if Porsche was to continue to exploit the promotional and engineering benefits gained from winning. Still, while there were rewards in terms of sales and reputation, Dr. Porsche and son Ferry understood well the tremendous costs involved, which could easily bankrupt a small, fledgling company such as theirs.

Hans Herrmann, two decades past his Mexican Road Race victory, displays the small sports car racing category trophy he earned at the 1954 Carrera Pan-Americana event from the seat of his restored factory 550 Spyder. In an era where there was virtually no commercial advertising connected with racing, the cars of the Carrera were among the most colorful. Indeed, outside of American oval track racing, about the only thing distinguishing one from the other was its national paint scheme. However, even though Porsche retained the traditional overall silver finish for its cars, it too indulged in accepting commercial sponsorship for its vehicles running in Mexico. *Porsche Werk*

While Porsche itself was reluctant to build full-fledged racing cars, others were not. This is Richard Trenkel's Porsche-powered Glöckler chassised sports racer from 1953. This lightweight car, especially in the hands of its creator, Helm Glöckler, was dominant in small-bore production racing during the early 1950s. Later, Glöckler would be instrumental in the creation of Porsche's own open-topped Spyder racers. Richard Trenkel continued to race his Glöckler Porsche through 1954, claiming a number of good places in the 1,100–1,500-cc category. The car's lines clearly reflect those of the later Porsche-built 550 Spyders that supplanted it. One of the Glöcklers found its way here to the United States in the early 1950s via Porsche's North American importer, Max Hoffman, who used it with great success in SCCA racing. *Porsche Werk*

The first 550 produced by the factory was completed in the spring of 1953. This car featured a 1,500-cc Volkswagen-based, pushrod, air-cooled, four-cylinder engine. It and its sister car were the only two of its type constructed. They featured a unique rear frame design that did not permit the use of the later Type 547 four-cam in-house Carrera Boxer Four. The two initial 550s enjoyed a spectacular but short career in the hands of the factory, winning among other things their class at Le Mans, as well as sprint races in the spring and summer of 1953 at the Nürburgring. *Porsche Werk*

There were resources Porsche could draw on, however. One was Frankfurt car dealer and competition driver Walter Glöckler. As Germany recovered from the devastation of World War II, Glockler began to field a series of lightweight sports racing specials. Initially, these were powered by Volkswagen engines. Later they received Porsche units. Indeed, by 1952, Glöckler was firmly on board with Zuffenhausen, his cars bearing the Porsche name and his team receiving assistance from the factory as well.

The Glöckler tie was one forged by Ferry Porsche himself. There was a new character on the scene who would further shape Porsche racing, this being Huschke von Hanstein. A prewar racer, von Hanstein's enthusiasm would take the company a long way toward its eventual place at the top of the sport. At the time, though, the competition tradition of Porsche was rather thin,

comprising in the main the successes of the Gmünd coupes. With Porsche, von Hanstein, and the engineers agreeing to the next step, a new era was about to begin. This would be the time of the spyders—small, sleek, open-topped sports racers on whose triumphs Porsche would build a legend that continues to this day.

With time at a premium, Porsche adopted the basics of Glöckler's 1951 mount, utilizing its twin-tube, ladder-type frame as the starting point for the first two spyders: 550-01 and 550-02. Unlike their siblings to come, these were to be powered exclusively by Porsche's VW-based 1,500-cc pushrod flat-fours. Additionally, their main frame rails were designed to pass underneath their swing axles, an arrangement that would be reversed from 550-03 onward.

Interestingly, Porsche built a pair of removable tops for these cars, the pair appearing in

Spyder 550-01, shown here, and its sister, 550-02, were fitted with removable coupe tops for the 1953 Le Mans 24-Hour. Although uncomfortable for the drivers, creating excessive heat and noise, these tops substantially reduced the drag figures for the two cars, helping them to sweep to a one-two finish in the 1,500-cc sports racing category. The cars were later sold in Central America, one of them winning its division that fall in the Carrera Pan-Americana Mexican Road Race. *Porsche Werk*

By 1955 Porsche's 550 Spyders were becoming common winners, dominating the small-displacement sports racing categories, both nationally and internationally. One of Zuffenhausen's successes came in the season-opening Argentinian race at Buenos Aires in 1955. Note the straight up and down headlights, which tag this as a preproduction 550 rather than a later customer car, whose headlights would be laid in at an angle. Porsche factory racers had long and hard careers before they were retired in favor of new equipment. *Porsche Werk.*

closed form at Le Mans in 1953, where they finished one-two in class. Later, in the Carrera Panamericana that fall, likewise beroofed, one claimed the small displacement sports car category win. As a roadster in the hands of Helm Glöckler, Walter's cousin, 550-01 scored the first triumph of the spyder era two weeks before Le Mans at the Nürburgring on May 31. Later, after the Sarthe, 550-02, this time piloted by Hans Herrmann, also won at the Nürburgring in spyder form. Following that, the two were sold to Jaroslav Juhan, a Czechoslovakian living in Guatemala, and shipped to that Central American country. It was Jose Herrate who took first with 02 in the Mexican road race after Juhan's 01 failed to finish.

While 01 would make an appearance in the Panamericana the next year, for Porsche the two cars were already passé. The reason for that was a young engineer named Ernst Fuhrmann, who was hard at work designing the Type 547 four-cam boxer four, which would come to be known as the Carrera engine. In various forms and displacement configurations, it would provide the motivation for virtually all the spyder line and beyond to the 904.

By the early summer of 1953, Fuhrmann's engine was developed enough to be ready for its first in-car, real-world trials. For this engine, Porsche had built a new spyder, 550-03. This open-topped machine differed significantly from 550-01 and 550-02, with its modified frame sweeping up over the swing axles and with the torsion bar being mounted ahead of rather than behind the axle. The Spyder was also clothed in a new body that was far closer to the eventual shape the 550 would assume as a limited production vehicle. Still, Porsche would fine-tune the 550 design, changing the chassis, engine, suspension and body details throughout the remainder of 1953 and almost all of 1954 before settling on a final set of blueprints for what was to become the 550/1500RS. That car began to be shipped to customers at the end of that year and the beginning of 1955.

Exactly how many 550s were built before the specifications were finalized is unclear. Karl Ludvigsen, in his book, *Excellence Was Expected*, claims that there were 8 prototypes and between 12 and 22 preproduction spyders constructed. The best guess from other experts is that 13 prototypes with two-digit serial numbers were

The contrast between purpose-built and modified sports cars can be seen here at Laguna Seca raceway during a Porsche historic event, as a Porsche 550 Spyder leads a Gmünd Coupe. Even though the Gmünd 356 SL is itself a relatively small car, it towers over its successor, whose tiny frontal area helped it dominate its segment of the motorsports universe for nearly a decade, despite horsepower outputs that today are considered puny. *Leonard Turner*

Above: Porsche French importer Auguste Veuillet drove this 1,100-cc Porsche 550 factory-entered Spyder to victory in its class at the tragic 1955 Le Mans 24-Hours. Veuillet was partnered on this occasion by Corvette's chief enginer, Zora Arkus-Duntov, who took time out from developing his GM two-seater to indulge in his passion for motorsport. Despite their excellent performance, there was little joy in their triumph, in the wake of the death of 80-plus spectators, who were killed when a Mercedes plunged into the crowd on the pit straight early in the race. *Porsche Werk*

Above right: The clean lines of Porsche's 1956 550A were not that much different from those of its immediate predecessor, the production 550 of 1955. However, despite its outward appearance and despite the fact that it was powered by the same Type 547 four-cam, four-cylinder, the 550A featured a new tubular, rather than ladder-based, chassis. The 550As would dominate the sports car scene both in factory hands and in the hands of Porsche's customers until the end of the decade. These cars set the standard for small-displacement racers and occasionally even shocked "the big boys." The 550A was introduced at the Targa Florio in 1956 on one of those occasions, as it scored an outright victory in that event—the first major overall triumph for Porsche in an international competition. *Porsche Werk*

Far right: One driver who got his start in small-displacement Porsches was Count Wolfgang von Trips, who drove this 550A in the 1956 Nürburgring 1,000-kilometer event with Umberto Maglioli, the winner of the Targa Florio earlier that spring in the model's debut. Von Trips, who would drive on and off for the Zuffenhausen factory, met his death in 1961 at the Italian Grand Prix in a Ferrari while contending with American Phil Hill for the Formula One World Driver's Title. This car, like the Targa 550A, appears to be unpainted, even though on this occasion, Zuffenhausen should have had time to apply a coat of its usual silver coloring. *Porsche Werk*

constructed, these including the 4 cars that were run by the factory at Le Mans in 1954. Beyond that, the factory did produce for itself additional cars with triple-digit serials.

While visually there were major differences among these early 550s, especially in the tail sections they wore, they all had vertical headlights—at least originally. And that is a major part of the numbers problem. Because of Porsche's financial situation in terms of the income it had to spend on motorsport, a number of these 1954 cars were retained by Zuffenhausen for racing in 1955, rebodied in the softer contours of the production 550/1500RS, complete with that model's sloping headlight arrangement.

The first 550 (chassis-03) to have the four-cam engine installed appeared for practice at the Nürburgring in August 1953. While the car and its powerplant were sound, the limited rev range of the early Type 547 flat four led to slower lap times than the pushrod-motivated 02, thus leading to the decision to park 03. It would appear later with Hans Stuck, Sr., at the Freiburg hillclimb, where the prewar mountain specialist would take a third place with it. With its sister, 550-04, it was subsequently transported to North America for a local Sports Car Club of America event in Georgia before being taken to Mexico to run in the 1953 Panamericana, where neither finished. However, the following year Herrmann would take 04 to the

"Spyders"

There are legends, and then there are legends. Trying to decide in which category Porsche's Type 645 Spyder fits is far less than clear. An obscure and brief excursion by Porsche's engineers off the main course of Zuffenhausen's overall development of the spyder genre, the irony is that the 645 may be one of the most widely recognized open-topped Porsches ever produced.

This dramatic divergence is due to what is known as "The Miracle of the Avus." Captured in Julius Weitman's great photograph and preserved today in a bronze sculpture by Larry Braun, the episode involved the spectacular exit of the Type 645, better remembered as the *Mickey Mouse*, and driver Richard von Frankenberg from Berlin's Avus circuit in September 1956. Both picture and sculpture capture the gravitational forces flinging the hapless von Frankenberg from the cockpit of the doomed vehicle as the *Mickey Mouse* stands vertical in thin air after launching itself from the track's north banking.

While the Type 645 crashed heavily to the ground in a public parking lot bordering the north curve, its magnesium body bursting into flame, von Frankenberg landed somewhat more softly in some bushes nearby. The miracle resulted from the fact that while the Spyder was totally destroyed, von Frankenberg emerged virtually unhurt. For all of this however, the Type 645 has remained very much a shadow; the car, whose public career covered a space of less than two months, was never again replicated in metal after its early demise.

The idea behind the Mickey Mouse was to both trim weight and reduce frontal area of the 550A. To this end the 645's track was set at 45.3 inches, some 5.5 inches less than the 550A, while the wheelbase was shrunk to 78.7 inches. Further, there was no conventional oil cooler, this task being taken over by making the hood itself a surface cooler and thus paring even more pounds off the Type 645.

Because of the reduction in wheelbase and to balance the weight of the driver, the fuel tank was placed on the right-hand side in the area normally allocated to the passenger seat. This also allowed the engineers to eliminate the right side door structure, giving added rigidity to the body and again removing weight. Even so, the biggest contribution to the Type 645's diet plan came from the decision to use magnesium rather than aluminum for the body material, the body itself being tightly drawn over the wheels and drive train components.

Similarly, the front suspension, except for being narrower, mirrored that of the 550A. The 645's rear suspension used unequal-length parallel wishbones and torsion bars. Although the same basic arrangement was later used for the Type 804 Formula One single seater, this very different design did little to curb the overly quick handling of the *Mickey Mouse* that made

One of the most unusual and short-lived Porsche spyders was the Type 645, better known as the *Mickey Mouse*. This short-wheel-based, narrow-track, magnesium-bodied car existed for less than 90 days and was driven only by Richard von Frankenburg. Although sleek, the Type 645 proved to be a handful before its eventual demise in a spectacular accident at the Avus track in Berlin in the late summer of 1956. The car flipped over the wall, crashing and burning to destruction, but throwing von Frankenburg free to land virtually without injury in the soft brush beside the track. *Porsche Werk*

the car extremely uncomfortable for von Frankenberg, the only man ever to drive it in competition.

This unfortunate situation appears to have stemmed from two causes, the 645's low polar moment of inertia and the subsequent natural tendency of the short-wheelbase vehicle to react extremely abruptly to changes in directional input, as well as the rear suspension's ability to generate far more initial grip than the front. This meant that the *Mickey Mouse* at first understeered strongly, this changing in a microsecond to an oversteer situation when power was applied.

The *Mickey Mouse* Spyder's short and rather unhappy career began with its appearance at the Solitude circuit on the outskirts of Stuttgart on July 22, 1956.

There the problems began even before the start, when first gear took an early vacation. Despite this, von Frankenberg drove on. Moreover, during the course of the affair, not only did he suffer oil temperature woes, but also encountered difficulties with the brakes that did little to improve his confidence. In the end, von Frankenberg and the Type 645 were forced to settle for fourth. The car made its second appearance at the Nürburgring several weeks later where it practiced for, but did not compete in, the sports car event run concomitantly with the German Grand Prix.

That brought *Mickey Mouse* to Avus. Although its handling was totally unsuited for the high-speed course, von Frankenberg chose to use it because of its top speed of 162 against 158 miles an hour for the 550A. It was a choice that at first seemed to be a good one, but ultimately turned out poorly when the *Mickey Mouse* got away from its driver and did its best to emulate an Olympic high diver. After it crash-landed in the parking lot, the crumpled magnesium remains of the Type 645 burned to ashes, most likely with the blessing and best wishes of von Frankenberg.

In one sense *Mickey Mouse* had been a design failure that, while bright in concept, gave off little light in the real world. In another, though, it created a heritage and a body of knowledge that were used to forge the next generation of Porsche racers.

Porsche's customer 550 was identical to the cars used by the factory. In fact, on some occasions, used factory cars were sold to Zuffenhausen's privateer corps. Today, restored examples such as this one shown at the Monterey Historic Event are not only highly prized, but extremely valuable. Despite their worth, these cars remain as they've always been: durable and reliable. *Leonard Turner*

Swiss engineer Michael May was years ahead of his time when he equipped his 550 with a wing in the mid-1950s. May, who would later go on to do the initial development work on turbocharging for road cars, proved that the aerodynamic device substantially improved performance, dramatically cutting his lap times with it. However, German organizers worried about safety, convinced Porsche's Huschke von Hanstein to get May to remove the device before the race. In 1966, American Jim Hall would recreate May's scenario with his Can-Am Chaparrals, changing the aerodynamics of the motorsports universe forever. *Leonard Turner*

First seen in practice for the Nürburgring 1,000-kilometer race was Porsche's new Type 718 RSK Spyder. Practiced by Umberto Maglioli, the car was not raced in the German event. However, it did subsequently appear at the Le Mans 24-Hours, where it retired following a crash. In various forms, the Type 718 would be raced by the factory for seven years, until replaced in 1964 by the fiberglass-bodied Porsche 904. *Porsche Werk*

1,500-cc class victory in the last of the Carrera road race affairs. There were numerous other triumphs to celebrate, as well, during the 1954 season, including class wins in the Mille Miglia and at Le Mans (where Porsche collected the 1,500 and 1,100-cc honors with a pair of sick-engined cars after its opposition dropped out).

Given its growing string of successes, Porsche and its 550 spyders were rapidly becoming the kings of the small displacement categories, so it was natural that the production 550/1500RS would prove to be popular with the factory's new-found customers. It would also prove to be a fast, reliable piece of equipment, capable of not only winning its division but, on the right day, challenging the "big boys."

For all practical purposes, the mechanical specifications for the production 550s reflected those of the later 1954 cars, with the brakes and transaxle still coming from the 356 assembly line. What was different was the body, whose shape was, as previously noted, far more rounded, with sloped headlights and lower, curved rear fenders. Underneath, additional steel bracing had been added to the ladder-type frame, transforming the structure into the beginnings of a traditional tube-frame configuration.

As with the previous cars, there were differences and changes among the production 550/1500 RS models. These included modifications to the drivetrain components, brakes, and frames. Additionally, as mentioned earlier, some of the 1954 spyders were rebuilt and rebodied to production standards. Regardless of the specifications, the Porsches continued their winning ways.

One triumph achieved with a distinct set of mixed feelings was at Le Mans, where the company again claimed the 1,500 and 1,100-cc categories, also taking the Index of Performance while finishing fourth through sixth overall. Unfortunately, those results were overshadowed by the deaths of more than 80 spectators killed when a Mercedes crashed into the crowd on the pit straight.

The 550/1500 RS would be involved in tragedy again several months later when actor James Dean died in his spyder after being hit by another car at an intersection while on his way to an SCCA race in central California. Indeed, if you wanted to win in the SCCA's smaller production

classifications, the only car to have in 1955 was a 550. So numerous were its successes that news was made when it didn't win, rather than when it did.

Interestingly, one car that did gain the upper hand over the spyders was the Cooper that Ken Miles, himself a 550 driver, modified to accept a Type 547 four-cam boxer four. As with most Miles-created specials of that era, and there were many, this one proved hard to beat.

Until this point, Porsche's spyder mainly had been a product of an ad hoc engineering process. In part this was so because of time constraints, and in part—perhaps even more so—because the funding for motorsport was sparse at best. While others might have been content to leave the 550

The Type 718 RSK was the first factory Porsche to use tack-on aerodynamic devices, these being a pair of fins mounted at the rear. Supposedly an aid to stability in crosswinds, these proved controversial, with some factory drivers liking them and others not. Even so, the car would be raced with them on more than one occasion, starting a trend that would continue to the present day. *Porsche Werk*

Frenchman Jean Behra was a Porsche stalwart during the 1950s. In 1958 he drove his Type 718 RSK to victory in the 1,500-cc division in the Le Mans 24-Hour enduro. The car finished an amazing third overall in the race, serving notice that Porsche was headed for things bigger than simply class victories. The car in the center is a Lotus 15 from Britisher Colin Chapman, who would later become a Porsche rival on the Grand Prix scene. The car farthest from the camera is a Deutsch-Bonnet, one of the small aerodynamic French entries that would one day become part of the Renault empire. *Porsche Werk*

alone, Porsche's engineers weren't. Over the winter of 1955–1956, they redesigned the spyder, keeping the same basic body lines, but completely redoing the chassis beneath the skin. This now became a true tube frame and had the added benefit of a revamped rear swing axle suspension that had a substantially lowered roll center. If almost impossible to tell apart from its predecessor, the new 550A's performance spoke for itself. With von Hanstein overseeing the operation, Umberto Maglioli used the first 550A to stun the

world by claiming the outright victory in the 1956 Targa Florio.

For the next two years the 550A would be the bedrock for the factory and its customers. At Le Mans in 1956 there were more victories, including the 1,500-cc and Index of Performance honors. There the winning car, driven by Richard von Frankenberg and Wolfgang von Tripps, wore a detachable coupe top like those fitted to the first 550s in 1953. The Le Mans triumph would be repeated in 1957, this time by a privately entered

The Type 550A is distinguished from its predecessor, the Type 550, most easily by the driver's headrest fairing. As with most rules, there were exceptions, and occasionally 550As would appear without the fairing. However, if one opened the doors or the rear deck lid and saw the tubular frame structure underneath, there could be little doubt as to the origin of this later model. *Leonard Turner*

Later factory Type 718 RSKs such as this one, shown in restored form at Monterey, featured shorter noses that were slightly more rounded than the original factory cars built in 1957. Rules and regulations would cause other appearance changes during the car's career. However, the basics of the Type 718 would remain, with the exception of the car's front suspension, which was also modified early in its career. *Leonard Turner*

550A Spyder. In fact, privateers would use their 550As for many years thereafter, winning with them even when Zuffenhausen considered them totally obsolete.

One interesting sidelight to the 550A story in 1956 was provided by a Swiss customer, Michael May, who added a wing to his battered Spyder and turned in the fourth-fastest time at the Nürburgring. Although von Hanstein persuaded May to take the device off his car for the race, May's adventure into aerodynamic downforce would be copied quite successfully a decade later by Texan Jim Hall, who would turn the sport upside down because of it. May would go on to develop a turbocharging

system for BMW's 2002 production racer, providing the foundation from which Porsche created the turbo system for its Can-Am 917 fleet.

It was during 1956 that Porsche engineers created a one-off spyder that was smaller and lighter than the 550A. This was the *Mickey Mouse*, whose pretty lines and wide use of magnesium alloys concealed the fact that it was an evil-handling little beast, a defect partly attributable to its short wheelbase. Meant to explore future possibilities, the *Mickey Mouse* spyder's life came to a spectacular end at Avus, when it flipped over the banked rim of the track, throwing von Frankenberg out of the car, amazingly with little injury.

Spyders— *Grossmutter*

If the role of the Type 550 and 718 spyders is at the heart of Porsche's racing legend, then the one remembered most of all is the last one built, a car that would come to be affectionately known at Porsche as *Grossmutter,* or grandmother. With the official designation of W-RS, chassis number 718-047 was perhaps the longest serving of any of the factory's racers. Certainly it has the most diverse history, having been used for a wide variety of purposes and a number of different venues throughout the world during the four years it ran under the Porsche banner. It is ironic that the W-RS, given its background, has come to be almost exclusively associated in recent times with the famed Edgar Barth who, in fact, only came to use *Grossmutter* in the autumn of its career.

The story of the W-RS began in the winter of 1960–1961. Built to accommodate the new Type 771 eight-cylinder being developed for both the Formula One and sports car scenes by Zuffenhausen's engineers, its wheelbase was lengthened from 866 to 906 inches. Unfortunately, neither the 1.5-liter 9P unit nor the 2.0-liter sports car powerplant was far enough along to be considered ready for racetrack usage that year. Thus, the W-RS left the factory with a four-cylinder Carrera four-cam installed.

The first appearance for the W-RS was the Targa Florio where, in the hands of Dan Gurney and Joachim Bonnier, it was second behind a Ferrari. At the Nürburgring, which came next, Gurney and Bonnier finished 10th overall.

There were few changes at Le Mans, other than the fact that Maston Gregory and Bob Holbert were assigned the W-RS. Holbert and Gregory brought the W-RS home as the 2-liter winner, with a fifth overall.

During the winter of 1961–1962 the W-RS received the Type 771 flat eight. It had a bore of 76 millimeters with a stroke of 54 millimeters, all of which produced a displacement of 1,982 cc. Taking the power from the engine was a six-speed gearbox, whose configuration allowed for different positioning of the halfshafts, depending on the chassis used.

Similarly modified, but never raced was the first coupe, 045. The revised W-RS appeared at the 1962 Targa where it had a hard time retiring after being crashed by Gurney. However, it

regained some measure of respect at the Nürburgring Hill and Herrmann driving it to third overall.

There would be no Le Mans for the W-RS in 1962, because it was pressed into service as Porsche's hillclimb contender by von Hanstein, who loaned it to Heini Walter for three events. While not as well known as some of the other Porsche contenders, Walter was a formidable competitor on the hillclimb tour. Still, he was no match for the Ferrari of Ludovico Scarfiotti, at least until the *Grossmutter* showed up. Even with the W-RS, the best Walter could do was a trio of second places before von Hanstein took it back.

By then, the Porsche team manager had a very different task in mind for the W-RS. Stripping much of its European gear, including the windshield, to bring it down to 1,368 pounds, von Hanstein shipped it to the United States, where it spent the next four months in the hands of Bonnier, competing in the SCCA's fall "Pro Series," the sports racing predecessor to the Can-Am.

For Bonnier, the results were definitely mixed. Fuel leakage difficulties kept him sixth at Mosport, while a broken engine eliminated him at Riverside and a broken transaxle did the same at Laguna Seca. The race at Kent, Washington, however, was much better. There, Bonnier scored a fourth overall and a first in the 2-liter division. At the conclusion of the informal SCCA championship, von Hanstein had *Grossmutter* taken to Nassau for the annual December Bahamas Speed Weeks, Holbert replacing Bonnier as the driver.

Holbert had already gained some experience with long wheelbase spyders the previous year. In spite of this, Holbert wasn't particularly fond of the W-RS itself, saying it handled like a pig. Nevertheless, he was able to finish second with *Grossmutter* in both the Nassau Tourist and Governor's Trophy events.

Holbert's complaints didn't go unheeded, as over the following winter the W-RS was rebuilt with new coilover suspensions replacing the parallel trailing arm originals. Additionally, it acquired a new fuel tank and steering gear. The W-RS was also given fiberglass doors and deck lids, the first time this material had been employed by Porsche, as well as full roll bar.

Revised in this manner, the W-RS appeared at the 1963 Targa, where it suffered gearbox problems and was forced to settle for seventh. The Nürburgring wasn't much better for the *Grossmutter*, as Barth retired with a broken halfshaft. That was the low point for the much-used car. At Le Mans, Barth and Herbert Linge, despite losing a wheel, easily outdistanced the opposition to win the two-liter honors in what was the last time a 718 of any kind would race at the Sarthe.

After Le Mans, Barth took *Grossmutter* hillclimbing once again, using it to win five out of his six victories that year (the first was scored in an Abarth Carrera) and the FIA championship's title. That should have been the fitting conclusion to the Spyder's career, especially in light of the fact that the new 904 was already well under development. But that wasn't to be.

The aged Porsche was rebuilt for the 1964 Targa Florio in the hopes that its durability would give it an edge over its rivals. Unfortunately, the new halfshafts installed in the process didn't last, putting the car out early.

Again that should have brought the W-RS's career to a halt. And again, fate had other plans. That was because Barth had decided early in the summer of 1964 that he didn't like the handling of his Elva-Porsche hillclimb car. As a result, the mechanics at Zuffenhausen once more dusted off the W-RS and pressed it into service. Barth and *Grossmutter* won five straight hillclimbs and captured what would prove to be his last-ever championship.

While not really an innovative car, the W-RS was the perfect transitional link between the Porsches of the 1950s and the Porsches of the 1960s and 1970s. As such, it truly deserves the title of *Grossmutter.*

This was the longest-lived factory entry of any Porsche. First run in 1961 with a Type 547 four-cylinder (as shown here before the Le Mans race that year), it finished in 1964 with a Type 771 2-liter flat eight. *Porsche Werk*

Along with the *Grossmutter*, Porsche produced two RS61 coupes. Unlike previous examples, these tops were permanent. As with the W-RS Spyder, in 1962 this coupe received a Type 771 eight-cylinder. The Type 771 flat eight, fitted to the W-RS Spyder and this RS61 coupe, was derived from the Type 753 1.5-liter Formula One boxer eight. This complicated engine was used by the factory to 1968, before being replaced by the far simpler Type 908 3-liter eight-cylinder. Equipped with the Type 771 engine, the RS61 finished second that year in the Targa Florio, painted in a flat red color scheme to make its German origins less obvious. *Porsche Werk*

Caught on film, the incident has come to be known as "the miracle of the Avus." As famous as the *Mickey Mouse* was, Porsche's engineers were not of a mind to build a replacement for it.

Even so, Porsche had plans for a 550A replacement. This would be the Type 718 Spyder, initially known as the RSK for the layout of its unique front suspension, the "K" referring to the shape formed by the downward-sloped upper tube at the front of the car. With a new frame and swoopier body, plus a newly designed rear suspension as well, the RSK first appeared as a test vehicle in the spring of 1957. Run at Le Mans, the new spyder

proved to be fast before it was eliminated in a crash with an Aston Martin.

The shape of the 718 was unique, although retaining some of the flavor of the 550s. The first cars had somewhat elongated noses, which were eliminated when the car finally went into production. In fact, the production shape of the 718 would remain essentially unchanged through the model known as the RS-60/61 except for rules-mandated alterations. Also eliminated before the car was sold to the factory's customers was the unique front suspension layout that had given it its name, this being replaced by a more conventional torsion bar design.

By 1958, the Type 718 was in full stride, finishing third overall at Le Mans while winning the 2,000-cc category as well as the 1,500-cc division. The car also found itself running in Jean Behra's hands as a center seater in the Formula Two race at Reims, where it won. Indeed, the range of the 718's abilities was confirmed by the fact that it was competitive in everything from hillclimbing to Le Mans and F2. It would also, in modified open-wheel form, provide the basis for Porsche's entry in F1 in 1961.

Changes in rules forced some modifications to the 718 for 1960, producing the RS-60, which had a larger cockpit area, a trailing arm front suspension, and a coil spring-based rear suspension layout. Although visually similar, the higher windscreen and bigger cockpit area did distinguish the open-topped car from its predecessors. What made the RS-60 even more distinctive was the fact that it was available to Porsche's customers in exactly the same form as it was raced by the factory. It also had one other distinction: it won outright the Sebring 12-Hour endurance race in 1960. Such an accomplishment, while in part due to the Porsche's dependability, was a measure of just how far the company had come in less than a decade.

In 1961, Porsche built one last spyder and a pair of similar but permanently roofed coupes. The longer bodies and reshaped snouts were the predecessors to what would eventually emerge as the 904, perhaps the prettiest racing Porsche ever produced. The spyder, which would become known as the W-RS, would race that season with a four-cam, four-cylinder. However, starting in 1962, it would receive a 2-liter Type 771 eight-cylinder, and with that engine it would create a legend.

From Le Mans to the Targa Florio and to the hillclimb scene, the W-RS was at home. Indeed, it is perhaps easier to list the places that it didn't win than to compile its lengthy list of victories. Kept in service through 1964, acquiring the affectionate nickname *Grossmutter* (Grandmother), the W-RS amassed a record that even in the storied history of Porsche is unmatched.

Despite this, the W-RS marked the end of an era. It was the last of its breed. The new generation of engineers, under Ferdinand Piëch, preferred to pursue what would become known as the "plastic" Porsche brigade.

The most famous driver of the W-RS *Grossmutter* was Edgar Barth, who drove it to victory not only in places such as Le Mans, but also in the FIA Hillclimbing Championship of 1964, just months before his death from cancer. With Barth's passing and the introduction of the new fiberglass-bodied 904, the *Grossmutter* was put out to pasture, or more specifically, sent to the Porsche Museum, where it remains today, having been restored by Barth's son Jürgen. *Porsche Werk*

Open Wheel

3

At the end of the 1960s, when Zuffenhausen decided to compete for the overall honors on the *Federation Internationale de l'Automobile* (FIA) World Makes Championship tour, it found itself facing Ferrari, which until then had dominated the prototype arena in the post–World War II era. The consequences of that decision brought about the golden age of the Porsche 917s and Ferrari 512s, whose speed and power changed the parameters of the sport forever. Despite the high profile of this famed "Porsche versus Ferrari" war, few realize that the 917/512 contest was the second battle between the German and Italian camps.

Porsche began its open wheel formula car adventure with a series of modified Spyders, the most famous of which were its center seater RSK Type 718s. These were simply standard RSKs with a steering wheel moved to the center line, tonneau covers for the cockpit, and a new rear deck lid. Jean Behra used this one to win the Formula Two race at Rheims in 1958. This was the first of a string of triumphs that would lead Porsche to the Formula Two Constructor's title in 1960 and into Formula One for 1961 and 1962. *Porsche Werk*

Although it looks odd today, as restored with an oversized roll bar, the advantages of the Type 718 center seater can still be clearly seen when compared to its normal spyder counterparts. The unique feature of these cars was their easy convertibility from center seat configuration to left-hand drive, which allowed them to be used in sports car racing as well. In most cases, the cars carried much of their standard sports car equipment even while running in Formula Two trim. *Leonard Turner*

The first came during the latter half of the 1950s, when Porsche squared off against Ferrari in Formula Two. For Europeans, F2 has a long and cherished history. Not only has it been an initial stepping stone for future international stars, it has also been a breeding ground for ideas that have shaped Formula 1. Indeed, F2 for many years served as a holiday playground for the Grand Prix set on off-duty weekends. Such was its place in the sport, that in 1952 and 1953, while rulesmakers worked to introduce a new 2.5-liter nonsupercharged F1 formula, the Formula 2 was run for the World Championship. The division then vacationed between 1954 and 1956 before returning in 1957 as a nonboosted 1.5-liter class.

Interestingly, while the rules for the reborn category specified a single-seat configuration, they didn't demand open-wheeled bodywork. That meant sports cars, such as Porsche's 1.5-liter 550A and 718 RSK could be configured for the formula with little effort, an opportunity not lost on the factory's management. Even as the 718 prototype was being prepared for Le Mans in 1957, plans were being made to take it to Reims for the F2 round, which followed the endurance classic at the Sarthe. Unhappily, the RSK was too badly damaged in a crash during the 24-hour race to be ready in time for Reims. Even so, a privately entered 550A did appear, finishing fifth.

The reason for Porsche's attention to the Reims event was the configuration of the circuit,

which encouraged speed rather than handling, a factor favoring the fendered spyders. In fact, it was at Reims in 1954 that Mercedes stunned the F1 world with a pair of streamliners that dominated the proceedings.

The French affair wasn't the only F2 round that Porsche had an interest in. The annual German Grand Prix at the Nürburgring included both F1 and F2 cars, the latter running with their faster brethren but for their own placings and prizes. Like Reims, there was a speed factor at the Ring, although handling was of equal importance. In the end, it was the spaciousness of the more than 14-mile mountainous course that tended to even-out the playing field.

Ultimately, though, the competitiveness of the barely modified Porsche sports cars rested on their midengined configuration. At the time of Formula Two's rebirth in 1957, only John Cooper had gone down the path taken by Porsche and produced midengined racing machines. During the 1950s, such layouts were considered odd, an attitude that would undergo a radical change by the start of the next decade, as midengined competition vehicles came to dominate the motorsports scene.

The Coopers were to be the benchmark for the F2 era that spanned the period from 1957 through 1960. Right behind them came the Porsches, the modified spyders eventually giving way to full-fledged open-wheel single-seaters. But we are getting ahead of our story. Embracing the

conventional wisdom of the time were Ferrari and a newly energized Lotus, then just beginning its formula car odyssey.

While Cooper with its advanced design was the most formidable opponent for Zuffenhausen, Ferrari and Lotus were not to be dismissed in terms of their competitiveness. The weapon for the Italians was a slightly downsized version of the Lancia-bred V-8 chassis Ferrari had inherited when the former company withdrew from motorsport following the death of Alberto Ascari and turned its equipment over to the House of the Prancing Horse.

With two seasons of refinement, the Ferrari-Lancia was fully in its prime. To power its F2 contender, the Ferrari camp had turned to Vittorio Jano, the legendary engineer, for the first of the 1.5-liter V-6s. Ironically, if the Ferrari had an elegantly created powerplant, the engines used by both Cooper and Lotus had far more mundane origins. This was the Coventry Climax four-cylinder, a unit intended originally for fire pumps. As for the Lotus chassis, unlike those that would follow,

it was entirely conventional, if lightweight, with a front-mounted motor and transmission mated to a rear-mounted differential.

If the equipment was strong, so too was the driver lineup in F2, with men such as Ferrari's Mike Hawthorn, along with Stirling Moss and future three-time world champion Jack Brabham, all listed as regular participants. Porsche had its own stars, however: Edgar Barth and Umberto Maglioli. For them, Porsche brought two 550As to the Nürburgring in 1957. According to reports, these were totally standard 1.5-liter-engined Spyders stripped of their right-hand seats and spare tires. Although Maglioli retired, Barth claimed the F2 win, with another private 550 coming home third. That ended Porsche's formula adventure for the year. However, it didn't conclude the company's long-term association with the F2 arena.

With the start of the 1958 campaign, Porsche again included F2 on its agenda. Once more the initial target was Reims. This time Porsche would make the show. Interestingly, though, Zuffenhausen would once again do this as cheaply as

After producing a number of customer and factory center seaters, Porsche engineers designed and built their first proper Formula Two car, the Type 718/2, over the winter of 1958–1959. The car, which featured a new frame and bodywork, used the same Type 547 engine and transmission as its spyder counterpart and much of the same suspension geometry. Despite high hopes, the car was not initially successful. *Porsche Werk*

Although this is a picture of the 1961 Formula One 1.5-liter Porsche chassis, little was changed from the initial frame design used in the 1959 and 1960 Type 718/2 Formula Two cars. About the only major difference was a lengthening of the wheelbase to help meet FIA weight requirements. In fact, what was so remarkable about Porsche's initial foray into formula car racing was the use of standard, or nearly standard, parts from the spyders, which remained virtually unchanged for several seasons until the arrival of the Type 804 in 1962. *Porsche Werk*

possible, using one of the first RSKs built, a 1957 model, which three weeks before Reims had won its class at Le Mans.

During the interim period, the engineers covered the headlights; added spats to the rear wheel openings; moved the instruments, the driver's seat, and pedals to the center of the car; and modified the steering to run on the vehicle's centerline. Finally, they fashioned a new deck lid, as well as a new tonneau cover with a single, wraparound centralized windscreen that fit over the original cockpit opening. Other than these modifications, the 718 Spyder was identical to its sports car siblings.

It was also fast. With Jean Behra at the wheel, it was 1.2 seconds quicker than anyone else, a major accomplishment considering it faced the latest Ferraris, a Cooper squad that had won three of the four F2 events prior to the French round, and Lotuses with lower engine installations and new Frank Costin-created bodywork that resembled the F1 Vanwalls of the time.

At the green flag, the affair at Reims immediately became a thrilling three-way contest between

Behra, Moss' Cooper and the Ferrari of Peter Collins. The ultraquick pace was too much for Moss' Coventry Climax engine, which lost its oil pressure on the 10th lap, leaving only Collins to challenge the silver Porsche. The 718's lower-drag bodywork proved to be the difference as Behra drove off to a 21-second advantage over the Ferrari by the end. Even that margin was small when compared to the fact that the first of the Coopers crossed the line more than two minutes in arrears (an OSCA was third).

The next appearance for the center-seat machine was at the Nürburgring, where, minus its fins and spats, it was raced by Barth to a second place in the F2 class behind the Cooper of future Can-Am and F1 titlist Bruce McLaren. The third and final event for the 718 RSK was at Avus, where, with fins, spats, and American Masten Gregory, it cleaned house among the F2 contingent.

The successes of the converted 718 weren't lost on Porsche's customers, several of whom ordered "convertibles." These had dual mounting brackets for the seat, steering and pedals, plus an extra set of bodywork to complete the transformation. Although the switch-hitter Spyders would occasionally do well, the pace or development had passed them by, and they would never again be a factor in determining the outcome of an F2 event.

A major reason for this was the announcement by the FIA at the end of 1958 that from 1961 onward Formula I would employ the same basic 1.5-liter regulations then governing F2. For Porsche with its potent Type 547 four-cam Fuhrmann Carrera four-cylinder, this was enough to spur the design of a 718, open-wheeled single-seater. The idea was that such a vehicle would form the basis for Porsche's entrance into Grand Prix racing when the new formula came into effect.

Using modified 718 running gear with a purpose-engineered tubular frame and overseen by Helmut Bott and Hans Mezger, the 718/2 was born. First tested in April 1959, the bathtub-shaped car made its debut with Count Wolfgang von Trips at Monte Carlo in May. Although quickest among the F2 contingent in the combined F1-F2 field, von Trips crashed out of the event on the second lap, taking two other F2 entries with him. At Reims, a pair of the new 718/2s were on hand for Hans Herrmann and Jo Bonnier. Facing them was Moss in a Rob Walker-entered Cooper powered by a Borgward engine.

Moss eventually led Herrmann and Bonnier to the checkered flag. With a pair of convertible Spyders in fifth and ninth, it still wasn't a bad day for Zuffenhausen. Only once more did a 718/2 appear that season, the occasion being Brands Hatch in England, where Bonnier took a fourth. The factory wasn't the only one, however, to run a Type 418-based single-seater. Behra had ordered such a car, using full 718 mechanicals, from Valerio Colloti. Although it didn't qualify for Monaco, Behra put it on the pole for the Grand Prix race at Pau, in his first event with it. Unhappily, the Frenchman spun out of the race. At Rouen, Herrmann used Behra's open-wheeler to gain another pole, although once more it failed to finish. At Clermont-Ferrand in France, Behra tried it again, getting up to second before retiring. This was the end of its career, as Behra was killed at Avus a week later in a sports car.

Even though Porsche had challenged in 1959, the field still belonged to Cooper. For 1960, the last year of the 1.5-liter F2 era, the Reims round gave way to a race at the Solitude Ring outside of Stuttgart. Meanwhile, Lotus introduced its Type 18, the first of its rear-engined cars, a vehicle which, like the 718/2, would carry over to the new

F1 tour the following year. Also introduced was Ferrari's 156 V-6, the midengined contender that would emerge as the F1 leader in 1961. That debut came at the Solitude round, after an early-season blitz by the new Lotus.

Porsche, which had lost von Trips to Ferrari, had bolstered its lineup with the addition of Moss, who ran a factory-loaned car throughout the year under Rob Walker's banner. All in all, the season would turn out well for Zuffenhausen. Even so, there were losses, like the Solitude Ring, where the battle turned out to be a full-fledged war between von Trips and Herrmann in his factory 718/2. The contest between the two as they passed and repassed each other kept the crowd on its feet before von Trips's Ferrari pulled away to a 3.6-second triumph. Behind them were the factory Porsches of Bonnier, Graham Hill and Dan Gurney. Porsche got its revenge at the Nürburgring-German Grand Prix which was run to F2 rules. There, Bonnier won and von Trips, temporarily back in a Porsche, took second.

The Italian GP, scheduled to be an F1 round, turned out quite differently when the F1 teams staged a boycott. With the F2 field promoted to the front, the day went to von Trips in the 156, with Porsche second. At the Modena F2 round that followed, Bonnier got revenge by winning. Surprisingly, second was taken by Richie Ginther in a front-engined Ferrari, while von Trips could do no better than third in his 156.

From the front, the torsion bar-suspended Type 718/2 Formula Two car looked more like an upside down bathtub than anything else. Although not especially aerodynamically efficient, the car nevertheless would go on to achieve success. In its 1960 version, it would give Porsche the FIA Formula Two title, a major milestone for Zuffenhausen at that time. *Porsche Werk*

From the side it is hard to tell a center seat Type 718 from a standard sports car version of the Porsche spyder. One distinguishing factor, however, is a rear deck lid that contains two small humps on either side of a larger center headrest fairing to cover the carburetor stacks of the Type 547 four-cylinder. Although covered over, the Type 718s often ran complete with headlights, jacks, and other equipment used in sports car races. *Leonard Turner*

Perhaps even more significant was the overall score for the year. With four additional victories by Moss, Porsche wound up with seven first-place finishes to three each for Ferrari, Lotus and Cooper. As a result, Porsche received the "Coupe des Constructeurs," the unofficial Formula Two World Championship for Makes. It was a more than promising way to head toward what Porsche hoped would be a new chapter in its tradition of success in 1961. Unfortunately for Zuffenhausen, that was not to be.

Based on its success of 1960, Porsche entered 1961 with solid expectations of being a major player in Formula One. Circumstances, however, would turn those dreams into nightmares, and ultimately, put an end to the factory's open wheel aspirations. From an overall viewpoint, the problems that forced Porsche to quit were of its own making, in that Zuffenhausen did not have the specialized experience in open wheel racing to ultimately compete at the highest levels.

Simply put, Porsche had been opportunistic and lucky in its initial fling with Formula Two, where, other than the Coopers, and later the as-yet undeveloped Ferrari 156, it largely was running against opposition wedded to obsolete front-engined technology. Although the format of the 1.5-liter capacity Formula One scene would be virtually identical to the old Formula Two, those contesting the new World Championship would be putting far more effort into it than they had when 1.5 liters meant a secondary series.

Although Porsche recognized it would have to step up its game for 1961, it didn't realize until far too late just how far up the ladder it would have to go if it were to build on what it had already achieved. Clearly, at the time, Zuffenhausen believed it did have what it would take to make its mark on the Grand Prix tour. Fueling this belief were two things, the first being Porsche's faith in the basic 718/2 chassis design, and the second the coming of its new Type 753 1.5-liter flat eight cylinder.

Even while von Hanstein was readying the team for 1961, adding Dan Gurney as a full partner for Bonnier in the wake of Moss's decision to race a Lotus 18, work was progressing on the 753 boxer eight. However, with Karl Rabe, the man in charge of race engineering, about to retire, internal politics, involving competition among those working on the new powerplant over who might replace Rabe, slowed the unit's development to the point where it would not be ready for use until 1962.

Thus, for 1961, Porsche would again be forced to use the Carrera four-cam four-cylinder, now fitted with fuel injection, but nevertheless still slightly inferior to the latest versions of the British Coventry Climax four-cylinder, and greatly inferior to Ferrari's 156 V-6, which during the course of the season would become even more potent when it appeared in 120-degree, instead of 60-degree, form.

Chassis-wise, the decision was taken to simply redo the 718/2, building on its strong points, while eliminating its weaknesses. What emerged was a tube frame quite similar to its 1960 predecessor, but with a 4-inch stretch in wheelbase that now was set at 90.5 inches. The car also had a new front suspension and a revised body, created by Butz Porsche.

The extra length was all to be found in the engine bay, so that the flat eight could be fitted, while the new front suspension now had combined spring and shock absorber coilover units, as well as unequal-length wishbones. All this gave the car a front track of 51.2 inches, and the rear was set at 50 inches. Also changed in detail was the front-mounted fuel tank. With all these revisions, Porsche redesignated the car Type 787. However, it would not appear until the first round of the World Championship in May at Monaco.

To start the season, Zuffenhausen used a pair of slightly modified 718/2s, which featured newly mandated roll bars and onboard starters. These appeared at the nontitle F1 events at Brussels and Siracusa, Bonnier taking the pole in the former and winning the first heat before being knocked out in the second.

This promising start, which came despite the fact that at just over 1,050 pounds, the cars were nearly 100 pounds over the minimum weight permitted, continued in the second nonpoints affair, where the Ferrari 156 appeared for the first time in F1 trim. Despite shifting woes, Gurney managed a second and Bonnier a third against the Ferrari.

While Porsche obviously hadn't achieved all that it might have wanted, it had done more than enough to be optimistic about Monaco. Bonnier would have one of the new 787s, Herrmann a revised 718/2 with the new body and other detail modifications, and Gurney would have Bonnier's new "stock" 718/2 from Siracusa. While they didn't qualify well, Gurney and Bonnier managed to get as high as third and fourth, before Bonnier's engine quit with dirt in its injection system and Gurney dropped to fifth.

Herrmann meanwhile, had a miserable day, eventually crossing the line in ninth.

For Holland, Porsche produced a second 787, Bonnier taking the new long-wheelbase car, and Gurney moving up to its slighter older sister. Herrmann had the same car he ran at Monaco, while Dutchman Carel de Beaufort was loaned a standard 718/2. If Monaco had been disappointing, Zandvoort was a disaster. The 787s never handled well, in addition to the fact that there wasn't enough power from the injected fours to stay with the opposition, even if the cars could have been made to corner properly.

All four Porsches qualified badly, and finished even worse, Gurney and Bonnier coming home 10th and 11th respectively, while Herrmann was beaten at the flag by de Beaufort's older-configured example. Such was the disappointment that

Jo Bonnier, right, stands beside his Type 718/2 at the British Formula Two race in Aintree in 1960, as Graham Hill, left, looks on. With the help of Stirling Moss, driving a similar car under the Rob Walker banner that season, Porsche surprised everyone by taking the manufacturers title in what was the last year for the 1.5-liter Formula Two Championship. The following season, Formula One would adopt essentially the same regulations, putting F2 out of business and Zuffenhausen onto the Grand Prix stage, where it expected to do extremely well. Unfortunately, success would elude the factory in F1. *Porsche Werk* von Hanstein and the engineers wanted to quit completely, a feeling pushed aside, ironically, by Dr. Porsche himself. At the end of the following year, Dr. Porsche would order his company's pull-out from Grand Prix competition, but for now he insisted the effort keep going.

Zuffenhausen regrouped, parking its new and revised cars in favor of its stored 1960 lightly revised 718/2s, which, with carburetor-equipped engines, ran the remainder of the 1961 Formula One schedule. Although Porsche didn't score a single Grand Prix victory, it did make itself felt. Gurney garnered three seconds and finished tied for third in the championship standings with Moss, while Bonnier collected a fifth in the British GP at Aintree for his best placing. One of Gurney's seconds came at Rheims, where both he and Bonnier battled Ferrari newcomer Giancarlo Baghetti for the win, Bonnier dropping out prior to the final lap, and Gurney being nipped at the flag by the Ferraris. Both Porsches suffered from high engine operating temperature.

In many ways, 1961 was an obvious failure for Porsche. Yet, von Hanstein, his drivers, and the factory engineers had accomplished enough to continue into 1962 when both the Type 753 flat eight and the new Type 804 chassis in which it would be housed came on line. Unfortunately, when it was all over, 1962 would turn out to be little better than 1961. Despite this, the year wouldn't be entirely lost, as the factory would be left with the legacy of the Type 753, which in its sports car Type 771 2.0-liter and 2.2-liter forms would power Porsche's proto-type fleet through the first part of 1968.

Taking a different approach than Ferrari, Porsche demanded that the Type 753 be high revving. (It would produce its maximum horse-power figures at 9,300 rpm.) Thus, the design parameters called for a compact, air-cooled unit with a forged, not machined, crankshaft; permanent instead of sand-mold castings; and symmetrical cylinders and heads. Ironically, when the 753 was finally completed, it turned out to be one of the most complicated engines ever to come from Porsche, a fact that ultimately led to its abandonment in early 1968 in favor of the far less complex 908 boxer eight.

With engineer Hans Honick in charge of its intended parameters and a young Hans Mezger

Jo Bonnier practices in his 1.5-liter Formula One four-cylinder prior to the Monaco Grand Prix in 1961. Bonnier would retire with dirt in his injection system. The victory went to Stirling Moss' Lotus 180. *Porsche Werk*

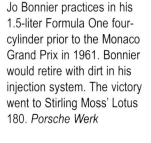

Joining the Porsche Formula One team in 1961 was American Dan Gurney, who in 1962 would go on to score the company's only victories during its 1.5-liter Formula One adventure with the Type 804 eight-cylinder. *Porsche Werk*

After much misadventure, Porsche returned to its 1960s-style Formula Two Type 718/2s for the 1961 Formula One season. These essentially remained in Formula Two configuration, with the exception of the newly required rollover bar hoops behind the drivers. They were further used through the beginning of 1962. Edgar Barth, left, and Jo Bonnier, right, are seen here prior to the start at the Grand Prix at Kapstadt in1962. *Porsche Werk*

responsible for the development side of things (particularly the camshafts), work began translating what was on paper into metal. From the start, the Type 753 was intended to be expanded to 2 liters. The enlargement carried with it the new designation Type 771. The displacement would later go up again to the 2.2-liter figure used in the 907s. All that was far in the future, though, as Honick and Mezger struggled to get the slowly evolving Type 753 to the dyno.

From a technical viewpoint, the boxer eight layout provided a good, low center of gravity, with relatively small, well-balanced reciprocating masses that increased its reliability. Further adding to the durability was the fact that the engine was "over square," its bore of 66 millimeters being substantially larger than its 54.6-millimeter stroke. These dimensions gave a total displacement of 1,494 cc. (The bore in the sports racing unit was increased to 76 millimeters for a 1,982-cc displacement.)

Honick was less successful in terms of the valve train, where the valves, which were widely angled, resulted in a deep, slow-firing combustion chamber. For a more even burn, twin plugs and dual distributors were used. Not so surprisingly, given the troubles in 1961, fuel injection was rejected in favor of four Weber carburetors with 38-millimeter venturis.

Although similar to the Type 718/2s, the 1961 Type 787 Formula One cars had some significant differences, including revised brakes and suspension geometry. However, the cars proved to be vastly uncompetitive and were withdrawn after the Dutch Grand Prix at Zandvoort being replaced by their predecessors.
Porsche Werk

To keep the weight of the 753 tolerable, the crankcase halves were made of magnesium, as were the valve covers, while the cylinders and heads were aluminum. Mezger figured that he would need 200 to 210 horsepower from the eight if it were to be competitive. What he got was far less than that, and he had to wait to find out the bad news.

Most people do not realize that all automobile manufacturers to some extent are dependent on outside suppliers. In the case of a small company such as Porsche, and particularly when specialized pieces are involved, the quality and timeliness of the pieces made by outside suppliers become crucial. In Germany during the late 1950s and early 1960s, outside suppliers were booked solid, a fact that meant Porsche had to wait nine months after ordering until it had the parts to assemble the first 753 unit. When it finally ran on the dyno in December 1960, it produced a disappointing 120 horsepower. Moreover, the torque curve was not as good as the 547s. In all, it was not a happy time, and it got worse. In large measure this was because of pressure from both inside and outside the company. The inside pressure came from Ferry Porsche's office, where he was beginning to have some serious doubts about where the program was going. Outside, it resulted from the fact that a new Ferrari, the 156, had appeared on the horizon.

Perhaps what upset Dr. Porsche the most was the lack of progress achieved with the Type 753 during the ensuing months as the output figures

for the engine failed to climb substantially from what had been seen in December. By June, the boss decided that the existing four-cylinder would not be replaced by the eight until the start of 1962. In fact, at one point, he almost canceled the new engine entirely, only relenting when told that there was no real reason why, with work, it couldn't be made competitive.

Among the things tried during the ongoing development saga was a roller crank, which was rejected after it proved to have no extra benefits over its plain-bearing counterpart. The biggest job, however, was the redesign of the cylinder heads, a task made more difficult by the departures of some key design team members.

Although by the time this happened, the engine and the new 804 Formula One chassis were running, it is obvious that the period constituted something less than an oasis of calm. Moreover, Porsche's limited staff was not only involved in the process of getting Volkswagen's new Type 3 air-cooled four-cylinder to market, but also was in the midst of work on its own Type 901 six-cylinder powerplant as well.

Over the winter of 1961–1962, Mezger and company created two new head designs for the Type 753. Both featured narrower valve angles, 73 degrees for one and 84 for the other. The intake valves were made smaller in both. Still, with a final 10.1:1 compression ratio, the company's official figures said the unit was putting out 180 horsepower, good enough, although barely, to take on the new British Coventry Climax and BRM V-8s that were in the 185–190 horsepower range.

There is suspicion, though, that the quoted figure for the 753 boxer eight might have been a bit optimistic, with some suggesting that it might have been closer to 165 horsepower. In fact, given that one of the new 804 chassis was fitted with a 547 four-cylinder as a backup, one can almost believe the truth of this contention.

Meanwhile, in creating the 804 chassis, Porsche used a standard tube-type space frame not dissimilar to its 718/787 predecessors. What was new was the "rocker" suspension with its inboard shocks and very low center of gravity. Indeed, compared to its progenitors, the 804, with its a six-speed synchromesh transaxle, might as well have come from the twenty-first century as any place else. With a wheelbase of 90.5 inches, it featured a front track of 51.25 inches and a rear track of 52.4 inches. The 15-inch diameter wheels were 5 inches wide at the front and 6.5 inches at the rear. Torsion bar springing was employed at all four corners, this in conjunction with a double wishbone suspension setup that also had disc brakes all around.

The main fuel tank, located between the driver and the engine in the cockpit and forming the underside and back of the seat, had a 19.8-gallon capacity, while a nose tank held a further 10.6 gallons. Interestingly, a series of pumps took the fuel from the main to the nose tank as the latter, from which the engine got its supply exclusively, emptied. This unique system helped maintain the same 46 percent front and 54 percent rear weight distribution throughout a race.

The aluminum body that covered a frontal area of the 804 weighed in at 55 pounds and had only 7.75 square feet. In total, the new Porsche came to the track at a hefty 1,100 pounds (1,016 dry without fuel or other fluids). While these figures were actually better when compared to the 1961 Ferrari 156, they weren't any better than those of the BRM of Graham Hill or the Lola of John Surtees, both space frame designs; and especially not better than Colin Chapman's revolutionary Lotus 25, which introduced monocoque construction to Formula One.

Indeed, it ought to have been easy for Lotus driver Jim Clark to score his first championship that year, but, as usual with Chapman, there was a lot of "breakage" on the Lotus. The Englishman

The Type 718/2s with their advanced Type 547 four-cylinder engines were quick in spite of their chunky appearance and sports car origins. Not only did they win their share of Formula Two events in 1960, but also delivered the F2 manufacturer's crown to Porsche. *Leonard Turner*

Bonnier, who would not have a good season, was given the first 804 built, 804-01, while Gurney sat in 804-02, the car that originally had been tested with a four-cylinder in it, but which had been converted to take the new 753 unit. Gurney's engine featured the 84-degree heads, while Bonnier's had their 73-degree cousins. To show how far things had come between the 1961 and 1962 campaigns, the pole time of the previous year, 1:35.7, was easily matched by Gurney's 1:34.7. Unfortunately, this achievement was completely overshadowed by Surtees' stunning 1:32.5 mark. (Bonnier's best was a slow 1:37.) As Bonnier struggled around, totally out of contention, Gurney pushed his way to third. Eventually, though, the American dropped back with and finally retired with shift linkage problems that cropped up after the first 10 or so laps.

Dr. Porsche, who had kept Porsche in F1 after its disastrous 1961 Zandvoort effort, decided he had seen all of Formula 1 he wanted for a while and ordered the team to stay in Stuttgart instead of going to Monaco, next on the GP list. Once again Gurney and von Hanstein "worked" on Porsche, eventually getting permission for Gurney to run solo at the street circuit. In the end the pair probably wished they hadn't tried. On the first lap, Richie Ginther's BRM, its throttle stuck wide open, slammed into a Lotus, which in turn rammed the rear of Gurney's 804, putting it out of the race. Its engine moved forward about 4 inches and its frame smashed, the wreck was taken back to Germany, where the boss immediately barred any further Grand Prix participation until things "improved." What Porsche meant by that was a troublefree, GP race-length test at the tough Nürburgring.

With Mezger working on the 84-degree heads to improve the midrange torque, Helmuth Bott put his talents into the chassis, reducing the main tank capacity to lower the driver and reduce the frontal area (meanwhile adding a cowl tank to make up the difference). Additionally, Bott used spacers to add a half-inch of rear track width to each side, bringing the total to 53.4 inches, and also modified the shift linkage. Thus refined, the Porsche team went to the Ring on June 18, having missed Spa in the process. There Gurney not only drove without any mechanical difficulties, he set a new lap record of 8:44.4 for the 14-plus mile circuit, a full 1.7 seconds under the 1961 quick time. Whatever else, Ferry Porsche was persuaded to let Gurney and Bonnier take their 804s to Rouen for the July 8 French GP, a decision that was to make all the previous problems worthwhile.

In mid-July 1961, the Type 718 came within a whisker of creating history at the French Grand Prix, when it lost that race by inches to Ferrari. The driver that day was Dan Gurney, who was forced to back off because of overheating; but for that, he might have scored Porsche's first World Championship victory. This restored Type 718/2 is virtually identical to the American's car on that afternoon. *Leonard Turner*

traditionally went for lightness over strength, and occasionally cut the line too thin. As it was, Clark was a fierce contender, while Graham Hill, a brilliant performer who never got the credit his rival did, was both quick and fast, turning these attributes into a world title for himself.

Against this backdrop, Ferry Porsche somewhat reluctantly agreed to let the Porsches run at the Dutch Grand Prix in Zandvoort, the opening round of the 1962 F1 title chase. Dr. Porsche made it clear that should the new 804s fail to be competitive during practice, they would be withdrawn. To underscore the point and ensure that the enthusiasm of von Hanstein and Gurney (whose drive to make the program work had been instrumental in the decision to continue) didn't cause them to override his orders, the boss accompanied the team to the North Sea facility.

Not far from the Normandy beaches, the Rouen circuit's start-finish line is at the top of a hill. From there, the track runs down in a series of high-speed straights and near flat-out sweepers to a 30-mile per hour hairpin at the bottom of a ride that could terrify even the most stouthearted. The course then proceeds up through a forest to another bit of high-speed highway, eventually returning to the hilltop's crest. This all takes place on public roads whose surface smoothness in 1962 was more akin to that of New York city's streets than a racetrack. It was then, and is today, a place for experts and few others.

With Porsche, still down on power but now much nearer the hoped-for 185 horsepower figure, von Hanstein and others still thought they had enough to keep on par with Porsche's leading rivals. The 3.9-mile Rouen facility was a far better place for Zuffenhausen to be, in spite of its problems, than Rheims, where all-out speed was king. Gurney appeared with 804-01 which now had 7-inch-wide rear rims, while Bonnier had the rebuilt 804-02 with 6.5-inch rear wheels.

If there had been hope after the Nürburgring, there was only disappointment after qualifying at Rouen. On the pole was Clark's Lotus at 2:14.8, with Gurney occupying the third row of the grid, 1.7 seconds back, and Bonnier in the row behind that, 3.1 seconds off Clark's pace. During the race Bonnier retired because of damage received in an early off-course excursion, an outcome dramatically different from that in store for his American colleague. Running sixth at the start, Gurney felt there was little hope of substantial improvement until the leaders encountered problems. Among those were Messrs. Hill, Clark, Surtees, and Gurney's future teammate, Sir Jack Brabham, all of whom had suffered either mechanical woes or had crashed out of the contest. In the end, Gurney found himself in the lead with more than a lap on the second-placed Cooper-Climax of Tony Maggs. It was a historic moment, and one that would not be repeated on the World Championship level until the heady 1984 season, when the Porsche TAG V-6 turbo-powered Marlboro McLarens began a three-year domination of the sport.

In 1962 Dan Gurney found himself with a much more potent Porsche than he had the previous season. This was the Type 804, which featured the new 1.5-liter Type 753 eight-cylinder. Porsche had hoped that this would be the instrument for its success in Formula One. Despite two victories by Gurney, including one at the French Grand Prix, the Type 804 was overshadowed by Collin Chapman's new monocoque Lotus 25.

Dan Gurney at work in the 1962 French Grand Prix at Rouen. Gurney was near perfect in his Type 804, which he described as "jewel-like." A week later he would use the same car to win the non-championship Solitude Grand Prix held in Porsche's backyard on the outskirts of Stuttgart. Despite these successes, Gurney would find the rest of the season a less-than-happy experience, later moving on to the Brabham Organization before founding his own Formula One team in 1966. *Porsche Werk*

Along with the win came something even more tangible and important for Zuffenhausen's F1 troops—a commitment by Ferry Porsche to complete the season. Now that they didn't have to worry about the plug being pulled, von Hanstein's band could finally concentrate on trying to beat its rivals on a full-time basis.

However, before heading to the British GP, the Porsche team moved down the road a few miles from the factory to take part in the hometown, nontitle Solitude race, which came a week after Rouen. There, Gurney drove the newly constructed 804-03, a car he would keep for the rest of the year. With 03, Gurney passed Clark's Lotus on the first lap and went on to score Porsche's second F1 triumph. Adding to the festivities was the second place posted by Bonnier in 804-02, despite the fact that Bonnier had lost a tailpipe along the way. Still, if Solitude and Rouen represented the summit, the British GP was a definite valley in Porsche's fortunes, Bonnier retiring with a ring and pinion failure and Gurney coming home ninth after overrevving the engine while challenging for second during the early stages.

All that was nearly forgotten at the Nürburgring when the Formula One circus arrived for the German Grand Prix. Again Bonnier was effectively out of contention, having chosen the wrong tires for the rainy start. Gurney, on the other hand, took the

pole. In spite of a loose battery cable that kept shorting out the electrical system throughout the affair, he wound up third in a near blanket finish that had Hill's winning BRM, Surtees and the American all within four and a half seconds of each other. It was one of the most thrilling races of the decade.

Bonnier took 804-01 to Sweden for his home F1 nontitle round, finishing fifth with it. Then the Swede redeemed himself at the unlikely venue of the Ollon-Villars hillclimb, where he and 804-01 collected a record-shattering victory.

While all of this was going on, 804-02 and 804-03 were back in Zuffenhausen being prepared for the Italian GP at Monza which, in those days, used the track's famed banking. As much weight as possible was removed from the cars, bigger cowl and nose tanks were added as well. The aluminum alloy nose section was replaced for this race by a modified fiberglass substitute, and the exposed top rear wishbones covered with aerodynamic fairings. The wheels themselves were covered with a German version of the popular California-bred moon discs, normally seen at the Bonneville Salt Flats speed trials. Finally, the cooling fan was given an electrical cut-out switch that allowed the engine to gain an extra eight horsepower for short periods of time.

Despite these efforts, the BRMs were never challenged, although both Porsches were there, fighting for third with the rest of the Fl leadership.

Despite several years of reasonable success with Porsche and a long future career in Formula One, Sweden's Jo Bonnier (shown here at the Nürburgring), was overshadowed by Gurney in 1962. In part, Bonnier made his own bad fortune, and in part it was made for him. The failure of the Type 804 lay not in its appearance, nor in its engine. Rather, its shortcoming was in its aging tube-frame chassis design. While Porsche engineers had utilized the most advanced tubular chassis technology, even that wasn't enough to keep up with the new monocoque revolution, epitomized by the Lotus 25. Bonnier's lack of success and that of the 804 contributed to Porsche's departure from Formula One at the end of that year. *Porsche Werk*

Still, the ending was less than spectacular, Gurney retiring with a broken ring and pinion, and Bonnier settling for sixth after suffering a slipping clutch. Watkins Glen wasn't much better, Phil Hill actually coqualifying Bonnier's car in case the sick-feeling Porsche regular couldn't take the green flag. Bonnier did make it after all, but was only able to collect 13th following a host of problems. Gurney meanwhile held third until his engine began to head for an early vacation, the team leader finally crossing the finish in fifth.

Although no one knew it at the time, the Watkins Glen race was to be the end of Porsche's Formula One involvement until the early 1980s when it rejoined a very different Grand Prix tour with its TAG-sponsored powerplant. While von Hanstein never gave up hope, and no real announcement was made, plans to go to the season-ending South African Grand Prix were canceled and Gurney and Bonnier released from their contracts. It was over. In this case, the finish had come not when the fat lady sang, but when the small man who ran the company, Ferry Porsche, said it was.

Dan Gurney, looking forward to more success following his victories in France and at the Solitude Grand Prix, found further wins totally elusive in 1962. With no further victories in sight, Dr. Ferry Porsche ordered the Porsche Formula One program shut down following the Italian Grand Prix at Monza, saying that Porsche should concentrate on its "core" interest—meaning sports car racing. Throughout the following year, Porsche would work on developing its fiberglass 904, the car that would start Zuffenhausen on its march toward center stage of prototype competition. *Porsche Werk*

The Coming of a New Era

4

For Porsche, the fiberglass-bodied 904 was a transition from what had been to what would be. Although generally referred to as the first of the "modern" competition cars produced by the factory, in reality the 904 took Porsche only part way into the future. Indeed, the 904, which would come to dominate 2-liter racing in both 1964 and 1965, possessed a split personality, combining the old with the new.

Intended as a platform for Porsche's about-to-be-released 911 Type 901 boxer six, the 904 wound up instead utilizing the Ernst Fuhrmann-designed Type 547 Carrera four-cam, four-cylinder that had seen already more than a decade's service. Likewise, while the 904 pioneered the use of a full fiberglass body, its advanced material shell was mated to a

---

To be approved as a production car, one has to manufacture it in series. In 1964 this meant Porsche had to build no less than 100 904s before the FIA would "homologate" it, or grant it such status. Here, in the factory courtyard along with a number of more mundane 356s, three 904s await delivery to their new owners. By that spring, all 100 had been sold. In 1965 Porsche planned a second batch of 100 to be ready for the 1966 season. These were canceled in favor of the upcoming 906. *Porsche Werk*

The prototype 904 differed from its successors in a number of ways, due to modifications made to correct defects found in testing. One of the easiest means of spotting the first cars built is to look for the small vents built into the sides of the rear quarter panels, as seen in this photo. These were later changed to scoop-like structures to improve cooling. The shape of the wheel openings was also changed. *Porsche Werk*

Just how extensive Porsche's testing work was can be seen in this photo at the Solitude Ring in late November 1963. Note the revisions to the wheel openings and the addition of scoops to the rear quarter panels. In addition, there were revisions to the suspension, brakes, and transmission. The frame and body structure also were strengthened. All this paid off with a victory two months later in the car's first race, at Daytona. *Porsche Werk*

low-tech perimeter box frame rather than the more costly tubular structures of previous competition Porsches. Despite these contradictions in its nature, the 904 was a milestone in Porsche's journey to the full domination of the sports car racing scene.

Throughout its involvement in Formula One and Formula Two, Zuffenhausen had continued to field factory entries in the sports car arena. However, given Porsche's limited resources, these were largely warmed-over versions of existing models such as the type 718-based W-RS Spyder and the Abarth-bodied 356 coupe.

In fact, other than dropping the 2-liter, Formula One-derived Type 771 flat eight into the W-RS Spyder and two sister coupes during 1962, there was virtually no meaningful work done to upgrade the sports car side of Porsche's house. That was about to change as Zuffenhausen's F1 efforts floundered, leading Dr. Porsche to redirect the funds spent on it toward the kind of racing that had brought such notice to Porsche in the past.

Unfortunately, given the lateness of his decision in the fall of 1962 to cancel the Grand Prix

Even though Porsche felt the Type 901 six-cylinder wasn't ready for competition, it wasn't content to simply stay with the Type 547 four-cylinder it provided to its customers. Thus, by the spring of 1964, only weeks after the 904's approval as a production car, the factory introduced its own "prototype" version. It featured the Type 771 eight-cylinder that it had developed in parallel with the Type 753 for its Formula One program. These 2-liter cars, which would do extremely well throughout 1964 and 1965, could be distinguished by the much larger scoops behind the doors. This particular example also shows evidence of having had its rear fenders widened, although this picture shows it with narrower standard rear rims. *Porsche Werk*

program, there was little Porsche's engineers could do for 1963, other than to again field the aging Abarth coupes and the equally well-worn W-RS Spyder. However, 1964 was another matter. During the winter of 1962–1963, the go-ahead was given to the project that would result in the 904. In charge on the mechanical side was Hans Tomola, who had been the father to many previous racing Porsches. Given the task of designing the body was Dr. Porsche's son, Butzi, then in charge of Porsche's styling department.

The idea to do the entire body structure, including the floor pan, in fiberglass arose from the factory's earlier successful experiences with various parts made from the material. In light of the complexities involved, however, Porsche went to the aircraft industry, choosing the Heinkel company to construct the bodies, these being fully trimmed-out before Heinkel shipped them to Zuffenhausen for final assembly.

Although the 904 would serve as the basis for the factory's own competition efforts, it was primarily intended to be a customer car, with the factory keeping only a small percentage of the 904s

The clean lines of this factory-entered 944 were the result of several years of development in the mind of stylist Butzi Porsche, the son of Ferry Porsche. Many of the elements were seen in the RS61 Coupes created by the younger Porsche's son that year, and in several subsequent vehicles as well. The small scoop on the rear corner panel indicates that this car was equipped with the Type 547 four-cylinder, which could be found in all customer versions. Originally it had been intended to power the 904 with a new Type 901 six-cylinder from the just introduced 911. However, Porsche felt that that powerplant was far too underdeveloped to be used in racing, particularly in the hands of its privateers. *Porsche Werk*

In 1965 Porsche made history when it decided to run not only its new 911 coupe but also its 904 circuit racer in the famed Monte Carlo Rally. Seen here in clean condition at the factory before heading to the start, the cars would make veteran rally watchers take notice. The 904 finished second and the 911 came in just slightly further back, in what were truly impressive performances. Both would go on to enjoy further rally successes, the 911's rally career continuing almost until the 1990s. *Porsche Werk*

Porsche always described its 904 as a "dual purpose car," meaning one that could be used on the street as well as on the racetrack. However, in January 1965 it took that meaning to new extremes when Eugen Böhringer and Rolf Wutherich drove their factory-entered example to a stunning second place in the Monte Carlo Rally. The snow and ice of this event was in no way an ideal venue for a midengine circuit racer such as the 904. Nevertheless, the pair came close to humbling their opposition with their fiberglass machine. Other than a slight increase in ride height, some winterized equipment, and the removal of the plastic head light covers (plus the addition of two auxiliary lights on the front hood), their 904 was virtually standard. *Porsche Werk*

for its own use. In fact, it was this commercial orientation and the subsequent need to keep manufacturing costs as low as possible that led to the abandonment of Porsche's traditional tube-frame layout in favor of the much cheaper box channel perimeter structure.

To achieve the necessary stiffness with this rather flexible arrangement, Tomola and his team came up with the idea of bonding the bodyshell directly to the chassis, this giving the 904 the same overall torsional rigidity as its tube-frame predecessors—quite an achievement in light of the fact that alone the 904's frame was just half as stiff as its ancestors. Specification-wise, the wheelbase for the 904 was set at 90.6 inches, with a front track of 51.8 inches and 51.9 inches at the rear. Suspension was of the double-wishbone type front and rear, and featured integrated spring-shock "coilover" units at each

corner, as well as nonventilated disc brakes. Initial rim size was 15x5 inches front and rear, these being shod with a variety of tires, depending on the intended use of the vehicle.

The transmission was the same basic five-speed found in the then-new 911, with the exception that the ring and pinion were reversed to accommodate the 904's midengine layout. As noted previously, the 904 originally was to have been powered by the 911's Type 901 six-cylinder. Unfortunately, in 1963 and 1964, the six was nowhere near developed enough to be raced by Porsche's customers with any degree of reliability. Therefore, Tomola and his engineers decided to use the classic Furhmann-designed Type 547 2-liter four. Changes to the aging powerplant included plain main and big end bearings, as well as lightweight alloy materials for the major engine components. Also used was a twin-plug ignition,

Porsche continued to race its eight- and six-cylinder cars as prototypes throughout 1965, while its customers dominated the production 2-liter sports car division. These special 904s garnered their fair share of victories, including taking their class at Le Mans in 1966. However, while the customer versions would enjoy continued success, the factory 904s were coming to the end of their time on center stage, about to be replaced by the upcoming lightweight 906. *Porsche Werk*

Not all 904s were silver. This red example was shot at the factory testing grounds in 1964. It was a standard model fitted with a Type 547 four-cylinder. Note the unique design of the front fenders, as well as the windshield wiper and very standard center-mounted rearview mirror. The fiberglass-bodied 904 with its perimeter steel frame broke new ground for Porsche. However, it was also an aberration, being the only factory-race car to employ such a frame design. *Porsche Werk*

with carburetion coming via twin-choke Webers, although some 904s utilized Solexes instead.

Barth and Herbert Linge debuted the 904 at Daytona Continental in February, racing as a prototype because it had not yet been produced in sufficient quantities to qualify as a production sports car. They placed sixth overall and first in the small displacement prototype category.

While there were clearly factory and private 904s entered in the two-year period marking its center stage service, the line between what was and what was not a factory entry was often blurred. That was evidenced next time out at the Sebring 12-Hour. There Briggs Cunningham and Lake Underwood again claimed the small-displacement prototype class in a car owned by Porsche, but sold afterward to Cunningham, who continued to race it as a privateer into 1965. Throughout this 1964–1965 period, it was not uncommon for nonfactory drivers to be found in "works" entries, and for factory chauffeurs to race with Porsche's customers in their own 904s. Meanwhile, Zuffenhausen's first eight-cylinder 904 made its appearance at the 1964 Targa Florio. Ironically, the best that the Type 771-powered works coupe could do was fifth overall. However the factory's honor was saved by its four-cylinder entry with Colin Davis and Antonio Pucci. They drove a nearly perfect race to earn Porsche its fifth Targa triumph. Second went to Linge in another factory 904.

Adding to 904's record in May were further class victories at Spa by Barth and company and at the Nürburgring via a privateer effort. June brought the most important event on the calendar for Porsche: the 24-Hours of Le Mans. There, despite its misgivings about the reliability of the Type 771 powerplant, two of the eight-cylinder 904 coupes were entered by the factory, both retiring because of failed clutches, which couldn't take the strain of the higher horsepower of the eights. Once more Porsche's honor at Le Mans was saved by a four-cylinder, this one driven by Guy Ligier and Robert Buchet. They were seventh overall and first in the 2-liter GT division. The rest of the 1964 season brought more triumphs for the Type 547-powered 904s, which dominated the small-displacement GT arena. In the end it wasn't even close, as the Porsche's privateers earned Zuffenhausen the 2-liter championship trophy with only an occasional assist from the factory.

While its customers were adding to the legend of the four-cylinder 904, the factory was continuing to develop the six-cylinder version, the prototype

of which was completed in the spring of 1964. As noted, the six didn't come out in public until that fall at the Paris 1,000Ks, where it retired with a broken transmission. The fall and winter of 1964 and 1965 saw Porsche's engineers put a great deal of effort toward getting the six to the point where it could be utilized as Zuffenhausen's principal weapon in 1965. Ironically, however, it was a standard four-cylinder that helped Porsche start off the year on a high note. This came when Eugen Bobringer and Rolf Wutherich, in an amazing performance, claimed second overall in the tough Monte Carlo Rally, an event not normally thought of as a venue for a car such as the 904. Even so, its versatility would continue to yield surprises. Regardless of its forays into uncharted fields, the 904's dominance of the production sports car scene continued unabated in 1965, Zuffenhausen's customers

The long nose and sharply raked windshield of the 904 were major factors in helping the car's aerodynamics. In turn, this contributed to good performance, even though its normal type 547 four-cylinder produced only limited horsepower. Not only did the car look good, but it followed the adage that what looks right is right. Attesting to that fact was its lengthy string of individual victories and season championships posted by both the factory and its customers. *Bill Oursler*

The 904s produced for the 1965 season and run by the factory can be distinguished from their predecessors not only by their generally wider fenders, but also by the small front vent windows that they sported in place of the two-piece sliding Plexiglas versions of the previous year. These days, many restored 904s feature Fuchs wheels. However, this factory example seen at the 1998 Monterey Historic Event retains its original pressed steel center rims and a rather colorful red front deck lid. *Leonard Turner*

In addition to the successes of the eight- and four-cylinder examples, six-cylinder 904s also produced their own list of wins. In the process they helped lay the groundwork for what would be one of the longest-running competition engines ever, the Type 901 existing in much-modified forms as a racing powerplant to this day. Much of the early development came in the 904, making it ready as the preferred unit for the Porsche 906, the car most experts believe is the progenitor of all modern racing cars from Zuffenhausen. *Leonard Turner*

easily winning the 2-liter crown for a second straight time. On the prototype front, the factory continued to enter its own cars, the majority of which were fitted with the Type 901 boxer six. The Type 901's newfound reliability translated into a number of wins for the works team. Chief among these successes was a tremendous performance by the 904/6 of Linge and Peter Nocker at Le Mans, where not only did they finish first in class and fourth overall, but garnered an upset victory in the prestigious Index of Performance contest.

However, despite its growing record of success, factory interest in the 904 was running out.

There were two key reasons for this. The first was that on the prototype front, the relatively heavy 904 was about to face a new challenger in the form of Ferrari's lightweight 166P V-6 Dino, a car which would turn out to be every bit as much a threat to the 904 as Porsche had thought it might. The second was the assumption of power by the ambitious Ferdinand Piëch (the nephew of Ferry Porsche) as head of Porsche's R&D operation. Piëch wanted to be his own man, an attitude carrying with it the winds of change. Over the years much has been made about the friction between the Porsche and Piëch branches of the family over how to manage Zuffenhausen. The

The Porsche 904, which had shown its potential even before its approval as a production car by winning its class as a prototype at both Daytona and Sebring, changed that into reality when it won the Targo Florio outright, after being approved by the FIA as a full-fledged production automobile. Interestingly, Porsche had decided to enter eight-cylinder examples for this event, but in the end it won the Targa with a standard Type 547 four-cylinder. It would be the 904's first and last victory in the mountainous affair, although certainly not the last triumph for Zuffenhausen. Number 32, shown here, manuevers at Le Mans *Porsche Werk*

One of the last Kangaroo racers was this example made in June 1965. These distinctive cars were an attempt at producing a competitive hillclimber from a standard 904, replacing the coupe body with a minimalist open-top structure. Although this car won a circuit event at the Solitude Ring, it never claimed victory on the FIA Hillclimb tour, being defeated solidly by Ferrari's 166 V-6 Dino. *Leonard Turner*

reality is that much of this can be attributed to Piëch himself, who disregarded any and all pleasantries in his determination to put his own stamp on Porsche.

Involved in all of this was the 904, which Piëch had inherited. Not only didn't he see room for much more development within the 904 design; his less-than-enthusiastic attitude toward it was heightened by the fact that he and his engineers hadn't created it. Indeed, it was Piëch who convinced his uncle to cancel the second batch of 904s—this even though a number of outside supplied parts such as frames and suspensions already had been produced. In the case of the latter, there were 100 sets delivered to the factory, a situation that would later compromise Piëch's ideas for what was to become Porsche's performance leader in 1966, the 906 also known as the Carrera 6.

Still, the 904 was also the car with which Piëch would begin his reign over Porsche's motorsport universe. The reason for starting with a car he disliked lay in the FIA's mountain or hillclimb championship which, with its 2-liter displacement cap, had been a Zuffenhausen preserve since its inception in 1957. In fact, Porsche had won the hillclimbing crown every year since, with the

While the Kangaroo Spyders scored no hillclimb triumphs, Gerhard Mitter took his eight-cylinder-powered example to a win in the middle of July 1965 at the Solitude Ring, less than two months prior to the car's retirement from factory service. *Porsche Werk*

exception of 1962, when Ferrari swept to the title. Now, with the very real prospect of having to fight off the lightweight and sophisticated 166P, Porsche was worried.

Without much competition, the 904 had proved an adequate, if not outstanding, hill-climber, helping Porsche to collect the mountain title in 1964. Still, even with a Type 771 eight, it would be no match for the Ferrari in 1965, at least in its rather heavy coupe form. Piëch's mandate then was to create a lightweight open-topped version, a goal tailor-made for him since, from the first, he has always been passionate about reducing unwanted pounds. The result of Piëch's efforts was the creation of five mountain, or *bergspyders*, collectively nicknamed "Kangaroos." The first

example, 906-007, featured the simplest—and the ugliest—body ever produced by Porsche. More-over, unlike the coupe shell, the body of 007 contributed nothing toward chassis stiffness, thus making the open-topped machine a truly poor handling flexible flyer. Such was the nature of 007 that even the factory's Jo Bonnier, who often displayed too much courage and too little common sense, refused to drive it at the 1965 Targa Florio.

Despite this, Davis and Gerhard Mitter gave 007 a good run in the Sicilian affair, overcoming its flaws to place second overall. The dune buggy-like spyder next appeared at the Nürburgring, where Mitter crashed it in practice. When 007 was subsequently rebuilt, Piëch's engineers took the opportunity to add a stiffening tube to the frame structure

The original Kangaroo was built by Dr. Ferdinand Piëch and his engineers in an attempt to produce a light weight Spyder from the relatively heavy 904 coupe. Using the 904 standard frame and drivetrain, Piëch and his people produced what must be Porsche's ugliest race car ever. The original Kangaroo is seen here on its way to the 1965 Targa Florio, where it finished second to a Ferrari P2. *Porsche Werk*

that not only increased its torsional rigidity, but also served as a pattern for the later examples of the 904 *Bergspyder* to follow. Initially, at least, other than use of needle bearings in their suspensions, these *Bergspyders*, like 007, were mechanically almost identical to the coupes. However, unlike the closed top 904s, they utilized both the six- and the eight-cylinder powerplants interchangeably. Moreover, the mechanical specs for the spyders were revised almost continually as Piëch's group sought to further improve their performance. Among things the hillclimbers acquired were larger rims, these growing from 15x6 inches at the front and 15x7 at the rear to 15x7 at the front and 15x9 at the rear. This, in turn, forced the addition of fender flares, which did little for their appearance, other than to cover their wider tires. Additionally, the Kangaroo fleet also acquired front and rear spoilers to improve their handling and grip.

Despite those efforts, the reconfigured 904 *bergspyders* would win only one hillclimb, that victory being garnered by Mitter in June at Rossfield.

In August 1965 Porsche, under Piëch's direction, constructed an all-new tube-framed spyder as a replacement to the Kangaroos. This car, which became known as the Ollon-Villars Spyder, featured the wheels, brakes and some suspension components from the Formula One Lotus 33. If Hollywood had provided a script, the Spyder would have won. However, a wrong tire choice saw it defeated in the event for which it was named. Success would have to wait until the following year. *Porsche Werk*

Due to rule changes, the Ollon-Villars Spyder was rebodied as a coupe for 1966, playing a major role in Gerhard Mitter's driver's championship. Mitter and the modified car also garnered the FIA Hillclimb manufacturer's honors for Zuffenhausen. *Porsche Werk*

The rest of the FIA mountain series fell to Ferrari. Still, Mitter took one of the Kangaroos to an unexpected triumph at the Solitude road race during the first part of August. That was it for the 904. By the end of 1965, the 904 Sspyders had disappeared, sold off with sixes installed to the privateers, who used them in a variety of events for a number of years.

Their fate had been sealed in July when Piëch, tired of their failure to stop Ferrari, had decided to build a completely new car. This was to be a full-tube frame machine featuring a state-of-the-art Formula One-like suspension design. Constructed

in just three weeks, using rims and other suspension components purchased from the Lotus Formula One team at the German Grand Prix, the car, 906-0010, was dubbed the Ollon-Villars spyder after its first event at the end of August. Although it didn't win there, it would go on to reclaim the mountain crown for Porsche the following season. However, its real importance rested not so much with its record of success, but rather in the role it played as the progenitor for a new era of Porsche racers that would lead the factory to the summit of the sport in less than five years.

The Ollon Villars Spyder uncovered. The Type 771 flat-eight engine nestles neatly within the frame structure, while the 13-inch Lotus rims and Dunlop tires lend an air of modern styling not seen on other Porsche racers of the time.
Porsche Werk

5

From the 906 to the 908

For Zuffenhausen, the early to mid-1960s was a turbulent period, marked by the introduction the 911 and the arrival of the often-controversial Ferdinand Piëch as the chief of its research and development department. Two years before he assumed his position, the company had introduced what may be the most beautiful competition Porsche ever built—the 904. Piëch had moved quickly in 1965 to put his own stamp on things by replacing the 904. And, in fact, he had some excellent arguments to support his position, because for all of its visual beauty, the 904 was not the most efficient motorsport vehicle.

In addition to its new model development, Porsche spent much time testing its current breed of cars. Here, the 906 is being examined during one of the engineering test sessions late in the spring of 1966 to check out new developments, such as the additional fuel injection and slightly different brakes. *Porsche Werk*

The 906 was unusual in its design when it came to its doors, which were hinged from the top rather than the front. This gullwing arrangement hadn't been seen on a race car since the famed Mercedes 300SL coupes of the early 1950s. The 906 also featured a fairly high fender line, a result of using the suspension pieces built for the canceled second run of 904s, complete with that car's 15-inch rims. Porsche factory 906s ran with varying drivetrains during their careers. Some remained in standard trim, while others featured fuel injection systems, and still others had the Type 771 flat-eight engine. From the outside, however, there were few visual differences that would mark them as factory prototypes, rather than approved production vehicles. The 906 made its debut in the 1966 Daytona 24-Hour endurance event. Even though the car had to run as a prototype, it brought Porsche success right off the bat, winning the small-displacement prototype division in the hands of Hans Herrmann and Herbert Linge. This would be the first of many such triumphs for the car, whose factory career would unusually span a season and a half, at a time when most Porsche racers lasted less than a year as front-line entries. *Porsche Werk*

Among the 904's problems was a lack of uniformity in weight, a difficulty resulting from the methods used in its construction. Unlike previous competition-oriented Porsches, the 904 eschewed the company's traditional tube-frame structure for a pressed steel chassis to which its fiberglass body was bonded, forming a single integrated unit. Because the resin for the body was pressure induced into the fiberglass, the amount of resin varied from car to car. With that variance came an inconsistency not only in the overall weight of the structure but, because the body was an integral part of that structure, in its torsional rigidity as well. Further, it was difficult to check or repair corrosion damage to the frame (not to mention accident-related kinks).

During the summer of 1965, Piëch began to truly make his mark when he decided to build a completely new spyder to combat the Ferrari 166 on the hillclimbing front. This turned out to be the famed Ollon-Villars tube framer with Lotus suspension components. It first ran that August after a three-week start-to-finish gestation period. The Ollon-Villars car is important because it is

Porsche began experimenting with longer-tailed cars at Le Mans in 1966, using a pair of 906s as rolling test beds. Equipped with fuel injection, these proved quite potent, winning their division. Future developments of the long-tail concept would result in a number of other successful models, including the 917, the 936, and the 956-962s. *Porsche Werke*

generally considered to be the progenitor for the first of a new generation of Porsche prototypes, the 906.

The advantages to replacing the 904 with the 906, from Piëch's viewpoint, were simple: with a tube frame, the exterior skin need not contribute to the car's rigidity, thus allowing the fiberglass to be much thinner. Further, although a pressed-steel chassis might be cheaper for a large run of vehicles, the new FIA regulations for 1966 had cut the figures needed to approve the 906 as a production vehicle from the 100 examples used in the days of the 904 to 50. At that figure, there was little to choose from costwise between a tube frame and a pressed steel design.

What the Ollon-Villars exercise did was to allow Piëch and his engineers to try out their concept of what the new 906 ought to be before actually having to begin the development of its design layout. In this sense, the hillclimb spyder performed a function similar to that of Boeing's Dash-80, often referred to as the prototype 707. Truthfully, the Dash-80 was a proof-of-concept vehicle with a great deal of similarity to the airplane it spawned, just as the Ollon-Villars spyder was in relation to the 906.

In brief, what Porsche's engineers knew from the start was that they would use the 911 boxer six as the main powerplant for the 906. Not only was the engine ready, but it also made an excellent promotional tie-in between the racer and the 911 street car.

Porsche had already worked on a competition version of the 911 powerplant, running it in the 904 during the 1965 season. During the career of the 904, as well as the 906, Porsche also used the 2.0-liter Type 771 flat eight-cylinder in some of the cars—a practice it would continue with the 906's successor, the 910, before it made the 2.2-liter version of the Type 771 the standard engine for the 907 in 1967–1968.

The changes to the 911 six were minimal, consisting of a different cam producing more valve overlap; forged pistons, which raised the compression ratio; larger valves (45 millimeters for the 906 versus 42 millimeters for the 911 on the intake side, 39 millimeters versus 38 millimeters for the exhaust); and a tuned exhaust system. Additionally, the 906's engine had a magnesium crankcase as well as titanium connecting rods and bolts. One other major departure from standard was the use of a twin-plug ignition system.

As used in the 906, the T-type 906 breathed through a pair of triple-choke Weber 461DA3C carburetors, giving the standard 906 approximately 210 horsepower at 8,000 rpm with a maximum torque figure of 146 ft-lb at 6,000 rpm. The Porsche engineers, also anxious to develop a mechanical injection system for the soon-to-be-announced 911S, used a Bosch mechanically injected setup on certain of its factory-entered 906s, running these as prototypes along with their Type 771 eight-cylinder-powered counterparts. The 906's five-speed gearbox was essentially the same one employed by both the 904 and

911. There were, however, differing ratios available to suit local conditions wherever the 906 was run and, as in the 904, the ring and pinion were reversed to let the unit sit behind instead of ahead of the engine.

If the drive train was a known quantity when the engineers started out, the rest of the car was much less so. While, as previously noted, Porsche's 550 and 718 spyders had been constructed around tube-frame structures, the chassis for the 906 was quite different, even though similar in basic design technique. What Piëch was striving for was a stiffer, lower vehicle with better drag figures than the 904. In terms of layout, this was partially achieved by storing the fuel in a pair of side or pannier tanks containing a total of 100 liters of fuel, these being mounted as low as possible in the frame structure.

As for the tube frame itself, that did in fact take its cue from the Ollon-Villars spyder with the exception that, unlike the hillclimb vehicle that had a 93.-inch wheelbase, the 906's was set at 90.6 inches, the same as that for the 904. Initially, the new 906 displayed a distressing lack of torsional stiffness, something cured by the addition of a pyramid structure at the rear, along with a removable diagonal brace at the top of the engine bay area. Ultimately the 906's tube frame, without any extra stiffening from the body, was marginally better in terms of torsional rigidity than the 904 with its combined body/frame platform.

Also retained from the 904 were the 15-inch diameter steel/alloy rims (although these were increased to 7 inches in width at the front and 9 at the rear). Likewise, the 906 used the 904's solid cast-iron disc brake with ATE calipers. Indeed, nearly all of the 904's front and rear wishbone suspension layout, complete with the 904's coilover Bilstein spring/shock absorber units on each corner, was kept for the 906. This was not what Piëch wanted, since it did not permit the use of the more modern 13-inch diameter wheel and suspension technology first seen on the Ollon-Villars machine. Piëch, however, was forced to accept this compromise by his Uncle Ferry, whose thoughts on seeing his son's 904 superseded by the 906 aren't fully known. However, his insistence that the extra suspension bits created for the aborted follow-on run of 904s canceled by Piëch be utilized in the new coupe was quite public. (Piëch did get what he wanted in the 910 that appeared first as a hillclimb vehicle in the latter part of 1966, that car using the 13-inch rim technology originally intended for the 906.)

Because of the added rim width, the track of the 906 came out to 52.7 inches at the front and 55.2 inches at the back. This represented a 1-inch increase forward and a 3-inch increase at the rear, compared to the figures for the 904. It also didn't do anything for the frontal area, which was now larger than the 904's and thus didn't help reduce the drag numbers either (the overall width of the 906 was 66.1 inches, some 5.5 inches more than the 904).

The design of the 906's body produced a much more chunky shape than that of its predecessor.

Succeeding the 906 was the 910, a virtually identical car but using 13- instead of 15-inch-diameter rims; this allowed a reduction in the height of the fender lines, producing a similar reduction in frontal area. The car, even though destined for circuit racing, was introduced late in the 1966 FIA Hillclimb Championship for testing purposes. The smooth lines of the 910 can be seen here. Ferdinand Piëch had always intended that his plastic tube-framed racers would use the more modern 13-inch rims employed in Formula One. But not until the 910 was he able to put that idea into practice. Ironically, because of its increased track width, the 910 would show little aerodynamic improvement over its 15-inch-wheeled predecessor, the 906. In profile the resemblance between the 910 and the 906 is clearly evident. Indeed the mechanical changes to the car were quite few, other than slight modifications to the frame to accommodate the modified suspension and smaller diameter wheels. The 910 would enjoy a number of successes during its brief stay on center court, including winning the Nürburgring 1,000-kilometer event outright in 1967. Its service as a factory entry would last less than a year before it was replaced by the 907. *Porsche Werk*

Still, despite a drop in esthetics, the 906 was the progenitor for the body designs that followed on through the 917. Unhappily, this was a time when the overall knowledge about aerodynamics was not nearly as great as it would become a decade later. The result was that the 906 as originally conceived, without spoilers, had a shape that created lift rather than downforce. Eventually a full-width rear-deck spoiler would be added along with trim tabs at the front to produce a fairly neutral handling vehicle that could be driven relatively quickly under almost all circumstances. Just how quickly can be seen in the 906's record during 1966, when it was employed as Porsche's front-line racing vehicle.

Barely had the first 906 been completed before it was shipped to Daytona for that year's 24-hour enduro (the first time the Daytona race had been run to that length). Driven by Herrmann and Linge, the new 906 topped the 2-liter displacement prototype category in which it had been placed until sufficient numbers had been built to qualify it as a production sports car. At Sebring, Herrmann, partnered by American Joe Buzzetta and Gerhard Mitter, again won in a 906. Up until this point, Porsche had used nothing but the standard Weber-equipped 906. For the Targa Florio, however, the factory brought two of its injection-fed cars along with a Type 771 906. In the end, however, it was the standard 906 driven by Belgium's Willi

The Porsche 910, like its predecessors, was a top contender at the Targa Florio. The car also achieved similar status at other events, including Le Mans, to such an extent that Porsche in 1967 came within a point of defeating Ferrari for the overall FIA World Manufacturers Title. *Porsche Werk*

Mairesse and Herbert Müller of Switzerland that emerged the outright victor.

Porsche was far less successful at the Nürburgring, where it entered five 906s: three injected sixes, one eight-cylinder, and one standard six. By the finish, accident and mechanically related woes had eliminated the 906s as contenders, leaving a Ferrari 206 Dino (a modernized, slightly larger displacement version of the previous year's hillclimb spyder) as the class winner.

Le Mans, up next, as always was a focus of attention for Porsche, and here, two weeks after the Nürburgring, Porsche had something special for the opposition in the form of three 906 longtails, all using injected engines. The idea of increasing the body length was based on a desire to decrease the turbulence and thus the drag of the vehicle by prolonging the point where the air separated from the rear of the car. This in turn produced a greater top speed along the 3.5-mile long Mulsanne straight, something which Porsche felt would reduce the lap times of the

906 while maintaining acceptable handling over the rest of the course.

In the coming years Porsche would expend considerable effort to refine this technique, eventually producing vehicles with more than adequate handling, that could at the same time achieve speeds of up to 250 miles per hour on the Mulsanne. However, it was a quest that, while ultimately successful, was filled with many wrong turns for the engineers and much danger for the drivers.

Of the five factory 906 Le Mans entries, four finished with virtually no problem. The long-tail example of Jo Siffert and Colin Davis took fourth overall, the Index of Performance trophy and the victory in the 2-liter prototype division. Only the top three 7-liter Fords, with more than double the Porsche's horsepower, were better. Adding to all of this were Gunther Klass and Rolf Stommelen, whose Weber-equipped short-tail 906 won the 2-liter production sports car category.

Admittedly, Ferrari, the chief rival for both Porsche and Ford, had problems due to labor strife

in Italy, which prevented the proper preparation of its vehicles. Also admittedly, there was rain for much of the time, something that lessened the stresses on the competing cars, and therefore increased durability. Nevertheless Porsche's success at the Sarthe in 1966 with its 906s was an achievement to be remembered.

Later in August at Hockenheirn, a local event but one very important to Porsche, Mitter led a one-through-three sweep of the overall standings in what was the last "official" appearance for the 906. So fast was the development of the 910, the follow-on car for 1967, that it was already running and winning in the hillclimb arena. Thus, even though it was at the top of its form, the 906 was "old hat" as far as Piëch was concerned. Happily, the 906, one of the last Porsches to be sold "new" to privateer teams, remained a formidable contender even in top endurance events for a number of years to come. (In 1967, despite the fact that it was no longer a lead entry for the factory, Porsche did enter a standard 906 for Ben Pon and Vic Elford at Le Mans, the pair using it to again claim the 2-liter sports car trophy for Zuffenhausen.)

In general, Piëch and his people were pleased with the 906. There was, however, the matter of its suspension. If Ferry Porsche thought in terms of bottom lines on profit and loss statements, Piëch's mind was far more occupied by pushing the barriers of technology forward. To him, the 906 was an unfortunate compromise, and in the early part of

1966 he set his engineers to correcting it. The result was the 910.

In many ways one could consider the 910 and its career accidental. Had not Ferry Porsche insisted on the use of the leftover 904 suspension components on the 906, it seems quite likely that car would have emerged looking very much like the 910, but carrying its 906 moniker. Had that been the case, most likely the 910 as a road race contender would have never existed, the engineers going directly from the 906 to the 907. Moreover, the 910, which followed the 906 into the 2-liter production sports car division, was never intended to fulfill that role. Rather, it had been conceived as a prototype, and even when the works cars were sold to Porsche customers at the end of the 1967 endurance season, the 910 maintained its prototype status.

Not until the spring of 1968, when the FIA again reduced the numbers needed to qualify for production-car status from 50 to 25, did that change. With Porsche's 1967-instituted policy of using only new cars for each major endurance event, no fewer than 28 910s had been constructed during that year. Thus, the prototype was transformed into a de facto production racer—not because of any planning on Porsche's part, but because of outside circumstances.

Indeed, the 910, unlike the 906, was not originally built to be sold at all. Rather, it was designed exclusively as a factory entry. The decision to use only new cars for major races, however, ensured what turned out to be a substantial run of 910s. Since it was not company policy to let investment in these vehicles go to waste, their eventual sale was almost certainly assured from the start.

In terms of its specifications, the 910 followed the engineering principles set down with the Ollon-Villars spyder and the subsequent 906s. The frame for the 910 followed the pattern of the 906, which, given the previously noted satisfaction with that element of the Carrera 6, was no great surprise. As expected, the primary differences

While Porsche was busy developing the 910 and the 907 during the 1967 season, it also produced a series of specialized 910 hillclimb spyders. These were powered by the now traditional Type 771 flat eight-cylinder and featured minimal bodies and equipment. The 910 hillclimb cars were among the first to employ a suspension-actuated rear spoiler. This design technology would find its way onto the long-tail 908 coupes and later the initial 917s. It was intended to increase rear end downforce, and thus traction, in a hillclimb setting, but it became crucial to total car control on the 908 and 917. One of the more successful of the hillclimb drivers was Rolf Stommelen, shown here at the Gaisberg Hillclimb in 1967. *Porsche Werk*

As finally developed, in 1968 the Porsche 910 hillclimber was an extraordinary vehicle, weighing just over a half-ton ready to race. Everything that could be lightened or removed from the car was. Note the minimal rocker panels on this example, as well as the suspension-activated rear spoiler. Such was the weight of these vehicles that Porsche had to construct a new car, the 909, moving the driver and engine forward to distribute the weight properly and achieve adequate grip at the front. *Porsche Werk*

came in the area of its suspension, which consisted of unequal-length wishbones and progressive rate coilover spring/shock units whose geometry was such that the outside wheels in a corner maintaining a neutral camber angle, creating a maximum amount of grip.

The standard 90.6-inch Porsche wheelbase was retained, while the front track was initially set at 1,430 millimeters (later being increased to 1,462 millimeters with the 13th chassis constructed), this being the same as the Ollon-Villars car and a 92-millimeter increase over that of the 906. At the rear, the track was reduced 1 millimeter from the 1,402 millimeters of the Carrera 6 to 1,401. The design weight the 910 met was 575 kilograms (1,268 pounds), this rising to 600 kilograms (1,323 pounds) when it was run with the 2.2-liter Type 771 eight in long distance events, beginning with the Targa Florio in 1967.

As previously noted, the 910 first appeared for the final two hillclimb rounds of 1966. Unlike the lightweight, mountain-dedicated 910s that would be used the following two summers, the initial pair of 910s built, 001 and 002, were fully representative of the breed that would carry Porsche's name in the World Championship of Makes for most of 1967.

In part, this was because of a change in the FIA's hillclimb regulations demanding coupe bodies and full-sized windshields. Thus, the shape

that would characterize the 910 was seen early when Gerhard Mitter used 910-002, powered by a Type 771 unit, to win the Schauinsland round of the mountain series, an effort that brought him the title honors as well.

Even though the new 910 was an obvious contender, the short-term circumstances of hillclimbing in no way matched the rigors of long-distance competition—the arena for which Zuffenhausen's new creation was ultimately intended. Thus, after the conclusion of the mountain tour, 002 joined 001 in an extensive early winter development program.

For this, the 2-liter boxer eights were removed, replaced by fuel-injected 901/21 flat sixes with which the 910 would begin the 1967 Makes campaign. As might be expected, a number of minor problems cropped up, especially in the area of frame strength. Although Porsche had increased the torsional rigidity of the 910 over the 906, its wider track resulted in about the same deflection numbers as its predecessor. In spite of the problems, the engineers had little difficulty in fixing the tubes that broke, as well as the other minor defects that came to light.

Also explored, but without the use of the wind tunnel, were the 910's aerodynamics. The car's lap times ultimately determined its shape. Designed from the outset with a removable roof, the 910 was tried in open and closed forms. Also used during the development period was a rear window similar to that of the 906's. Eventually it was determined that the 910 was quickest with the roof but without the window—the way it was to be raced most of its career. Tall drivers such as Udo Schutz, who essentially looked over the 910's windshield, raced it in open topped form.

Surprisingly, even though one might have expected better drag figures for the 910 in light of its much lower fender line, its added width compared to that of the 906 gave it similar drag statistics. In fact, at the 1967 Daytona 24-Hour season-opener, a not-quite-up-to-snuff six left 910-003 1/10 of a second slower in qualifying than the quickest of the two factory 906s in attendance. Nevertheless, when the flag came down to end the affair, Hans Herrmann and Jo Siffert found themselves first in the 2-liter prototype category and, perhaps more importantly, fourth overall behind three Ferraris.

The next time out was the 12-Hour at Sebring, where the Fords, which had failed so miserably at Daytona with a spate of transmission woes, took the first two spots. Here, the 910 of Mitter and American Scooter Patrick, which had grabbed the 2-liter lead early on, finished third overall.

At this point, with two good showings and with Ford and Ferrari having split the championship honors, Porsche was a surprising contender not just for division honors but for the overall Makes crown as well. Meanwhile, at Monza there was more of the same, as Mitter and Jochen Rindt took third, with Herrmann and Siffert finishing fifth to the Ferrari contingent.

The real break for Porsche came at Spa. There, local hero Jacky Ickx piloted his modified John Wyer Gulf Ford GT-40 to the win over Siffert and Herrmann's 910. Had the victory been recorded for Ford, things might have been different. However, since the victorious car was officially listed as a Gulf Mirage, the FIA refused to award the points to Dearborn, giving them instead to a somewhat embarrassed Wyer, thereby improving Porsche's own title hopes.

Things got even more interesting at the next two events, the first of which was the Targa Florio. Here, Porsche entered six 910s, three of the traditional six-cylinders and three with 2.2-liter eights. In the end, Porsche finished one through three

with the 2.2-liter of Paul Hawkins and Rolf Stommelen leading the parade. At the Nürburgring, which followed, the six-cylinder 910 of Schutz and U.S. resident Joe Buzzetta garnered the victory.

Le Mans saw the introduction of the 910's successor, the 907, fitted for the only time in its history with a six instead of the 771 eight. This was a Ford-Ferrari show, however, with the Americans beating the Italians, while the 907 took fifth and a 910 sixth. After that, there was the 41-mile mountain course that constituted the circuit of the July Mugello affair, won by Mitter and Schutz with Stommelen and Jochen Neerpasch second, both in 910/8s.

That brought Porsche and Ferrari to Brands Hatch with the overall title in the balance. Whichever make finished in front of the other would take the crown. For the occasion, Ferrari hired Scotsman and future World Champion Jackie Stewart. Although Stewart's P4 V-12 was defeated by the Chaparral of Phil Hill, it did claim second and came home ahead of third-place finishers Siffert and Bruce McLaren in a 910/8. Thus

When first tested at Hockenheim during the winter of 1967, the long-tail 907 was an extremely clean car devoid of scoops, spoilers, and the like. However, despite its low drag numbers, it proved nearly impossible to drive. Thus, it acquired a rear end spoiler and ducting to cool its transmission and brakes. Porsche introduced its new long-tail 907 model at Le Mans in 1967. The car featured an aerodynamically wind tunnel-tested body shell, but was otherwise similar to the 910 in its mechanical specifications. At Le Mans this car won its class. *Porsche Werk*

Porsche, which had a lock on the 2-liter crown, lost to Ferrari by a single point for the overall honors. It was a disappointment, but Porsche's time would come just two years later.

With the 907 in the wings, and with the long-distance season over, the 910s, most of which had done but a single event, were refurbished, fitted with six-cylinder engines and sold to privateers. For many years thereafter, 910s could be seen in a host of endurance venues, as they provided good value for the money to their new owners. Still, the 910's career as a factory racer wasn't quite over, as it would resume its duties as Porsche's mountain representative.

Even though by now, Porsche had not only proved all that it could in hillclimbing, the fact that the mountain series allowed Piëch to pursue his dietary loss exercises meant that Porsche wasn't through with this upwardly mobile form of competition. For 1967 Piëch had four special 910 chassis constructed. Three, 910-030 through 910-032, appear to be fairly straightforward, if specially lightened, variants of their 771-engined circuit racing counterparts. Unfortunately, given the pace of activity, a number of the details surrounding these vehicles have been lost in the less than totally complete records that remain at the factory.

Perhaps one of the more interesting mysteries is the material used for their tube frames. According to most major Porsche historians, they were steel. Yet the sole remaining hillclimb 910-031 is listed by Porsche as having an aluminum chassis. Whatever the confusion, there are a number of known facts about these three cars.

In their hillclimb trim they featured tissue-thin spyder bodies with doors and a low plexiglass windscreen. They had small, 3.2-gallon fuel tanks, and transaxles that featured Guibo flexible rubber joints in place of the more normal universal-jointed halfshafts. Titanium stub axles were employed as well. All were fitted with 2-liter 771 flat eights using fuel injection, but without oil coolers for their dry sump systems. Through the first two events at Montseny and Rossfeld, the cars were left otherwise standard, running the same brakes and wheels as found on other 910s. In all, the trio at this point weighed in at around 1,100 pounds each, about 220 pounds less than the standard coupes.

After Le Mans, Piëch gave the go-ahead to further reduce the poundage—provided the cost didn't exceed $30 a pound. One immediate result was the use of beryllium brakes on 032, which Mitter ran at Mont Ventoux after his regular car, 031, was damaged in practice. That affair, however, went to Rolf Stommelen in 030, with Mitter taking second. At Trento-Bondone, both had their normal spyders back, although the cars were now using special lightweight wheels. Mitter emerged the victor, as he did at Cesana-Sestrière and Freiburg (where Stommelen had 032—both cars having their original cast-iron brakes reinstalled).

For Ollon-Villars, Mitter had a new hillclimb 910. This was chassis 910-025, allegedly raced at the Targa Florio and Mugello, where it had won both times. The problem was that 025 had been a full-fledged steel chassis coupe for those affairs. Now, at Ollon-Villars, it boasted of an aluminum tube frame and was in complete *bergspyder* open cockpit trim. In fact, it had a few new weight-saving measures of its own, such as a smaller 2.2-gallon oil tank for the dry sump system, the extensive use of magnesium castings in place of the previously employed aluminum ones, and new titanium screws and nuts where possible. As with the other hillclimbers, a new body with reduced sides was used.

These measures brought 025's weight down to 925 pounds. (In contrast, 030 tipped the scales at 1,002 pounds.) Handling difficulties now began to reappear as the weight distribution moved more and more toward the rear of the car, forcing some fairly drastic changes in the suspension settings in order to cope. Mitter used 025 to win at Ollon-Villars, while Stommelen took it to the victory at the Gaisberg season finale. The result left both men with four wins and three seconds, although Mitter claimed the title on the basis of his third at Rossfeld.

Piëch retained 025 for 1968, but renumbered it 033, replacing the rest of the *bergspyder* fleet with a pair of new aluminum chassis spyders, 034 and 035. All three featured changes based on the lessons learned the previous year. While the rear suspension remained much as it had been (except for the use of titanium springs), Z-shaped torsion bars replaced the front coil springs, and an antisway bar was used to control roll resistance. At the rear of the body, Porsche had added the same movable, suspension-activated flap arrangement seen later on the long-tail 908 coupes, and later still on the early 917s. This was supposed to provide downforce without affecting straightline speed.

Another weight-reducing measure was the elimination of the alternator, as Porsche discovered the battery would survive one run without recharging (the batteries being changed between heats). Surprisingly, some of the more exotic lightweight materials were discarded in favor of less expensive alloys. Reportedly this was done with a view toward developing these pieces for Porsche's street cars, although one suspects this was more a lip service designed to appease Dr. Porsche, who was becoming alarmed about the costs involved with Piëch's motorsports efforts.

By the end of the 1968 season, the 910 hillclimb spyders weighed an average of just over 900 pounds. Unfortunately, even with perfect suspension setups they were still quite tricky to drive, a fact made tragically clear at Rossfeld, where Stommelen was seriously hurt in 033, and Scarfiotti, who had just come over to Porsche, was killed in

The ultimate Porsche hillclimb car was the Type 909. The major difference between this car and its predecessors was the fact that the driver and engine were moved as far forward as possible to create better balance and grip. The driver's legs would hang over the car's front axle line. The Type 909 formed the basis for the 908/3 Spyder, which would first appear in the Targa Florio of 1971. *Porsche Werk*

035. While 035 was a total loss, both Stommelen and 033 were seen again. Fortunately, Mitter was undeterred by all of this, winning every event he entered to claim his third consecutive (and last) mountain title.

Aware of the weight distribution problems (only 300 of those 900 pounds rested on the front wheels), the engineers created a new hill-climber whose principle change was to move the driver forward, so that he sat partially ahead of the front axle line. The weight distribution was also helped by putting the five-speed gearbox between the engine and the differential instead of hanging it out back. Called the 909, the new car, which used 12x13 rear rims and 8x13 rims at the front, also had a special pressurized fuel injection system when it appeared at Gaisberg. Stommelen used 909-002 to finish second behind Mitter, who drove his usual 910 after refusing 909-001.

While Mitter had no problems, Stommelen suffered from fuel injection woes that left him with a severely underpowered engine. He was second again at the season finale in Mont Ventoux. There he drove 909-001, now fitted with a standard injection set up. Once more, Mitter was first, using the 910. Its record aside, the 909 should not be dismissed, since its configuration was the foundation not only for the 908/03 but the 936 and 956, which followed.

While the 910 was enjoying the center stage spotlight on the endurance scene in the spring of 1967, its successor, the 907, was getting ready to make its entrance at Le Mans. The Le Mans cars would be long-tails, whose shape would be applied virtually unchanged through the subsequent 908 and early 917 models. It and its short-tail counterpart, unlike the 910, benefited from wind tunnel testing. Despite this, the short-tail 907s didn't look much different from the 910. They were, however, much lighter.

Although the layout, frame, and running gear of the 910 were carried over, there were some changes in the mechanicals of the 907, dictated by the need to save weight and retain its aerodynamic integrity. One of these, suggested by development engineer Peter Falk, was the reduction in the angle between the lower front wishbone and the combined coilover spring and shock unit. By so doing, Porsche was able to reduce the

The Hans Herrmann, Jo Siffert long-tail 907 was the meat in a one-two-three Porsche sweep of the 1968 Daytona 24-Hour long-distance event. Leading the way up front was Britisher Vic Elford, who just days earlier had won a very different affair, handing Porsche its first victory in the Monte Carlo Rally. The 907s would form the basis for their successors, the 908s, whose only difference would be a new, more simplified 3-liter, eight-cylinder powerplant. *Porsche Werk*

number of actual coils in the spring without affecting the spring rate, thus saving some badly needed pounds. The second was the use of ventilated discs for the front brakes. With four instead of two surfaces available for cooling, there was no need for ducts to bring air to the front brake assemblies, which helped to keep the outside air flow over the body smooth and drag-free.

In sum, the statistics for the 1967 Le Mans 907 showed it with the standard 2,300-millimeter wheelbase, with a front track of 1,462 millimeters and a rear track of 1,403 millimeters. Overall length was 4,839 millimeters, while the overall width was 1,720 millimeters. The weight was about 370 kilograms (1,477 pounds). Interestingly, while the 907 was always designed to take the Type 771 eight in its ultimate 2.2-liter form, for Le Mans the two cars prepared (907-003 and 907-004) were powered by the injected 911 boxer six-cylinder, 004's induction system having the new space cam metering design, which substantially increased its fuel economy.

While 003, with Gerhard Mitter and Jochen Rindt aboard, retired with an overrevved engine, 004, in the hands of Jo Siffert and Hans Herrmann, took a fifth overall and first in the Index of Performance as well as a victory in the 2-liter prototype division. It was a stunning justification for Piëch's decision to develop the car, particularly

since the 910 had been a winner as late as the Nürburgring event two weeks earlier and would continue to be a contender well into the prime of the 907's life. That fact was demonstrated clearly in the final Makes round at Brands Hatch. There, not only was an eight-cylinder 907 (007) entered for Herrmann and Jochen Neerpasch, but a 910 with Siffert and Bruce McLaren also started.

For 1968, things were to be quite different. After the 1967 Le Mans race, the FIA decided hurriedly to change the rules to exclude the big Fords and Ferraris and limit the prototype division to a maximum displacement of 3 liters (which happened to be the size of the V-12s being raced by the French Matras). Because of the short notice, 5-liter "production" sports cars were allowed to take part as field fillers. Eventually, Porsche and Ferrari would use this loophole to totally frustrate the FIA by manufacturing the 917 and 512 models in the proper quantities. That, though, would come later.

At the beginning of 1968, it was the 907's turn on center stage. Its stay, though, was to be short, since Piëch had decided to build a full 3-liter car, the 908, for introduction late in the spring prior to Le Mans. Knowing that the car was coming, Piëch's engineers reworked the 907 so that when the 3-liter flat eight was ready, all that would have to be done was to drop it in the 907's

chassis, thus creating the "new" 908. While the engineers worked on the new powerplant over the winter months, the rest of Piëch's people were preparing the 907 for its 1968 duties.

Among those revisions was the shape of the windshield where it met the roof, the windshield being cut down and the roof extended forward into what was to become the configuration used through the 917 era. Additionally, the oil cooler was moved from its position in the front deck lid to the nose for better efficiency (this allowed for the anticipated expansion of the cooler's size for the 3-liter eight).

Other than the windshield change and the relocation of the oil cooler, the long-tail 907 remained unchanged from the previous year (although it would grow rear fins by the time the postponed Le Mans 24-hour race took place in September). The short-tail coupe had a slightly different rear deck configuration, adapted from the 910 and designed so that it could be swapped for its longer cousin without any changes to the rest of the 907's bodywork.

With Porsche beginning to experiment with the use of aluminum as a frame material, one 907

chassis (907-011) was built with the lighter weight metal. The aluminum-chassised car was part of a Porsche 907 one-two-three sweep of the opening round of the Manufacturers series. Leading the way was the steelframed entry of Elford and Neerpasch. However, in an unusual show of graciousness, team manager von Hanstein put Siffert, Herrmann, and Rolf Stommelen in the coupe as well so they could also claim a share of the victory. Of interest was the now standard "line abreast" finish. One man not sharing in the glory was Mitter, who had flipped coming off the banking at 150 miles per hour after a slow leak caused a tire to go flat.

Next came Sebring, where Siffert, again partnered by Herrmann, took the win, their short-tail 907 being followed home by the similar Neerpasch/Elford example. Brake problems delayed the 907 contingent at Brands Hatch, handing the honors to the Gulf Ford GT-40 of Jacky Ickx and Brian Redman. Brands Hatch was followed by the Targa Florio, where Elford and Maglioli brought their 907 coupe home first in what turned out to be the type's factory swan song. Starting with the next event, the Nürburgring 1000-kilometer race,

Porsche used the extra time after the 1968 Le Mans race was delayed from June to September to further develop the 908. The long-tail version was virtually identical to its 907 predecessor. The main difference between the two was the suspension-activated wing mounted between the side fins that had been added to the 907 in the spring of 1968. The 908 gained added stability with its new wing/spoiler setup, but not so much that it couldn't be driven with the airfoil locked in a single position, when ordered to do so by the FIA at Le Mans in 1969. *Porsche Werk*

the Porsche banner would be carried by the 3-liter 908.

Unfortunately, the relative simplicity of the new 3-liter engine was no guarantee of reliability, for while the 908 won twice (including in its debut appearance), it was far from race-ready. There would be a number of changes to the engine, as Piëch's group struggled to cure the bugs. Not until the following year would the 908 become the contender Zuffenhausen had hoped it would be.

Because of this, when the postponed Le Mans 24-Hours got under way in September, the 907 was present as a back-up to its newer sibling, even though the three 2.2-liter cars on the grounds were technically entered by private teams. Mechanical ills took their toll on the 908 Porsche camp, allowing the John Wyer-entered GT-40 to claim the race and the title. Second, however, went to the 907 of Dieter Spoerry and Rico Steinemarm in what would be the latter's last event before taking over as Porsche team manager from von Hanstein. While they missed the overall triumph, the pair was credited with the win in the prototype category.

For a number of years thereafter, the 907 continued to be raced by private teams as a class contender as well as an occasional hillclimber. Surprisingly, it was competitive, winning its category at Le Mans as late as 1971.

Turning to the 908, its story as noted is one of obvious logical, progressive development, from the 907. Initially, there was little performance difference between the 907's Type 771 engine and its 3-liter successor. Instead, the real advantage was the fact that since the 908 unit was designed to form the potential basis for a future production engine, it was tremendously simplified compared to the 771. Where it took an average of 225 man-hours to put together a Type 771, only 25 were needed to assemble the 908 boxer eight.

Designed by Hans Mezger and his team, the 908 3-liter dispensed with the 771's all-gear-driven accessory system, using a chain drive for the double overhead cams, and belts for such things as the alternator. That cam drive arrangement saw power taken off the crankshaft through an intermediate shaft to the cams themselves. At the 1969 Daytona 24-Hour enduro, Porsche tried a lightened intermediate shaft that had not been adequately tested and broke during the race itself, allowing the Lola-Chevrolet T70 Mark III coupe of Mark Donohue and Chuck Parsons to take the victory.

In terms of dimensions, Mezger initially conceived a dry-sump unit with an 84-millimeter bore and 66-millimeter stroke, which used aluminum cylinders with chrome-plated bores, titanium connecting rods, a magnesium crankcase and two-valve

The 908 finally came right in the spring of 1969, scoring an impressive victory in the Targa Florio. The car now was bodied as a Spyder, which saved considerable weight over the coupes of the previous year. This was possible because of FIA regulation changes that essentially did away with weight limits. With the spyder came a change in designation, the car being known as a 908/2. *Porsche Werk*

cylinder heads (this latter feature again in keeping with the idea of the engine forming the basis for a future production unit). The compression ratio was 10.4:1, while the valves were set at an included angle of 71 degrees to get enough space for the necessary cooling passages in the heads, the intake being 47.5 millimeters in diameter and the exhaust 40.5 millimeters. Feeding fuel to the cylinders was a Bosch mechanical injection unit.

The 908 eight-cylinder was slightly larger in terms of overall dimensions than its predecessor, which meant that the driver's compartment bulkhead of the 907 chassis had to be moved forward slightly on the passenger's side to allow the new unit to clear. Additionally, the pannier fuel tanks were moved forward as well. Overall, the

908 engine was only 40 pounds heavier than its predecessor, achieved through the careful attention to weight-saving measures. In terms of power output, Mezger's newest creation pumped out a healthy, if not overwhelming, 320 horsepower at 8,500 rpm when first run on the dyno.

By the time it was tested at Monza in the early spring of 1968, this had been increased to 335 horsepower and would eventually rise to a solid 350 horsepower. This latter increase came during the summer of that year when Mezger decided to increase the bore to 85 millimeters, thus increasing the displacement from 2,926 to 2,996 cc.

While it actually took only four months for the 908 to go from paper to the dyno, it took

another four months before it was ready for racing. Moreover, throughout its first year, the engine produced an excessive amount of vibration, causing a number of accessory failures (largely centered around the alternator), which led to numerous retirements during that period.

To cure the problem the engineers tried a number of things, the first of which was to change the firing order. Where the 771 had a 1-7-2-8-5-3-6-4 order, the 908 began life with a 1-8-2-6-4-5-3-7 order that allowed each cylinder bank to be treated as a separate four-cylinder engine for exhaust system purposes. Unfortunately, with the twin-plane crankshaft design, the secondary forces were multiplied instead of canceled out, resulting in a very rough-running unit. By late spring, the order had been revised to 1-5-2-7-4-8-3-6 in an attempt to reduce the problem. Later other changes to the belt drives and even the mounting brackets (the alternators having a rubber cushion inserted between the engine and the bracket) were tried with some limited success to keep the cars running.

By the beginning of 1969 the engineers had come up with a more permanent solution, in the form of a flat crank in which the secondary forces were canceled out and the firing order returned to the sequence used in the 771 powerplant. Tested during the first months of 1969, this revised boxer eight was first used at Sebring that season where it acquitted itself well, even if the car did not.

The failure at that event, which we will cover later, was due primarily to frames that were too light to take the pounding handed out by the rough Sebring course. On balance though, it must be said that Piëch's attention to weight-saving often gave Porsche the edge against its rivals.

One example of just how far Porsche was prepared to go in this area concerned the gearboxes used by the early 908s during 1968. Given the extra horsepower and torque of the 908 eight, Zuffenhausen decided not to use the five-speed transaxle employed by the 907 for the Type 771 engine, but rather a new six-speed unit thought to be more durable. The problem with the six-speed was that while it did its job admirably, it was, at least as far as Porsche was concerned, vastly overweight. In fact, according to Porsche's calculations, the gearbox put the 908 some 44 pounds above the minimum throughout the season. When they got the chance over the winter of 1968–1969, the engineers took the opportunity to create the Type 916 transaxle, which reverted back to five forward speeds. (The 916 designation used for the 20 or so limited edition 914 models was a marketing title, not a design type number.)

With all this focus on weight saving, it is ironic that initially the 908 coupes were constructed using steel tube frames, the first aluminum chassis being 908-012. Still, with everything that was happening during that period, it is easy to see why some things took just a little longer than others. The aluminum cars were ready at the end of the summer of 1968 for the postponed Le Mans race, which was, in reality, less than five months after the 908's in the spring.

For the most part, Porsche had earned a well-deserved reputation for quickly being able to turn its newly minted debutantes into race-winning contenders, particularly during Piëch's reign. Such was not the case with the 908 (nor in fact with the subsequent 917), which took the better part of a year to sort out. The heart of the problem so obviously centered on the new eight-cylinder. One has to wonder why it took the engineers so long to come up with the final revised crank. Still, the overall pace of development was frenzied to say the least. Beyond this, in the 908, Porsche was beginning to explore areas of performance and speed that not only they, but most of the automotive community, had not explored before.

Porsche began testing the 908 in the spring of 1968 at the Nürburgring, Monza, and Le Mans trials before entering two cars along with the usual 907s at the Italian track for the 1,000-kilometer race in April. In addition to a number of electrical problems caused by the heavy engine vibrations, other stability, suspension, and throttle-related difficulties emerged with the new cars, most of which were attended to with a fair amount of success. At Monza, however, the vibration problems caused one of the two 908s entered to retire with a broken alternator, while the other, piloted by Siffert and Herrmann, finished 19th. The 907s also had problems at Monza, leaving the win to John Wyer's Ford GT-40 team. However, at the Nürburgring in May, the 908's more-than-26-percent horsepower advantage was finally harnessed enough not only to make it slightly quicker than the 907, but enough for its first triumph with Siffert and Vic Elford at the controls.

Although Siffert went on to win the Austrian GP and also take a third at Spa with the 908, the mechanical problems continued. Fortunately for Porsche, political troubles in France forced the postponement of Le Mans, leaving more time for the development, which was clearly needed. At Watkins Glen all the 908s, with the exception of Siffert and Herrmann, who was sixth, again retired. This time the culprit was a series of wheel bearing failures due to lubrication difficulties, which were subsequently corrected. Wheel bearings, however, would continue to be a source of problems during 1969.

By the late summer of 1968, the 908s had been considerably refined, now featuring aerodynamic movable rear spoilers, 15-inch diameter wheels (at least in short-tail form) and, starting with 908-012, an aluminum tube frame that brought the weight of the car, despite the "heavy" gearbox, down under 1,500 pounds. One interesting point concerned rear spoilers, which were attached to the suspension itself through a system of rods, the suspension's travel activating the system. Originally, the 908 had presented a "clean" appearance without the devices. When the engineers added the aerofoil units, they fully expected the drag factor of 0.345 to increase. Instead, it remained exactly the same, the spoilers actually smoothing the air flow over the rear of the car.

For Le Mans, there were four aluminum-framed 908s (013 to 016) entered. All the 908s had the then-latest engines with revised firing order and 85-millimeter cylinders. With their long tails and extra equipment, the 908s weighed 50 kilograms over the minimum for the 3-liter prototype classification. After 24 hours of racing, Neerpasch and Stommelen brought their 908L home third behind the winning Wyer Gulf GT-40 and one of the "private" 907s, the 908 suffering three broken cooling blower belts along the way. The rest of the other 908s retired, ending their races in the paddock for a variety of reasons, ranging from a broken gearbox casing to alternator failures. It was, perhaps, not exactly how Piëch and company would have liked to end the official season, for not only did Porsche lose Le Mans, but also the coveted Manufacturers title, which went to the aging GT-40s of the Gulf team. Some honor was salvaged, however, at the subsequent nonchampionship Monthléry 1,000 Kilometers just outside Paris, where Herrmann and Stommelen were first with their short-tail 908 entry.

For 1969 the rulesmakers, recognizing that the 5-liter sports cars such as the GT-40s had an unforeseen edge in performance, revised the regulations concerning the 3-liter prototypes, eliminating minimum weights as well as such equipment as the spare tire and luggage containers (boxes supposedly capable of carrying one's theoretical bags should one, for any reason, be crazy enough to have them in such a vehicle). Porsche's designers went back to work.

While Mezger and the engine department were working on the new flat crank, the chassis and body groups were reviewing their areas. The result was to leave the 908 long-tail coupes largely as they were at the end of 1968, but to scrap the short-tail closed versions in favor of an open spyder configuration which we will look at in a

moment. The first test for Porsche in the new year, however, came at Daytona, where all five long-tails retired with the previously noted intermediate shaft failure (this after suffering earlier exhaust system problems). Had not the engines expired, Porsche would have scored an easy triumph at the North Florida speedway, the final car out having an hour and a half lead over its nearest rival at the time it withdrew from the event.

If Daytona was unpleasant, Sebring wasn't much better. For the central Florida airport enduro, five of the new spyders were entered. Although they had much higher drag figures than their long-tail counterparts, their light weight (just over 1,300 pounds) made them very competitive. All were fitted with the new flat-crank engines using the latest firing order, and all had the new, lighter weight Type 916 five-speed transaxle.

What Porsche had apparently forgotten about Sebring was the roughness of the crumbling circuit, and that was to prove to be the team's undoing. When designing the new spyder frames, the engineers had decided to eliminate the rear pyramid structure as a weight-saving measure since the open-at-the-rear fiberglass body didn't need it for support. The result was a host of chassis breakages and another Gulf Ford GT-40 victory. Of the five 908s, American Buzzetta, partnered by Stommelen, was third, the highest placed of the three cars that finished. It was, again, not the most pleasant time for Porsche.

Moreover, it was during this period in 1969 that Zuffenhausen was struggling to complete the 25 917s necessary for the homologation permits that would allow them to run in the sports car category starting at the Spa race, only weeks away. Despite having to ready the 917s, the engineers revised the aluminum frames once more, restoring the rear pyramid structure. With this latest revision, the 908 finally reached maturity, a fact dramatically shown by the 1-2-3 win (led by Siffert and Brian Redman) at Brands Hatch, the next event on the 1969 Manufacturers schedule. That triumph was the first of a string for the 908/02s, as the spyders were known, and the 908L coupes—victories that would include Monza, the Targa Florio, Spa, and the Nürburgring. At that latter event, a new body shape was approved for the spyder, which was flatter and smoother than its predecessor. Even so, spyders with Siffert and Redman again driving, eventually won. In the new incarnation, the plastic windscreen was eliminated and, all in all, the car looked quite sleek. Unfortunately, its improved aerodynamic drag did little for its handling characteristics. Two of the new cars were destroyed at the Ring, while the third, in the hands of Herrmann and Stommelen, was second. After spoilers were added, the handling was improved greatly, making the "flounder" a formidable contender.

At Le Mans, though, three of the four primary Porsche entries were long-tail coupes. The fourth

The Flounder had the fender lines raised so that it ran virtually flat throughout to the rear tail section, as was the custom with the then-current crop of American Can-Am racers. By raising the center section, the Porsche factory substantially increased down-force and grip over the 908/2. These lines were replicated in the 917 PA spyders, making the 917 an aerodynamically passable vehicle.
Leonard Turner

908 for Siffert and Redman was an experimental "flounder" spyder with slightly extended and enclosed tail, which would retire due to gearbox overheating. The story of this event is well known, as two of the 908 coupes and both of the 917s entered, then retired, leaving Herrmann and Gérard Larrousse to defend the company's honor against the Gulf GT-40 of Jackie Oliver and Jacky Ickx.

Unfortunately, the Herrmann/Larrousse 908L had its own problems, being delayed when a wheel bearing failure forced the replacement of an entire front upright. With Herrmann piloting the car in the final stages, the brakes became suspect (indeed, the pad warning light was on for most of his final stint). Meanwhile with Ickx behind the wheel of Wyer's 910 the scene was set for the dramatic conclusion. On the final lap, the two swapped the lead back and forth a number of times before the Ford crossed the finish line, a mere 100 yards or so ahead of the 908. Despite losing Le Mans, Porsche had secured its first Makes title with its spring winning streak, something that took away much of the pain from the defeat at the Sarthe.

Later that summer, Siffert and Redman led another 1-2-3 sweep at Watkins Glen, the last major event the 908 was to win in 1969 (the later Austrian GP going to the 917). With the conclusion of the 1969 campaign, Porsche as a factory officially bowed out of racing, selling off its 908s and turning over its competition program to the Wyer and Salzburg teams for 1970 (this latter being owned by the Piëch family, making its "private" status somewhat suspect). Still, anyone who thought Porsche had retired from motorsports was greatly mistaken, as Piëch's engineers continued their work at the same speed-driven pace. Likewise, those who thought the 908 saga had come to its conclusion were similarly wrong, as the 908 line was actually just about to get its second wind, one that would last for more than a decade, long after the departure of Piëch's influence on Porsche's racing effort.

In fact, in the normal course of events, the 1969 season would have been the last for the 908 as a front-line factory car for Porsche. However, this was a different kind of era, when a number of varying avenues toward a single goal were examined and pursued. In evaluating the 917 it was determined that two events on the 1970 calendar posed a problem for the powerful, relatively heavy machine: the open-road Targa Florio, and the winding, 14-mile Nürburgring circuit. From Piëch's viewpoint what was needed

For the Targa Florio and Nürburgring rounds of the 1970 FIA Manufacturers Series, Porsche produced the 908/3 Spyder. This lightweight, squared-off vehicle was based on the 909 hillclimber, with the driver moved so far forward that his feet overhung the front axle. Claiming the win at the 1970 Targa Florio was Jo Siffert, whose entry is seen here behind its Porsche factory counterpart. For this race, the 908/3s utilized 13-inch-diameter rear rims. These were discarded for the next event at the Nürburgring in favor of 15-inch rims, which became standard for the rest of the car's factory career. *Porsche Werk*

to win in each of these venues was maneuverability, not raw horsepower.

Interestingly, such a car existed, or almost so, in the form of the 908/69 project. This was an attempt to produce a new ultralightweight version of the 908, which subsequently was shelved after the company decided that the 908/02s could achieve the goals set for Porsche's motorsport program. Based on the very lightweight 1968 909 2-liter hillclimb spyder, the 908/69 spyder had an all-new aluminum frame, which, like the layout of the 909, moved the engine forward far enough to place the driver almost over the front axle assembly. In fact, with a revised suspension, the gearbox placed between the flat 908 powerplant and the differential, and a totally new body, there wasn't much left over from the 908 design except for its powerplant and its numerical designation.

Given all the circumstances during 1969 in trying to sort out both the original 908 and the new 917 at virtually the same time, it was not surprising that the 908/69 program languished as a potential plan of attack while those other more pressing matters were attended to. But in the summer of 1969, the decision was made to take the 908/69 out and use it for the Targa and Nürburgring the following spring.

By that fall the first of two development cars was completed with the second coming together around the first of the year. After further work, particularly in the area of its aerodynamics, the design was finalized and seven "production" cars constructed. When it emerged into the public light, the new two-seater carried a markedly different body shape than its predecessors and a new designation, 908/03. Where previous 908s tended to be curvaceous, the 908/03 featured a blunt nose and a flat upper body, all intended to reduce drag and generate increased downforce. At 1,200 pounds, the 908/03 Spyder was the lightest 908 yet. The engine remained the same as the previous season except that the cooling blower assembly had a fluid coupling to reduce the strain on the V-belt drive. The previous 2,300-millimeter wheelbase was also retained.

At the Targa, four 908/3s were entered, three under Wyer's Gulf banner, and one for Porsche Salzburg. In the end the work was justified, Siffert and Redman winning handily after their Ferrari opposition dropped out. Adding to the factory's joy, Pedro Rodríguez and Leo Kinnunen came home second, while Dick Attwood and Björn Waldegaard were fifth.

At the Targa, 13-inch diameter rims were used all around, however, for the Nürburgring, the rears were replaced with 15x15-inchers. There Elford, now partnered by Kurt Ahrens, got his revenge and the victory, while Attwood and Herrmann finished second. Siffert and Redman went out with an engine failure, while Rodríguez crashed during a battle for the lead. After this race the cars were stored by Porsche, their tasks having been completed.

With the start of the 1971 season, Piëch decided to use their stored 908/03s once more for the Targa and the Nürburgring. While the cars were gathering dust, Porsche had started work on a four-valve, water-cooled-head version of the 908 boxer eight, primarily with the idea of contesting the "3-liter-only" World Makes title chase scheduled to come into effect in 1972. To this purpose, a fully functioning engine was constructed before the project was dropped because of the company's commitment to its 917 Turbo Can-Am program, and because the rulesmakers had placed a 650-kilogram (1,433-pound) minimum weight restriction on the sports racers for the new Manufacturers tour.

Thus, when the 908/03s emerged from their hibernation for the 1971 Targa and Nürburgring affairs, they were little changed. Among the minor differences were a front splitter to further reduce airflow-induced drag under the car, large side fins (similar to those fitted to the 917s), a heavier roll bar, and an improved on-board fire extinguisher system. The drivetrain components remained the same, although for the Nürburgring the width of the rear rims was increased from 17 inches to take advantage of the new tire technology available in that size.

At the Targa, the fortunes of the 908/03 brigade were terrible. All three spyders entered (two for the Gulf organization, one for Martini) retired. The Siffert/Bell and Rodríguez/Müller Gulf Porsches went out because of accidents; the Elford/Larrousse car failed because of suspension damage caused by two blown tires while contesting first place.

For the Nürburgring, Porsche built two new chassis, entrusting them to the Wyer crew. Unfortunately, the outside supplier that actually welded them together, failed to follow the blueprints accurately, causing both to suffer cracked frames. One piloted by Siffert and Derek Bell was forced to retire. The other, which was started by Rodríguez and Jackie Oliver and now in the hands of Siffert, just managed to hold off the older 908/03 Martini

example for second. Taking first place was the Martini entry of Elford and Larrousse, which ran without problems.

After the Ring, the factory wasted little time in selling its 908/03 fleet off. However, if anyone believed these vehicles would fade into some sort of sunset under their new owners, they were wrong, as the cars raced and won through the remainder of the decade into the 1980s.

Interestingly, despite the lack of power, the chassis had aged well. Thus, while many at Porsche were uncertain, enough insiders agreed that when Jöst and some others came asking for the 2.1-liter, turbo six-cylinder that had powered the experimental RSRs of 1974, they were sold to them at just over $36,000 each.

There were three cars converted in this way for the 1975 season: one from Jöst, one from the Spanish team (which accomplished virtually nothing with it), and a third purchased from the Porsche museum by Dr. Herman Dannsberger for his newly formed Martini operation that had Herbert Müller as its driver. All three were reno-vated by the factory's sport department and all

featured revised bodywork which included a modified version of the 917/10 Can-Am tail sec-tion. Among the three, there were differences in air intake locations to accommodate the inter-cooler, but these had relatively little effect on their overall aerodynamics.

Although the Martini entry was usually the quickest, it was also plagued throughout the year with engine and transaxle problems. Nevertheless, Müller was able win the European version of the Can-Am, the Inteserie, with it in 1975.

Jöst, on the other hand, with Casoni as his codriver, was second at Monza and Dijon, and was then fourth at Le Mans, having added Jürgen Barth as a third driver. There, he substituted the original nonturbo eight-cylinder for its boosted six-cylinder replacement, as well as a 917/30 tail (minus the wing). Additionally, Jöst's car, again fit-ted with the turbo and 917/10 tail, came in fourth at the Osterreichring and at Watkins Glen.

For 1976, when the prototype arena was divided into the production-based Group 5 classi-fication that ran for the Makes championship, and the full-blown, custom-built Group 6 sports racers,

In its final factory form, the 908/3 may have lacked outright horsepower, its 3-liter flat eight producing no more than 360 horsepower. However, the car's nimble handling made up for the deficiency, and even though it squared off against more powerful automobiles, in the end it proved successful, winning the Nürburgring for the second year in a row. In later years, after the 908/3s were sold to Porsche customers, they would acquire turbocharged six-cylinder engines and more elaborate deck lids that included full-width wings and spoilers. *Porsche Werk*

which competed for their own World Sports Car crown, Jöst once more reworked his 908/03. This time it had the same turbo-six as the new 936 factory cars, as well as a new nose, which resembled that of the factory prototype and a full 917/30 tail, including its wing. Using this car, Jöst scored the first Group 6 win ever when he finished first at the Nürburgring, after the factory 936 and the French Renaults all dropped out (the 936 with throttle cable problems, and the French cars following a fratricidal accident on the opening lap).

For the next several seasons, that win was to be the highlight of the revived 908/03's career, as sports car prototype racing wound down to just a single "outlaw" event, the Le Mans 24-hour classic, which was not a part of any championship. Then in 1979, after officials realized they needed something to spur interest in their sagging Group 5 series and allowed Group 6 cars to compete (although not for points), interest in the 908s increased once again. This time, the aging 908 emerged with another new body, whose tail combined the 917/10 wing with the engine cover of the 936. Additionally, the refurbished cars also had the latest twin-turbo flat-sixes and a new designation: 908/04.

Jöst, who was a leader among the 908 proponents, had an outstanding if somewhat shortened season, entering four races and winning two:

Dijon's 1,000 kilometer (with Volkert Merl and Hans Ketterer) and the Brands Hatch six-hour (with Merl). In 1980 the Jöst 908/04, with Rolf Stommelen and Barth as drivers, again triumphed at the Nürburgring, the last-ever win for a 908 (although Merl had some successes in the failing Interserie with the car).

The other campaigner of the 908/04 was Sigi Brun's team, which took its spyder, the ex-Spanish machine, to a third place at Silverstone in 1981. Unfortunately, only a few weeks later, the car was destroyed and Herbert Müller killed when he crashed and burned at the Nürburgring.

With the introduction of the new Group C cars in 1982, the long-winded 908s were finally headed into retirement. Their achievement, however, will always remain one of the most remarkable in the sport. Conceived in 1968, the 908 raced and won under not just a single set of rules, but under three different scriptures in international endurance competition. Moreover, its record in other venues such as the Can-Am and the Interserie have endowed this multifaceted design with the kind of reputation from which legends are carved. Designed, developed, and raced for the most part in the shadow of other supposedly more important and faster cars, the 908 survived to show just how far good, basic engineering can go in motorsport.

The Porsche 917

6

Whether Englishman Vic Elford was very brave or very foolish remains open to debate. Certainly in 1969 he was very determined. "The only car I wanted to drive at Le Mans that year was Porsche's then-new 917," noted Elford in a mid-1990s interview. "Helmuth Bott, the man immediately overseeing the 917 project, was much less enthusiastic. But in the end I was able to get my way."

Bott, working at the time under Piëch and later to replace him as head of research and development at Porsche, had good reason to be nervous. The 917, although using the proven building blocks of its successful predecessors, explored new and uncharted territory for Porsche. With nearly twice the horsepower and an estimated top speed of more than 230 miles per hour, there were serious problems to be sorted out, a fact of

---

The most famous photo ever taken of the Porsche 917 was this one of the 25 cars needed to qualify it as a 5-liter production sportscar lined up together in the factory courtyard during the spring of 1969. The nearly 600-horsepower endurance coupe was a bitter surprise to Porsche rivals, as well as the FIA, which never believed a company would complete 25 examples of a single model simply to qualify for the World Manufacturer's Series. But Porsche did, and the 917 became a legend. *Porsche Werk*

In the late summer of 1969, Porsche produced a special 917 Spyder for Jo Siffert to race in the North American Can-Am series. This car, 917-028, had a raised deck lid for improved downforce. Nevertheless it needed add-on spoilers front and rear to give it adequate grip. By the race at Riverside, Siffert's spyder had a new nose, much flatter in shape. Porsche hoped this would eliminate the need for the front trim tabs that were continually being ripped off in combat. Unfortunately, the nose still generated insufficient downforce, resulting in the addition of slightly smaller tabs that were still vulnerable to race-bred damage. In spite of a late start and his problems, Siffert still managed to finish fourth in the standings.
Porsche Werk

which Elford was well aware. "In truth," he confessed, "the handling wasn't all that one might have wished. Going through the kink on Le Mans' Mulsanne straight where you were at the limit, you had to be very gentle or otherwise the back end would start to steer the front. I think it is a measure of Porsche's engineering capabilities that the following year, in 1970, I was able to go flat out through that same kink—at night, in the rain."

The story of the 917's transformation, indeed, of its very existence, is filled with political intrigue, technical drama and, in the end, success in such measure that it changed forever the face of international motorsport.

The environment which the 917 would come to dominate was created on short notice in June 1967, just after Ford had won its second consecutive 24 Hours of Le Mans. Then, as now, the importance of the Sarthe event transcends the rest of the prototype sports car scene. Winning Le Mans is the summit. All the rest is merely part of the climb. For years, Le Mans had been the province of Europeans in general, and Italy's Ferrari in particular.

When Henry Ford II found he could not buy out Enzo Ferrari as a means of bolstering Dearborn's performance image, he decided he would beat him on Ferrari's own playing field—Le Mans. At first the European contingent scorned the simplistic nature of Ford's chosen weapon, the GT-40. When Ford steamrollered its way to victory at Le

Mans in 1966 and 1967 with its seven-liter versions of the car, that attitude changed to a fear that Europeans (especially the French) would be cut out of the glory that comes from winning the 24-hour classic. The FIA quickly decided in the wake of Ford's second Sarthe triumph to ban the unlimited prototype displacement regulations that had permitted the Fords to run in the first place.

The new formula, which was to take effect on January 1, 1968, capped the engine size at 3 liters. Realizing that the notice was extremely short, however, the FIA also allowed "production sports cars", whose displacement limit was set at 5 liters. These were to be drawn from the ranks of the small-block GT-40s and the Lola T-70 coupes, which had been produced in numbers exceeding 50 units each, and were intended to bolster the potentially slim starting grids.

However, the tail and not the animal quickly became dominant. John Wyer, the crafty ex-Aston Martin man who had played a key role in the development of the Ford, now brought forth two updated versions of the venerable GT-40 coupe and, with the backing of the Gulf Oil Company, proceeded not only to walk away with the Manufacturers' title, but Le Mans as well.

The shock was unpleasant, but nothing like what was to come. At the insistence of McLaren and Lola, the FIA decided to liberalize the rules for its Makes tour in the spring of 1968, the changes to take effect the following January. To stimulate the 3-liter corps, minimum weight scriptures were done away with and the bodywork regulations substantially relaxed. As for the 5-liter cars, the production numbers were cut in half from 50 to 25. It was a decision the FIA would come to regret.

Moreover, the source of that emotion came not from America, but rather from Zuffenhausen. With the 908's inaugural race more than a month away, the decision by the FIA in April 1968 to reduce the production requirements of the sports car category started the first stirrings that would come to be the 917.

At the time, there was some doubt about the feasibility of building a large-displacement air-cooled engine. This was of considerable importance to the West German government, which was interested in acquiring a new, air-cooled-engine battle tank. The primary source for this tank, as far as the government was concerned, was Porsche. There were, therefore, research funds available to investigate the needed powerplant technology. These were used to help create the 917's flat 12-cylinder engine, known officially as the Type 912.

The finalized shape of the 917 short-tail included raised rear fenders with a valley running down the centerline of the car. The only failure for Porsche's 917 during the 1970 and 1971 World Manufacturers Series came at Sebring in 1970, when both Gulf Wyer cars suffered front hub failures while leading. The Siffert/Redman entry shown here retired late in the race, while its sister limped to the finish behind Mario Andretti's winning Ferrari 512S. *Bill Oursler*

Often it is hard to pinpoint the key component of such a complex package as the 917. There is little doubt, however, that this 12-cylinder propulsion unit was the heart, if not the soul, of the 917. Developed by Hans Mezger's group, which was keenly conscious of the costs involved, the Type 912 was a blend of proven parts and new technology.

To keep the budget under control, it was decided to use the same head design for the 912 as had been employed in the 908. Still, Mezger did take the opportunity to reduce the included valve angle from 71 to 65 degrees in order to produce a more compact combustion chamber. Other than that, the 908's configuration design with its sodium-filled 47.5-millimeter intake and 40.5-millimeter exhaust valves was retained, along with the same basic fuel injection system. Also carried over were the 908's 85-millimeter bore and 66-millimeter stroke, giving the 12-cylinder an initial displacement of 4,494 cc, with the capability for further expansion.

If the upper end of the boxer 12 was familiar, the bottom was not. Worried about vibration problems, Mezger and his engineers not only paid careful attention to the placement of the eight main crankshaft bearings, but also came up with a central power take-off system that essentially divided the crank into two shafts. All the accessories, including the horizontal cooling fan, were driven off this center crankshaft gear arrangement. Unlike other aspects of the 917, the engine design proved to be nearly perfect from the start. Moreover, the decision not to go the full five-liter route also proved to be wise, the 912 producing a healthy 580 horsepower at 8,400 rpm and a stout 376 ft-lb of torque at 6,800 rpm in its initial 1969 race form.

Far less perfect were the 917's aerodynamics. For Porsche, the ultimate goal had been to reduce the drag coefficient of its cars, thus maximizing the limited power on hand. The idea was to give them a fighting chance against their rivals, almost all of whom were more amply endowed in the engine compartment area. A primary consideration in this equation was the creation of a vehicle able to run at the highest speed possible on the Mulsanne straight at Le Mans, since Zuffenhausen felt this was critical to achieving its ultimate goal of winning the Sarthe outright. Because of this,

Helmut Flegl, who was in charge of the 917's chassis, kept the same track dimensions (58.6 inches at the front and 57.2 inches at the rear), which were used by the less powerful 908.

As a result, the 917 was initially fitted with 15-inch diameter wheel rims, which were only 9 inches wide at the front and 12 inches at the rear, far narrower than they could have been. Further, the 908's 90.6-inch wheelbase was retained. The reason for this latter decision, according to Flegl, was weight. While a longer wheelbase might have been preferable from a handling viewpoint, Flegl felt it would have weakened the rigidity of the chassis. To bring back the rigidity, the engineers would have been forced to add extra frame tubes, increasing the weight and reducing overall performance.

For the 917, Porsche used as a basis the aluminum chassis and fiberglass body of the 908, the major change being the need to move the driver forward so that the pedals were ahead of the front axle line in order to accommodate the somewhat longer 12-cylinder engine. Fitted also to the 917 was the suspension-activated movable rear flap arrangement, first seen on the 908, that was designed to increase downforce. One other change to the body was the detachable rear section, which allowed the car to be run as a "short-tail" vehicle if conditions warranted it.

Completing the mechanical specifications were the 12-inch diameter ATE four-puck disc brakes, the coilover double wishbone suspension, and the Porsche-designed rear transaxle that could be used either in four- or five-speed form, both with the company's patented synchromesh system. The three-plate Fichtel and Sachs clutch used initially was later replaced by a Borg and Beck unit. Additionally, the upper front suspension wishbones were adjustable, while at the rear, both the upper and lower wishbones had this feature. The springs were titanium, while the shocks were of gas pressure design from Bilstein.

A 37-gallon tank was installed, as were adjustable sway bars. In all, the package, excluding fuel and oil for the engine's dry sump system, weighed in at 1,763 pounds. Given this figure and the 580 horses found in the engine bay, the 917 was awesome in a straight line. Unfortunately, it was far less so when it came to cornering. Indeed, its handling, although substantially improved over the years, was never spectacular, especially under braking where it had a tendency to wander.

If Elford wanted the 917, his countryman, Brian Redman, was far less convinced. He still remembers the time when Porsche called him at his Yorkshire home, asking if he could come to Germany to test the new car: "It occurred to me that there were a

The shape of the 917 short-tail as it finally evolved was aggressive yet somehow pleasing. This was one of the Porsche Salzburg cars run under the Porsche-plus-Audi banner at Sebring in 1970. It retired with engine problems after its sister entry failed to finish following a crash with Vic Elford at the wheel. Porsche Salzburg would only win once during the season with the 917. That triumph came at the most important race for Porsche, the Le Mans 24-Hours. *Bill Oursler*

Despite a coming together at the start, with teammates Jo Siffert and Brian Redman, Pedro Rodriguez and Leo Kinnunen posted an easy victory in the 1970 Watkins Glen six-hour enduro. Note the small rear wing added between the fenders to improve downforce. This solution was not employed by the rival Salzburg operation. *Bill Oursler*

In 1970, Porsche made severe modifications, intended only to be used at Le Mans, to the long-tail 917s. The new body shell had a permanent tail section. Except for its final paint scheme, this 1970 long-tail is all ready for Le Mans. While not perfect in terms of downforce and handling, the low-drag car was quick enough that it could be driven flat out at 240-plus miles per hour on the 3.5-mile Mulsanne Straight at night in the rain. Despite its potential, the best one of these cars could do was second place in 1970. *Porsche Werk*

In 1971 Pedro Rodriguez seemed set to contest for the victory at Sebring. However, the Mexican driver, in one of his lesser moments, came together with the Ferrari 512M of Mark Donohue and David Hobbs. The resulting carnage put both cars out of contention. The race went to Vic Elford and Gerrard Larrousse. *Bill Oursler*

number of drivers much closer to Zuffenhausen than me. So I telephoned my teammate Jo Siffert, who strongly suggested that we let someone else sort out the 917." At Belgium's Spa circuit several months later, Redman was forced by Bott to keep his date with the 917. Never considered safe, Spa that day was awash in rain, a fact that caused Redman to keep a low profile in the pits.

"I was doing my best there to be like the invisible man," recalled Redman, "when Herr Bott said I should drive the 917. Noting that since it was raining, I suggested postponing my taking the car out. Bott's reply, as I recall, was to 'drive slowly.' My confidence wasn't improved when I turned on the windshield wiper, and it flew off. Again I suggested that patience was a virtue and again Bott told me to 'drive slowly,' I believe that lap may have been one of the longest in Spa history."

Ultimately, Redman and the 917 would become a formidable combination, but that was much later, after a test in the fall of 1969 at Zeltweg where some distinctly ad hoc body modifications were made. In the spring, though, the story was quite different. Then the 917 was almost impossible to keep on the road. So bad was the car that none of the regular Porsche team members wanted to use it in a race. At the Nürburgring, which immediately preceded Le Mans, outsiders Frank Gardner and David Piper were drafted as its crew. Despite some anxious times, they kept the 917 out of the scenery to finish eighth.

It was not the kind of situation calculated to improve Porsche's image, particularly since it had gone to so much effort to get its super car into action. In a real sense, Porsche had sprung the 917 on the FIA. Not until the Geneva Auto Show in March 1969 did the rumors of the 917's existence turn to reality, when the company displayed the first complete example. The FIA never imagined that anyone would go to the trouble of actually building 25 race cars just to get a new design homologated as a "production sports car."

When the FIA realized that Porsche had done exactly that, it insisted Zuffenhausen adhere to the letter of the rules and actually assemble all 25 917s before it would give their blessing. Although it was a time-consuming process, Porsche pushed to complete the cars, not only producing the vehicles, but lining them up for the now famous courtyard photo used by so many in telling the 917's story.

That dramatic lineup at the factory courtyard on April 21, 1969, represented the beginning of a new era in motorsports. Just as Ettore Bugatti ruled the racing world in the 1920s and Mercedes in the 1930s, Porsche's big new racing coupe would usher in the Zuffenhausen epoch in sports car competition that now has continued so long.

Having met its requirement, the 917 received the sanctioning body's blessing in time for Spa on May 11, 1969. Because it was not ready for serious usage, Porsche continued to rely on the 908 as its primary tool in its quest for the Manufacturers' title. However, with Elford successfully lobbying for the 917's inclusion at Le Mans, some hurried modifications were made. Primarily these were confined to the front end geometry, where the aim was to substantially reduce its antidive properties.

Four 917s were prepared for the French classic, two for the factory (Rolf Stommelen and Kurt Ahrens in one, Elford and Dick Attwood in the other), one for privateer John Woolfe of England, and the fourth as a spare. As difficult as the 917's

position was at Le Mans, it got worse before the start, when officials insisted on the deactivation of the movable rear flaps.

Several weeks earlier, after a rash of wing failures in Formula One, the FIA had banned all movable aerodynamic devices, including those on the sports car scene. To convince the officials that the 917 was undriveable without the flaps, Stommelen was sent out in a lurid demonstration with the flaps set in a fixed position.

Afterward the authorities struck a compromise. The 917 could keep its flap mobility. In exchange, the 908s would lose theirs. Porsche accepted the decision, Stommelen proving the wisdom of the action by putting his 917 on the pole. Nine hours into the race, though, Stommelen and Ahrens were out with a broken clutch. Elford and Attwood fared somewhat better, the pair leading for a good portion of the event before a leaking oil seal did in their clutch as well, this coming at the 22-hour mark.

Sadly, the third 917 crashed on the first lap, when Woolfe lost control in the White House curves, subsequently succumbing to his injuries. (Woolfe's was the only death to be recorded during the 917's career. The Ferrari 512, the 917's main rival in 1970 and 1971, also listed a single driver fatality. Ironically, it involved Pedro Rodríguez, the famed Porsche pilot who was running Herbert Müller's 512M in a German Interserie event when he was killed.)

In August 1969, Ahrens and Siffert gave the 917 its first victory with their win at Austria's Osterreichring after Jacky Ickx's Cosworth V-8 Gulf Mirage broke. For Gulf team owner John Wyer, it was a unique occasion—the end of one era and the beginning of another. At Sebring the previous March, Wyer had been approached by new Porsche team manager Rico Steinemann about running Porsche's racing effort in 1970. That had come at the insistence of Ferry Porsche, who was worried about the amount of money Zuffenhausen was spending on its competition programs. Always

conscious of the profits and losses in the company's ledgers, Dr. Porsche was not happy with the ever-increasing resources being used by Piëch for racing. His solution was to find someone suitable who could help foot the bills and, at the same time, put Porsche at the forefront of the sport. With strong support from Gulf, and with a winning record (that would come to include that second Le Mans victory at Porsche's expense), Wyer's British-based team seemed perfect.

After lengthy negotiations, Wyer and Porsche came to terms on a two-year agreement, which ought to have made the Gulf organization Porsche's primary representative on the World Makes tour in 1970 and 1971. That it did not is part of the intrigue of the 917 program and the apparent clash of personalities between Wyer and Piëch.

As far as Piëch was concerned, Wyer was a far too independent individual. Used to having near-total control over motorsport, Piëch found it difficult to hand part of that responsibility over to the Englishman. Under the agreement Wyer would manage the actual operational side of things, while Piëch's engineers took care of the design and development aspects.

What Wyer desired was a car with which he could win. What he did not want was to be Piëch's experimental conduit. If Piëch decided to try

A near disaster occurred at Daytona in 1971, when Rodriguez brought his Gulf 917 into the pits with a broken transmission while in the lead. When the Mexican left more than an hour later, he found himself a lap behind the Ferrari 512S of Tony Adamowicz and Ronnie Bucknum. Rodriguez calmly ran the Ferrari down to score the win. However, the same transmission woes would again plague the Gulf team at Le Mans that June. *Porsche Werk*

The John Wyer Gulf team runs in formation at the beginning of the 1971 Sebring 12-Hour enduro. While Wyer had captured the win at the Florida long-distance affair in 1969 with a Ford GT-40, he was destined never to triumph there again. In 1970, his two 917s suffered hub problems, and in 1971, Pedro Rodriguez tangled with Mark Donohue and Jo Siffert was penalized for receiving outside assistance on the course. Both incidents in the 1971 race assured the team's final status as noncontenders. *Bill Oursler*

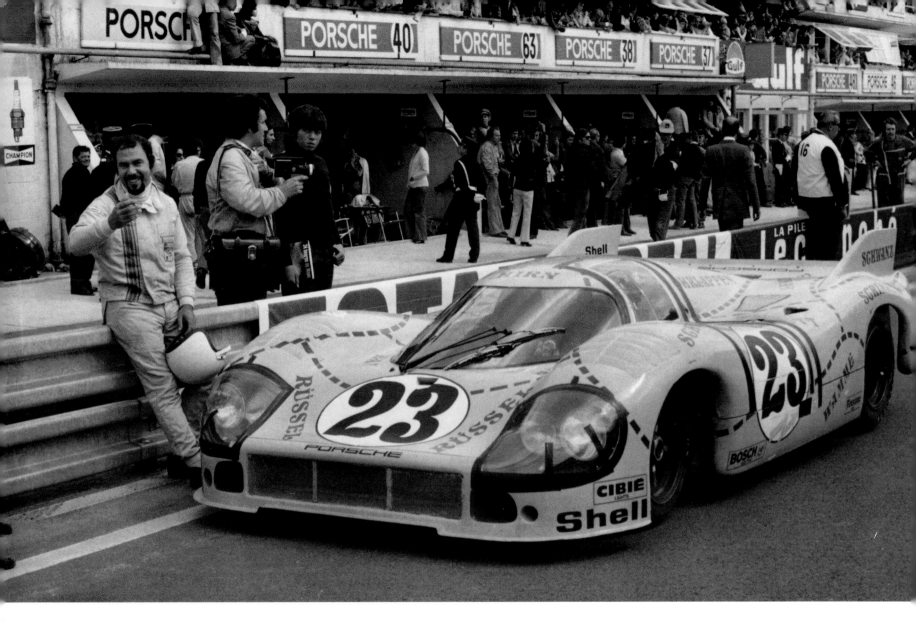

For the 1971 Le Mans race, Porsche created the unique 917/20, better known as the *Pink Pig*. This extremely noticeable car had an extrawide body in an attempt to marry the handling qualities of the 917 short-tail with the aerodynamic benefits of the 917 long-tails. Painted pink and decorated in the manner of butchers' cuts for pork, the car was less than successful, eventually crashing out of the event while driven by Reinhold Joest. *Porsche Werk*

something new, Wyer preferred that it be proven in testing first. On the other hand, Piëch saw clearly that the common ground between the two men was racing as an engineering exercise to prove new pieces.

There were further personality differences that increased the gulf between them as well. Still, it was Piëch's basic refusal to accept his uncle's dictum that Zuffenhausen leave the business of racing the company's products to others that soured his relationship with Wyer. Indeed, throughout the two-year association between Wyer and Porsche, Piëch not only introduced new parts and cars as he saw fit, but also, on occasions when he desired, raced them as well.

Beyond this, there was the back door or, in this case, the other side of the Porsche family. While no one knows who said what to whom, when the

1970 season began, Wyer found that Piëch's mother, Dr. Porsche's sister Louise, was going to field her own two-car 917 team. This would run under the banner of Porsche Salzburg, the importers for Porsche and Volkswagen in Austria, an enterprise jointly owned by the Piëch and Porsche families, but controlled by the Piëches.

During 1970 the Porsche Salzburg coupes were serviced by Porsche in its customer racing department, located at Werke 1. This technicality may have kept Porsche from breaching its contract with Wyer, but it did little for his humor, since he had believed he alone would be the factory's racing representative. The distinction concerning the privateer status of Porsche Salzburg was a fine one. Not only did Piëch use his mother's operation to try out new developments rejected by Wyer, but also, as previously noted, to race the special cars he wanted to control himself. Included in this latter category were the 1970 long-tail 917s designed for Le Mans that had proved to be so difficult to tame. The aerodynamic problems associated with these 917 *langhecks* were a continuation of those encountered with the first of the 1969 cars. Indeed, throughout the endurance phase of the 917's career, a battle between increasing downforce and reducing drag, not always mutually inclusive goals, was waged by the engineers.

On an overall basis, one can see a pattern during Piëch's tenure that tended to emphasize low drag numbers at the expense of downforce. Up through the 908, this was controllable, at least to the extent that the handling was acceptable. The 917, with its vastly increased performance, was another matter. Even though the 917 had been able to win in Austria, its handling remained problematic, a fact that was evident during the October 1969 test session at Zeltweg, where the Wyer group got its first chance to try out Porsche's coupe. On hand, in addition to the closed-top examples, was 917-027, the prototype Can-Am spyder. There have been any number of stories about how the coupe's aerodynamics were considerably improved during this test. Most, however, leave out the important part played in the equation by 917-027. Unlike the coupe, the origins of the spyders' body shape could be found in Tony Lapine's 908/02 "flounder" Spyder, from which its lines had been lifted almost intact.

Where the coupe's tail dropped down toward the rear, 027's rose slightly in a fashion not only common to its 908 brethren, but also to the then-current CanAm contingent. At Zeltweg, the differences in the lap times between the coupe and the Can-Am prototype were about four seconds. If Porsche's upper management had been there, things might have been different. As it was, Piëch stayed home, leaving Flegl and Peter Falk to represent the company, and that changed everyone's approach to improving the closed topped cars.

Deputizing for Wyer (who remained behind in England because of illness) were David Yorke and John Horseman. It was the latter who decided to examine the coupe more closely in light of the lap time differential between it and the spyder. He discovered that the air flow was separating from the rear of the coupe's deck lid when he noticed that the rear body was clear of the insect carcasses that covered the front of the 917. Also present was Wyer's (and later Ferrari's) master mechanic, Ermano Cuoghi, who with Peter Davies then went to work to raise the top of the tail.

Using bondo, screws, and aluminum sheeting, the pair turned the curves into a wedge. The result was a transformation in the handling and an improvement in lap times that made the coupe the equal of the Cam-Am sports racer. There is little doubt that both Falk and Flegl probably would have been more cautious in their approach than the irrepressible Cuoghi. But Piëch, who probably would have opposed making the modifications, was absent and Flegl and Falk didn't have the authority to stop the ad hoc alterations, those changes were made. Later, Piëch's engineers, with the help of wind tunnel data, further improved the body shape, creating the final "wedge" silhouette for which the 917 would become famous. Engine-wise, Porsche increased the stroke from 66mm to 70mm, creating the 4.9-liter version first seen at Monaco in 1970. Ultimately, the engineers enlarged the cylinder bores from 86.0 millimeters to 86.8 millimeters, bringing the displacement up to 4,998 cc. They also exchanged the Cromal cylinder lining material for a Nikasil alloy, a move that helped give the 5-liter powerplant another 30 horsepower and 15 ft-lb more torque. This final endurance variant produced 630 horsepower at 8,300 rpm and 427 ft-lb of torque at 6,400 rpm.

Other than a switch to Girling discs for the cars were run by Wyer, the 917 coupes underwent few other changes. Still, there were some aerodynamic modifications. Again these involved the tail section. During the course of 1970, Wyer, with the aid of the British aircraft industry, came up with a small winglet, which he mounted at the rear of the valley between the rear deck fenders. This

Porsche's 1971-winning 917 was a Martini entry driven by Dr. Helmut Marko and Gijls van Lennep. From the outside, the Martini Porsche looked normal. However, underneath it sported a lightweight magnesium frame similar to that which Porsche would use for Mark Donohue in the 1972 Can-Am series. When first tested Porsche was so worried about driver confidence that it told no one that it was using a car whose chassis was made from its lightweight material. *Porsche Werk*

allowed the two small lip spoilers on the tail to be run at a reduced angle, in turn decreasing the drag coefficient while maintaining most of the downforce. Until Porsche produced its own tail with a flatter wedge angle and huge side fins. As with the Wyer tail, it also reduced drag without any great sacrifice in downforce. With its aerodynamics finally set, the time had come for the 917 to turn hopes into reality. That would come in 1970 at the Daytona 24-Hour, where the 917's remarkable winning career would start.

Although the basics of the 917 may have been set by 1970, the intellectual curiosity of Piëch led to the exploration of two other areas of technology, which not only affected the 917, but also the future of the sport. The first of these was the development of the *langheck* body shape, while the second was the transformation of the endurance coupe into a Can-Am contender. Ever since the first long-tail Carrera 906 appeared at Le Mans in 1966, Porsche had been working on the development of this feature as a means of improving speed without degrading handling. It was a difficult task. One of the key figures in this exploration

was Norbert Singer, who would later gain fame with the 935 and the 956/962.

Over the winter of 1969–1970, Singer revised the shape of the original long-tail 917. The new design, with its larger side fins and longer nose, was visually attractive. However, it proved almost impossible to drive. In fact, during testing on Volkswagen's high-speed track, one car was totally destroyed and another badly damaged when they left the pavement and headed into the woods. By the time Le Mans arrived, Singer had made some further changes, adding a wing between the fins and getting rid of the plastic cover over the engine as well as making the shape of both the nose and tail slightly concave.

In terms of performance, the Porsche Salzburg example, with a 4.9-liter for Vic Elford and Kurt Ahrens, not only took the pole but also led occasionally until it retired with a broken valve spring. The other *langheck*, assigned to the new Martini and Rossi team, used a 4.5-liter engine. It came in second despite a persistent engine misfire in the hands of Larrousse and Willi Kausen.

While the long-tails were about two seconds

quicker on the Mulsanne than their short-tail cousins, they weren't consistently faster in their race lap times, a fact that seemed to justify John Wyer's decision not to accept them for the Gulf Porsche team. In the end, Porsche's first overall Le Mans victory went to the standard 4.5-liter 917-023 of Attwood and Herrmann from the Porsche Salzburg stable. Although not as quick as Wyer's short-tail entries, the car ran without problems, taking the lead when the Gulf 917s retired following a series of mechanical problems and accidents.

The *langhecks* were further revised for 1971, after a visit to the French aerodynamicists at SERA. These revisions included their partially covered rear wheel wells and their new nose sections, which now featured a front splitter. Again, the long-tails were quick, but not durable, all retiring in the race after leading. The improvements were such that this time Wyer included two on his team roster, the third going to the Martini camp.

There was one other unique 917 participant in 1971, the rather ugly *Pink Pig,* otherwise known as 917/20-001. While from the front it resembled the long-tails, it kept the short rear deck arrangement. What really set the Reinhold Jöst/Kausen coupe apart was its extra wide fenders, these giving the pink-painted machine a bloated, distinctly ugly look.

The intention was to see if the long-tail's aerodynamic advantages could be incorporated in a short-tail design by reducing air turbulence around the wheel well area. In reality, this did not prove to be the case of the race. Jöst crashed the car out of the race around the three-quarter mark, after a rather mediocre performance.

With the *langhecks* and the 917/20 on the sidelines, Porsche's second Le Mans win went to 917-053, driven by Helmut Marko and Gijs van Lennep. The standard-looking coupe (entered by the factory under Martini's name) had a definitely nonstandard magnesium frame, developed as a test prototype to see whether the knowledge gained could be used in Porsche's upcoming Can-Am program.

The idea of participating in the North American unlimited sports racing championship came from Volkswagen of America's Josef Hoppen, who wanted to publicize his company's newly established Porsche Audi Division. The result was the entry of 917-028, better known as the 917 PA spyder, for Siffert in the latter part of the 1969 Can-Am.

Although Siffert fared surprisingly well, it was clear that the spyder was not up to the task of beating the then dominant McLarens. Further, with all that was happening on the endurance

In the fall in 1971, driver Mark Donohue first tested the nonturbo-charged version of the 917/10 Can-Am Spyder he would drive the following year in the Can-Am series for Roger Penske with sponsorship from Liggett and Myers tobacco. The car was identical to one run by Jo Siffert in the 1971 Can-Am, with the exception of a revised nose section and a wing between the rear tail fins. Porsche would keep this car at its Weissach test center until it was sold to privateer Willie Kausen in 1972. *Porsche Werk*

A key figure in Porsche's early Can-Am efforts was Swiss Jo Siffert. In 1969 he finished fourth in a series with his 917 Spyder, despite starting the season late. In 1971 Siffert and his 917/10 opened-topped car also impressed the Porsche factory, again taking fourth in the points, this despite another late start and his tragic death before the end of the year. *Bill Oursler*

Jo Siffert introduced the 917/10 Can-Am car to the series at Watkins Glen. When it arrived at the track, the Porsche was painted white; by race day, however, it had been converted to the Day-Glo colors of the STP corporation from whom the Swiss had sought and got sponsorship backing. After Siffert's death, the car would be returned to Porsche and used by Willie Kausen in the European Interserie, painted in Bosch Yellow. *Bill Oursler*

front, Hoppen was unable to get Porsche interested in returning to the Can-Am for 1970. However, neither he nor Piëch forgot the SCCA's prestigious tour. In the spring of 1970 Hoppen opened a dialogue with Roger Penske. Meanwhile Piëch set his people to designing and building a 16-cylinder version of the Type 912 engine for possible use in the series.

Interest in the Can-Am picked up when the FIA announced it would ban the 5-liter cars. As far as the French-dominated FIA was concerned, the 917s and their Ferrari 512 counterparts not only violated the spirit of their intentions, they also eclipsed their 3-liter counterparts, including the Matras on which so much hope had been pinned.

If the FIA wanted the 917s out, the SCCA had no objection to them coming in. As far as it was concerned, the pushrod Detroit V-8s were more than equal to the task of keeping pure-blooded racing engines like the Type 912, that powered the 917 in the role of backmarkers. The SCCA was wrong. In fact, after Porsche took over as the dominant car in the Can-Am, the SCCA adopted a posture quite similar to that of the FIA. Instead of barring the Porsches outright, however, the SCCA chose the path of crippling them through fuel and restrictions that made them unable to compete with any hope of success.

Having made its decision to end the 917's international career, the FIA removed virtually all regulatory restrictions on the five-liter brigade for the 1971 season. This allowed Piëch to try out some of the technology he wanted to use in the forthcoming Can-Am campaign. The magnesium chassis of the 1971 Le Mans-winning 917-053 was part of that exercise. It is ironic that the only other use of the hard-to-deal-with material was in the chassis for 917/10-001 used in the first Can-Am of 1972 by Mark Donohue and subsequently destroyed two weeks later during a Road Atlanta testing mishap.

The form and the participants in Porsche's Can-Am adventure were determined both by decision and circumstance. While the 16-cylinder offered one possibility toward the improvement of the 917's North American competitiveness, the ultimate route chosen toward that goal was turbocharging the existing 12-cylinder. Development began under Mezger in the fall of 1970, with the first unit ready for installation in 917/10-001 by the late spring of the following year. It wasn't until April of 1972, however, that the bugs in the powerplant's injection system were eliminated, producing an awesome engine that would come to turn the Can-Am upside down. Later the technology would be used to turbocharge the 901 flat six,

creating the basic motor for the 934, 935, 936, 956/962, and 911GT1 competition models, as well as the 930 street turbo version of the 911, from which the 934 and 935 were derived.

Parallel with the engine work, Porsche was revising the 917's coupe chassis into the 917/10 spyder, the first two examples of which were on their wheels by June 1971. While 001 was kept as the test mule at the just-completed Weissach complex, 002, using a normally aspirated 5-liter motor, was handed over to Siffert to run in the Can-Am as a prelude to 1972.

By this time, the summer of 1971, Porsche and Hoppen had a fairly clear picture of who would be the factory representatives in the series. Although Wyer had sought to be among the finalists, in the end it was decided that Penske and Donohue would run one team, while Siffert would field a second. The death of the Swiss star at Brands

Hatch that October altered the plan. After much negotiation, Penske and Donohue became Porsche's only team, fully justifying that choice with two Can-Am titles. The second of these, earned in 1973, came with the extended wheelbase 917/30, which featured the largest 912 engine, a 5.4-liter unit with a 90.0-millimeter bore and 70.4-millimeter stroke, producing a consistent 1,100 horsepower and flash readings of up to 1,500 horsepower. During the initial tests of the 917/30, Donohue and Flegl then in charge of the Can-Am program, found that 917/30-001, was no faster in a straight line than the 917/10. Willing to accept less downforce, Donohue convinced Flegl to graft the tail of one of the Le Mans *langhecks* onto the back of the Can-Am spyder. This boosted its top speed over 240 miles per hour. Interestingly, variations of this tail stayed with Porsche through the 936 and 956/962 eras.

George Fullmer in the Penske L&M Porsche 917/10 Turbo leads Greg Young's blue McLaren MF at Watkins Glen in 1972. Although Fullmer didn't win at the Glen, he did go on to capture the Can-Am honors for himself and Porsche that year. Ironically, at the Glen, the official McLaren team garnered its last Can-Am win after having dominated the series since 1967.
Bill Oursler

The business end of the Penske L&M Porsche. With its deck lid removed, the complex turbo charging system fitted to the 5-liter 917 Type 912 12-cylinder can easily be seen. This version featured log manifolds and butterfly valves, an arrangement that was modified for 1973. During that latter season the 12-cylinder displacement would grow to 5.4-liters, giving flash readings of 1,500 horsepower on the dyno rather than the 1,100 seen with its 5-liter counterpart. *Bill Oursler*

As January 1970 approached, however, all this was in the future. For the present there was only the upcoming Daytona 24-Hour to be considered. Porsche had done a great deal of testing for the event with 917-011, the car that would become the Porsche Salzburg entry in the Florida affair. There were no major problems encountered, a good thing since Daytona would mark the debut of Ferrari's new 5-liter V-12 512.

Although potent, the record of the 512 was as dismal during 1970–1971 as the 917's was brilliant. In all, Ferrari won only one championship race, the 1970 Sebring 12-Hour, after the Gulf 917s came down with a rash of failures in their revised front hubs. Otherwise, the 917s totally dominated the season, with the exception of the Targa Florio and the Nürburgring affairs, where the 908/03s triumphed.

At Daytona, the first place laurels belonged to the Gulf Wyer pair of Rodríguez and Finland's Leo Kinnunen. Together they would also win at Brands Hatch, Monza, and Watkins Glen. Siffert and Redman would further add to the Wyer team's performance with firsts at Spa and the Osterreichring. In addition to these victories and the brilliant Porsche Salzburg triumph at Le Mans, Jürgen

Neuhaus used his standard 917 coupe to win the 1970 Interserie crown (the championship that would evolve the following year into the Can-Am's European counterpart).

If 1970 was relatively easy for Porsche, 1971 was somewhat less so, although the 917 again as the dominant car was at the season opener at Buenos Aires, Siffert and his new Gulf Wyer partner, Derek Bell, were the victors in a sad affair that saw the life of the talented Ferrari driver Ignazio Guiunti snuffed out in an unnecessary crash with one of the Matras. Then at Daytona, Rodríguez and his new Gulf teammate, Jackie Oliver, finished ahead of the field following a lengthy pitstop that saw their gearbox rebuilt in the final hours. Later the two would also win Monza and Spa, while Rodríguez, with Attwood as his partner, would take the honors at the Osterreichring, a week before his tragic death.

Meanwhile, at Sebring it was the turn of Elford and Larrousse in their Martini entry to enjoy the fruits of victory. With the 917 corps retiring at Brands Hatch, the win there went to Alfa Romeo, a performance the Italians would repeat at Watkins Glen. Once more the 917s stayed away from the Targa and the Nürburgring, reappearing

at Le Mans for their second straight Sarthe triumph. On the Interserie front, Kinnunen used a modified version of the 917 PA Spyder to win the first of his three Interserie titles (the last two with a 917/10).

Müller, in whose Ferrari Rodríguez perished, gave the 917 one final moment of glory when he collected the 1974 Interserie crown with Donohue's adjustable wheelbase 917/30-001 test mule, now set to 917/10 specs. In 1975 Miffler again won the Interserie, using his 908/03 Spyder for the majority of the events. Tim Schenken added, however, a postscript to the 917's saga that season by scoring several victories with his Georg Loos 917/10.

In North America, Porsche's Can-Am efforts became serious with the agreement between Zuffenhausen and Penske. The tentative steps taken earlier by Siffert, first in 1969 with the 917 PA, and then in 1971 with the second 917/10 Spyder built, had shown potential. The Swiss driver finished

fourth in the points in both seasons with a series of top-five finishes. That potential was fulfilled in 1972 with Penske's L&M Cigarettes-backed operation, although in the beginning both Porsche and the American had to be wondering whether they would ever achieve their goals. At the Mosport season opener, Donohue and his 5-liter 917/10 were dominant over the previously vaunted McLarens until a stuck butterfly valve in the induction system dropped him to second, handing the victory to McLaren driver Denny Hulme.

Then, while testing at Road Atlanta for the next race, Donohue badly injured his knee when he flipped and destroyed his magnesium-framed Spyder, after he lost the tail section in an accident he was lucky to survive. With Donohue out of action, Penske brought in George Follmer to drive the aluminum-chassised back-up car, 917/10-003, which had served throughout the winter as the team's test mule.

Mark Donohue, on his way to his first victory of 1973 at Watkins Glen, leads the factory-owned Porsche Carrera RSR 911 long-tail of Peter Gregg. Gregg's car had been brought to America to run the Glen six-hour, but was also entered in the Can-Am. Donohue, who had lost the first two races of the year, crashed his primary car in practice and was forced to use the backup during the event. It didn't matter, as he utterly dominated the field in an impressive display of engineering and driving skill.
Bill Oursler

George Follmer was called in to substitute for Mark Donohue who was injured in a testing accident at Road Atlanta. Follmer proved a wise choice, winning the 1972 Driver's Crown for himself and the manufacturer's honors for Porsche. *Bill Oursler*

Despite his unfamiliarity with the unique machine, Follmer, nevertheless, went on to win at the North Georgia track, thus validating all the effort put into the program. Despite his success, there were many involved in the program who wanted to replace Follmer with a better known driver, such as Mario Andretti. Those pressures increased after Watkins Glen, where Follmer lost to the McLarens in a disappointing performance witnessed by most of Porsche's top management, including Dr. Porsche himself. Penske, however, stood behind Follmer, who rewarded that faith with successive triumphs at Mid Ohio and Road America. By this point Donohue had recovered enough to return to the series, a fact that presented some complications for both the factory and Penske. In part these were an outgrowth of the complicated negotiations of the previous fall, which were made even more convoluted by the departure of Piëch as head of R&D as part of a family pullout from the day-to-day management of the company. What had been a clear mandate had become clouded as Bott, named as Piëch's successor, and Ernst Fuhrmann, the company's new

president, settled into those positions. Fuhrmann, as a young engineer, had designed the famous Type 547 Carrera four-cam four-cylinder.

Meanwhile, according to Penske's contract, he was to receive two cars for the 1972 campaign, and now, he wanted a third 917/10, something with which neither Bott nor Fuhrmann was comfortable. On the other hand, with Follmer leading in points, Penske was not willing to throw him out to accomodate Donohue.

Ultimately, a compromise was reached, Penske receiving a third chassis, 917/10-005 around which the team built a new car for Donohue using most of the spares the team had on hand. The new teammates appeared at Brainerd in September, where Donohue, after qualifying on the pole, retired following a minor off-course excursion. Follmer in turn, headed up Porsche's charge until he ran out of gas in the final stages, letting François Cevert claim the win in his year-old, privately entered McLaren.

That was it, however, for the opposition, as Penske took the rest of the races, Donohue finishing first at Edmonton, and Follmer doing the

Mark Donohue leads a Porsche parade at Road Atlanta. Following behind the Penske driver Number 16 is George Follmer, running for Bobby Rinzler's RC Cola team; Hurley Haywood in the Brumos Number 59; and Jody Scheckter in Vasek Polak's Number 0. The latter three are all 917/10s, and Donohue's Porsche is a 917/30. *Porsche Werk*

same at Laguna Seca and Riverside to garner the season honors for himself and the factory. Over the winter of 1972–1973, 003 and 005 were sold to Bobby Rinzler's team who procured Follmer to go with them as a partner to Charlie Kemp under the sponsorship of the RC Cola soft drink brand.

Donohue would go it alone in 1973, using the stetched wheelbase 917/30 in what was supposed to be a Penske walkaway. While things eventually went according to plan, as was the case in 1972, Donohue found the "hills" filled with trouble for the opening events. First he tangled with a back-marker at Mosport where Kemp won, and then was slowed at Road Atlanta when an improperly closed fuel tank allowed gasoline to wash over him during the race, the victor on that occasion being Follmer.

After that it was all Penske, as the blue-painted, Sunoco-backed Donohue "panzerwagen" didn't lose another race, Porsche claiming its second manufacturer's crown, and Donohue his first and only driver's title. After the Riverside season finale, Donohue announced his retirement, the 917s going with him after the SCCA made them uncompetitive by reducing their fuel capacity to below a critical point.

The 917/30 would appear only twice more, once as the original Can-Am was dying at Mid Ohio in 1974, where it finished second in the hands of Brian Redman, and again in 1975 at Talladega, where an unretired Donohue set a new closed speed record of more than 220 miles an hour just 10 days before his death during practice for the Austrian Grand Prix.

So advanced was the 917 that in 1981, when a rules loophole beckoned for its return, a one-off endurance coupe was constructed by the Kremer brothers, proving to be very competitive despite the age of its design. These days the legend of the 917 remains so strong that the vintage racing examples often draw more attention than their newer Group C or IMSA GTP counterparts. After more than two decades, the 917 is a car that still stirs the soul.

The true historical importance of the 917, however, is the profound change it caused in international endurance competition. From the moment it first appeared until its final mile in the World Makes Championship, it was the benchmark by which all others were measured and in some ways, still are.

Production Factory Racing and Rallying

7

While the Porsche factory may have started its racing efforts with production cars, in the decades since its official involvement with them has been limited, Zuffenhausen preferring to let its customers carry its banner in the production car field. Only sporadically has Porsche itself raced assembly line-based vehicles, something particularly true in the time since the 911 was first introduced in the early 1960s.

It is somewhat ironic, therefore, that one of the factory's early experiences with the 911 came just as it was going on sale in 1965, when Herbert Linge and Peter Falk drove one to a top-five finish in the Monte Carlo Rally. After that it was the turn of Porsche's customers, at least until Piëch introduced the lightweight 911R in 1967.

Porsche introduced its 911 into competition at the 1965 Monte Carlo Rally. Driven by Herbert Linge and Peter Falk, the car finished a credible fifth overall. The prestigious event would later prove to be fertile ground for Porsche, Zuffenhausen winning it on numerous occasions. *Porsche Werk*

In 1967, Porsche, under the direction of Dr. Ferdinand Piëch, designed and built what many consider to be the progenitor of Zuffenhausen's "factory hot rod." Using lightweight materials throughout, including fiberglass doors, hood, and deck lid, this special Porsche was dubbed the 911R. It formed the foundation for all future lightweight, competition-oriented 911s. However, because of marketing considerations, the car never made it into production status, since fewer than 25 were built. While the Porsche 911R did not compete as a production car, it did enjoy a rather extensive competition career. One unique episode in its motorsport history came when Dieter Spoerry, Rico Steinemann, and Jo Siffert drove this example to a series of record speed runs at Monza in October 1967. *Porsche Werk*

The proposition that more weight means extra mass was of prime importance to Porsche, given the limited displacements and power outputs of its engines at that time. Ultimately, Porsche would join the ranks of the "big boys" with units, in turbocharged form, reaching as high as 1,500-plus horsepower. Back in the mid-1960s, though, 250 horsepower was the goal, and 300 horsepower a dream.

Almost lost in the 1966–1971 period of frenetic activity that saw Piëch push Zuffenhausen to the forefront of the sport was a special, lightened 911R. In many ways, but for different reasons, this unique Porsche not only shared the same short-term fate as Zora Arkus-Duntov's Corvette Grand Sport racers, but that car's long-term legendary place in history as well.

The Grand Sports were the original "wolves in sheep's clothing." Looking very much like their standard 1963 street-bred Corvette counterparts, the Grand Sports were in actuality, full competition vehicles with special frames, running gear, brakes and engines all intended to take on and beat the Ford-powered Shelby Cobras. Unfortunately, the management of General Motors canceled the program after only five cars had been completed, leaving the Grand Sports to run in the prototype arena where the pitch of the field was definitely in favor of the opposition. Even though orphaned, the GS crowd had its moments, some impressive enough

Porsche produced the first of its lightweight 911 coupes, the 911R, in 1967. Considered to be an experiment, the car was never made in sufficient numbers to qualify as a full-fledged production automobile. Despite this, it enjoyed considerable success. This example won the Tour de France in 1969. *Leonard Turner*

to make people wonder just how good the cars could have been if they had run as production-based vehicles instead as prototypes.

Unlike the Grand Sports, there was initially no real thought given to making the 911R a production racer. Rather, it was an exercise to see just how light a 911 could be produced with motorsport in mind. To this day, while there are achievements to be pointed to, the principal legacy of the 911R is the door it opened to the future.

In all, according to experts, Porsche would construct 24 911Rs: 4 prototypes and 20 "production" machines. The project began in the second quarter of 1967 when Piëch's engineers pulled four 911S bodyshells from the assembly line and stripped them down to bare metal. What they put back was far less than what they took out.

Replaced by fiberglass look-alike components were the front and rear deck lids, as well as the front and rear bumpers, and the two front fenders. On the prototypes, aluminum was used for the doors (on the production cars, these would be in fiberglass also), while plexiglass was employed for the side and rear windows to go along with a windshield of thinner glass. The stripped interior was fitted with a pair of Scheel lightweight seats and not much else other than a roll bar (even the

window winding mechanisms were omitted). In terms of the suspension, the 911 R followed the standard 911 design, except for its 2-inch lower ride height, Koni racing-type shocks, and nonproduction brakes. These latter units featured ventilated discs and calipers with a greater swept pad surface. The front track was set at 54.3 inches, and the rear at 53.7 inches. Although the 15-inch diameter wheels appeared standard, they were wider, being 7 inches at the rear and 6 at the front.

The engine originally fitted to the 911R was a variant of the unit used in the 906. It retained the same camshafts, timing, dual ignition, and enlarged valves (45 millimeters versus 42 for the intake side and 39 millimeters versus 38 for the exhaust) of its 906 sibling. It also retained the chrome-plated cylinders of the 906 engine and its twin, triple-choke 461DA3C Weber carburetors. Likewise, it had a smaller fan (225 millimeters versus 245 millimeters) than the normal 911 unit.

Unlike the 906 engine's magnesium crankcase, the 911R's was aluminum. With a 10.3:1 compression ratio, the unit pumped out a healthy 152 ft-lb of torque at 6,000 rpm, and 210 horses at 8,000 rpm. Given a weight of just over 1,800 pounds, that made the 911R one of the hottest production-based cars of its day. Transmitting this power to

Gérard Larrousse drove this 911R to victory in the 1969 Tour de France. Today this car survives in restored condition as a part of the Miles Collier collection in Naples, Florida. It is one of several 911Rs now residing in North America. *Porsche Werk*

the rear wheels was essentially the same strengthened five-speed transaxle unit used in the 906.

Having that gearbox in place was useful to Piëch's engineers when later, they decided to transplant an even more potent engine into their factory racer. This was the fuel-injected Type 916 dual-cam boxer six that for the first time employed tappets between the cams and the valve stems. Although innovative, the powerplant was not particularly popular, having less than desirable motivational capabilities in the 3,000–4,500 rpm range. Even so, the significance of the Type 916 engine lay not so much in its existence, as it did in the fact that with the addition of two cylinders it would become the boxer eight used in the 908 and later, with four additional pistons and a central drive pickup system, the basis for the 917's 12-cylinder unit.

All that came later. When Porsche assigned the task of building the 20 production 911Rs to the Karl Baur Company in Stuttgart, the engine of choice was the modified 906's. It was at this point in the late summer and early fall of 1967 that Porsche's legendary Huschke von Hanstein became involved in the 91IR story, suggesting to the company's marketing experts that given the relatively low cost of producing the car (it was about the same money as a 911T), it might well be possible to construct a run of 500 to qualify it as a legitimate production machine.

The conservatism of the marketing department, which would later almost scuttle plans for the Carrera RS and RSR in the 1970s, led to the decision not to produce the 91IR in such large numbers. Some claim that since there were new Rs remaining at the factory into the 1970s this was a wise decision, but most believe it was a mistake.

Yet, like so many lost chances, the possibilities will always remain nothing more than speculation. What was real, though, was the impressive, if limited, record the 911R achieved during its time on stage. That began in July 1967 when one of the factory's lightweight 911s went to Mugello, where in the hands of Vic Elford and Gijs van Lennep it came home third behind a pair of Porsche 910s. What made the occasion even more impressive was that the car behind it in fourth was a full-blooded, 7-liter V-8 Ford Mark IIB GT-40—the same kind of long-distance racer that had won at Le Mans in 1966, and would win again in 5-liter form in 1968 and 1969.

Life wasn't over for the Mugello 911R, either. No sooner had it returned to Zuffenhausen than it was summoned to Monza to help Rico Steinemann set a number of international speed records.

Steinemann had the sponsors (British Petroleum and Firestone) but he lacked a car, that problem cropping up when the front suspension of his team's 906 had collapsed after 10 hours of pounding on Monza's extremely bumpy banking. Steinemann's call to Stuttgart set in motion one of the more unusual episodes in the factory's competition efforts.

Under the FIA's regulations, Steinemann and his partners could restart the run with a new car, but only within 48 hours. The tight time limit produced quick action: the Mugello car, hurriedly checked and lightly refreshed, along with a second 911R destined to be a spare parts source car, were dispatched by road from Stuttgart to Monza. There, with the second 911 stripped of the needed spares (including front suspension units which would be fully utilized), the attempt began a second time. Before it was over, Steinemann and company had set 11 time and distance marks over a period of six days, including one for 20,000 kilometers (12,420 miles) at an average speed of 130.2 miles an hour.

However, that wasn't anywhere near the end for the 911R's growing reputation. In November Elford and his navigator, David Stone, took a 911R to the Corsica Rally, a full pavement event, where the pair came in third. Shod with the latest radials, the 911R proved to be quite tail happy, the word "oversteer" taking on new meaning. Still, Elford appeared to like his cars that way, and was more than comfortable behind the R's wheel.

Even so, given its continuing "prototype" status, there were few practical places to race the coupe. One was back at Mugello where in 1968, it scored a fine third. In 1969 Gérard Larrousse and codriver Maurice Gelin ran the Tour de France in a 911R, turning in a spectacular performance, winning the event outright. After that, they took the same car to Corsica, winning the FIA-sanctioned rally over a host of factory teams with their outcast entry.

The previous year, the results of the Corsican event had turned out far less happily for Porsche. It was at that rally the factory decided to debut the 916 engine in the 911R. None of three entered finished. One retired after an accident, while the second went out because of a broken differential, and the third failed after experiencing oil system difficulties.

Indeed, while Larrousse would subsequently drive a 916-equipped 911R in rallies throughout 1969, he would win only a single event. That was the Rally *Neige et Glace* in France. In sum, Larrousse said that the lack of low-end torque hampered the 916-engined 911R in rallying, where low-end torque is exactly what is needed.

For Larrousse, his successful and less successful times with the 911R in 1969 would be his last association with the car. However, the future director of Renault's racing fortunes wasn't quite through with lightweight Porsches. In 1970, the factory again decided to go after the overall prize in the Tour de France. This time it built the lightest-ever 911, starting with a 911ST and using many of the bits and pieces from the 911R's parts bin. Larrousse had promised the crew that if the car weighed in at under 1,760 pounds he would buy them a case of good French champagne. When it tipped the scales at 1715 pounds, Larrousse paid off. Unhappily, 1970 was the year the Matra prototypes decided to tackle their home country's event, leaving Larrousse third at the finish.

Many of the lessons learned in the design and construction of these first lightweight 911s were passed on to the other, more standard 911s used in motorsport, particularly in international rallying where Zuffenhausen created a tremendous record for itself. Similarly, 911s didn't do all that poorly in circuit racing, especially in the United States,

Britisher Vic Elford and his partner David Stone gave Porsche its first Monte Carlo triumph in 1968 with a 911T. Elford had nearly won the event the previous year for Zuffenhausen, but lost because of a bad tire choice in the final stages. A week after the Monte Carlo performance, he would be part of the Porsche winning team at the Daytona 24 Hours in a 907 long-tail coupe. *Porsche Werk*

Björn Waldegaard piloted his 911T to a second straight Porsche Monte Carlo triumph. Unlike the previous year, the weather conditions varied from springlike to the more normal snow and ice found in the January affair. Waldegaard repeated his 1969 performance at Monte Carlo in 1970, with Lars Helmer as his navigator. The car was now a 911S, running on Fuchs forged wheels and featuring a 2.3-liter type 901 flat six-cylinder. *Porsche Werk*

where they cleaned house in the SCCA's Under-2-liter division of the Trans-Am—until being ruled out in 1970.

In spite of this, the factory did not pay a great deal of attention to its production coupe as Piëch and his engineers concentrated on creating the legendary for-racing-only fiberglass-bodied Porsches, which eventually led to the famed 917 and its turbocharged Can-Am successors. However, in 1972 after internal family pressures resulted in the exit of Piëch and his cousins from Porsche's direct management structure, the new man at the day-to-day helm of the company, Dr. Ernst Fuhrmann, knew that something had to be done with the 911 in terms of its on-track capabilities.

For Fuhrmann it was a simple matter of economics. Although Porsche's commitment to competition has always been a means of developing new engineering technologies, it has also always served a second function: that of being the most efficient means for a small firm such as Porsche to promote its products with its potential customers. It was this latter consideration that caused

Fuhrmann to order a program to breathe new life into the 911, seeing it as a way of focusing new attention on the then nearly 10-year-old vehicle, which he intended should stay in production through the best part of the 1980s.

Under Norbert Singer, the engineers set to work during the late spring and early summer of 1972, just months after Fuhrmann's arrival, to create what would eventually become the Carrera RSR. Again, Singer and his staff placed the basic 911S, Porsche's top performer of the time, on a strict diet, reducing its homologated weight to 1,985 pounds, 210 less than the previous 911 customer-oriented racer minimum.

For the street, the interior of the road-going Carrera RS was largely stripped, with virtually no sound deadening and a pair of lightweight bucket seats. Similarly, the bumpers were fiberglass, as was the rear deck lid, which now incorporated the soon-to-become-famous ducktail rear spoiler. This was designed to reduce by 75 percent the rear aerodynamic lift that caused the 911's excess in undesirable high-speed oversteer instability.

Underneath the fiberglass was a new 2.7-liter engine with its bore enlarged to 90 millimeters and the coating for its cylinders changed to Nikasil.

It should be pointed out here many street 1973 RS models found themselves converted to racing specifications, something not all that difficult to do since the road-going version was intended as the basis for its on-track counterpart. The factory homologated the initial 1973 RS as a nonmodified Group 3 car, and its RSR counterpart in the more lenient Group 4 category. Indeed a number of the so-called street RS Carreras found themselves doing almost exclusive duty as Group 3 racers, adding to the record being earned by their Group 4 RSR brethren.

In late 1969 Porsche produced a batch of lightweight body shells featuring thinner metals throughout and no sound deadening. These cars, approximately 35 in all, would form the basis for all 911 competition vehicles through 1972. Officially listed as 911Ss, they unofficially carried the designation "ST." This is one of the 2.4-liter examples seen in 1972 and run by the Kremer Brothers in Germany. Other examples made their way to the United States for such Porsche notables as Peter Gregg and Michael Keyser. *Porsche Werk*

The 1973 Daytona 24-Hours marked the first appearance Porsche's new Carrera RS/RSR series. Not yet approved as a production machine, the Carreras ran as prototypes. Nevertheless, the factory-loaned example driven in Brumos colors by Peter Gregg and Hurley Haywood won outright. *Bill Oursler*

One area receiving immediate attention for Group 4 competition was the engine, whose cylinders now sported a 92-millimeter bore, bringing the displacement up to 2,806 cc. In addition the compression ratio was raised to 10.5:1. Further, the valve sizes were increased, the intakes now set at 49 millimeters and the exhausts 41.5 millimeters. (The size of the ports was accordingly increased as well.) The engineers retained the provisions for twin plugs, while simplifying the Bosch butterfly injection system.

For reliability, a crankshaft damper was fitted and the camshafts modified so that a fourth bearing could be added. Except for the crankshaft modifications, the rest of the bottom end remained much as it was in the RS. Still, the changes, which also included a regrinding of the camshaft lobes, pushed the horsepower up from the 210 mark for the standard six to a healthy 300-plus, the first time this figure had been reached by the 911's Type 901 six. Moreover, the maximum torque rose to 217 ft-lb, a figure that ensured the RSR would be quick off the corners.

The brakes for the RSR came from the 917 program, complete with finned calipers and cross-drilled, ventilated rotors. The brake system used twin master cylinders and was fully adjustable front to rear. Initially, the RSR was fitted with 9x15-inch rims at the front and 11x15s at the rear to provide an adequate tire contact patch for racing purposes.

To cover the wider wheels, the fender flares were extended, providing one of the main visual differences between the competition and street models. The other visible difference was the inclusion of an oil cooler in the center of the front bumper, plus an additional front air dam that was attached to the bottom of the bumper unit. This latter change turned the car's 77 pounds of front lift into 60 pounds of downforce, but only at the expense of increasing rear lift from 92 to 126 pounds. This despite the presence of the ducktail spoiler. After testing in December 1972, Singer and the engineers took the advice of driver Mark Donohue and raised the spindles on the front struts, thus lowering the car without sacrificing

Following Daytona, where the factory had loaned Peter Gregg a Carrera 911S, Zuffcnhausen decided to come out of the closet and run its own Carrera program, with Martini sponsorship. These, as well as the customer cars, would now carry the full competition designation "RSR." However, the factory entries were subjected to continual experimental modifications, which put them in the prototype category. The first change was an expansion in engine size to a full 3 liters. *Porsche Werk*

any suspension travel. The diagonal rear suspension arms were shortened, being mounted 47.5 millimeters further back on the chassis and 15 millimeters outward. Other changes included the replacement of the standard plastic bushings with solid, metal-based substitutes, and the addition of heavy-duty front and rear sway bars. Finally, the RSR Carreras were supplied with Dunlop fuel cells, the optional 31.7-gallon capacity (a 29-gallon unit was standard) coming with a Dunlop fuel cell.

The 1973 RSR also acquired coilover springing, but this was not fitted to the first three Carrera racers, which appeared in the United States in the early months of 1973. The lack of coilovers had led some to describe these cars as RS rather than RSR models, although in reality they were somewhere in between the two. Later, in the fall of 1973 a series of similar "half-breed" Carreras were shipped to the United States. These latter cars, constructed that summer, were competition vehicles that bridged the gap between the 1973 and 1974 on-track RSR Carreras, featuring the narrower tires of the earlier model along with the original ducktail spoiler and simplified internal

roll bar of the 1973 RSR. On the other hand, they also had the full 3-liter engine of the 1974 racer, as well as its revised front bumper layout.

In fact, as with so many other competition Porsches, the factory made a number of running changes, most of which were first applied to the factory's own entries and later offered to its customers. What complicates the history of the Carrera RSR is the existence of the many variants produced during its long career. Not only were there customer RSRs as well as customer RS models, there were also the several different factory-entered versions, as well as the Carreras built by Porsche, especially for the Roger Penske's International Race of Champions ABC television series.

The difficulties with those vehicles is that when they were sold after the February 1974 IROC finale, those who purchased them did not always bring them up to full customer racing specifications, leaving a number of oddball cars running in both the Trans-Am and IMSA Camel championships. One more problem is that during 1974 Josef Hoppen, Porsche's North American competition boss at the time, ordered a further batch of 25

121

The unique "Mary Stuart" Martini Carrera RSR of 1973 was an attempt by Porsche engineers to provide the car with better grip and handling with the use of wider wheels and large spoilers. Although forced to run as a prototype, the unique coupe did achieve better than reasonable results, usually running among the top five.
Leonard Turner

similar cars for the 1974–1975 series before Penske and company decided to switch to Chevrolets instead. These cars then had to be put into the "customer" system as well, emerging as standard RSR models.

All that was far in the future when the first two factory-prepped Carreras appeared for the Daytona 24-Hour enduro in late January 1973. Since not enough had yet been produced to qualify them for homologation in the production categories, the two were forced to race as prototypes against the 3-liter Matras, Mirages and Lolas present. By midnight the 3-liter sports racers were gone, leaving the two Carreras—the blue-colored Penske entry of Mark Donohue and George Follmer and the white Brumos example of Peter Gregg and Hurley Haywood—to battle each other.

Although Donohue and Follmer forged ahead during the predawn hours, by early morning a machining fault had caused a piston to burn through, forcing their retirement. This left Gregg and Haywood to cruise to a stunning inaugural victory for the new model, establishing themselves in the process as key players in the future of Porsche's competition programs. As Gregg, Haywood, and Porsche celebrated, they could not have known at the time that massive changes in motorsport were coming, and that the Carrera RSR would emerge from them as a foundation for what was to follow.

At the time of Daytona, even though the international prototype arena was not as strong as it had been, Ferrari and Matra were still pouring money into their sports racing efforts in an attempt to establish superiority. While this tended to overshadow the production cars, by the end of the 1973 year Ferrari would be gone, preferring to concentrate on Formula One, leaving the prototypes on an increasingly long, and downward slide.

With the decline in the interest in prototype racing and the 1974 demise of the Can-Am, suddenly production cars such as the Carrera RSR were elevated to headlining status and the factory went out of its way to help its customers. Porsche not only took care of the RSR's construction, it also handled a continuing development program that produced for 1974, among other things, the definitive 3-liter engine, center-lock wheels (14 inches wide in the rear and 10.5 in the front), and the whaletail flat rear spoiler that would come to characterize the RSR for the rest of its career and which, in modified form, would be applied to the 934 that succeeded it.

While the first two Carreras—the ones run by Penske and Brumos at Daytona—were standard cars (indeed, technically these two 2.7-liter machines were RSs rather than RSRs) even though they ran as prototypes, the factory would actually field a pair of its own Carreras with backing from Martini throughout the remainder of the 1973 season as Group 5 prototypes. These cars, heavily modified, were in fact test beds not only for items that would appear on the 1974 Carrera fleet, but also for advanced technology parts, especially in the area of aerodynamics, which Singer and his engineers wanted to explore for future factory programs.

From the start, the factory Martini RSRs were equipped with 3-liter sixes as part of a development exercise before they were installed in customer cars. Also, rim widths were widened, again reflecting a trend that would occur among the privateers over the course of the RSR's career. This latter exploration created visual changes in terms of much larger fender flares that clearly separated the Group 5 Martini entries from the normal RSR brigade. However, it wasn't the use of extra wide flares that made the look of the factory coupes so memorable. Rather it was a proliferation of ever increasingly large and complicated spoilers, especially at the rear, which truly left a lasting impression. These devices were part of an effort by Singer to find extra grip through increased downforce. By the time the Targa Florio came around, the Martini RSR's sported extensions to the rear ducktail unit that were incorporated into the rear fenders, fitting flush against the sides of the original deck lid. This modification was further perfected, producing what is called the "Mary Stuart" design for its "high collar" like appearance, reflective of the Scottish queen's dresses.

Later, Singer's team would come up with an extended tail section, featuring what amounted to a biplane wing arrangement, which, although a preview of the 1974 RSR's whaletail arrangement, was far more radical than that "production" innovation. Surprisingly, as had happened at Daytona, these "prototype" RSRs enjoyed more than their share of success against the full-blooded Group 5 sports racers, Herbert Muller and Gjis van Lennep, taking their Martini entry to victory in the Targa. At Le Mans in June, the same pair used the in factory entry to claim fourth overall, a remarkable

achievement given the fact that the then-ultrafast Sarthe circuit greatly favored the sports racing Matras and Ferraris over what was basically a modified street car. For Watkins Glen, Porsche entrusted two long-tails to Penske and Brumos, Donohue and Follmer finishing one place ahead of Gregg and Haywood as both cracked the top 10. That was it as far as factory RSRs were concerned, but not for production-based factory racing programs from Zuffenhausen, as Singer and his team would go on to field a turbocharged Carrera RSR in 1974 as a development exercise for the boosted 934s and 935s which would appeared in 1976.

For Gregg, and to a lesser extent Haywood, 1973 was a heady year. The Trans-Am, which had lost its exclusive support from Detroit, was opened up to all forms of GT cars for 1973 and he and the factory lost little time in exploiting that decision

A further modification to the factory's Martini-backed Carrera RSRs was the extension of the rear spoiler. This earned it the nickname "Mary Stuart," for the similarity to the high collars worn by the sixteenth-century Queen of Scots. This photo was taken at the Nürburgring, where Gijs van Lennep and Herbert Müller drove their "Mary Stuart" entry to fifth overall. *Porsche Werk*

At Le Mans 1973, van Lennep and Müller again drove a 3-liter factory-entered Martini "Mary Stuart" Carrera. The pair brought considerable honor to Zuffenhausen by finishing fourth overall behind a group of full-fledged Matra and Ferrari prototypes. The next modification to the RSR would be the addition of a full rear wing and improved, smoother front spoiler.
Porsche Werk

by the SCCA, Gregg taking delivery of a new full-spec RSR for the season-opening Road Atlanta Trans-Am, which he won. Although Gregg would not finish first again on the shortened Trans-Am tour (there were only six events), his consistent top-five placing gave him the crown over the up-and-coming Al Holbert. Still it was on the IMSA-sanctioned Camel GT tour that Gregg and his Porsche-supported RSR really displayed their talents when everything was said and done. Gregg led a decisive Porsche RSR victory brigade, the Brumos driver also collecting the top honors in the Trans-Am for himself and Porsche.

For 1974, Gregg and the rest of the Porsche contingent hit the racing trail with the newest whaletail RSR Carreras, which featured not only the revised rear spoiler, but also a new throttle side injected 3-liter boxer six and the wider tires introduced by the factory late the previous year. Under increasingly liberal IMSA scriptures, those rear rims would grow even more, eventually reaching a rear width of 17 inches.

With the SCCA's Trans-Am series haunted by a lack of money and the fuel crunch, the 1974 championship was reduced to just three rounds: Lime Rock, Road America, and Watkins Glen. Through the efforts of Hobart and Gregg, Porsche easily dominated the failing series.

While Al Holbert's Carrera won the opening Trans Am of 1974 at Lime Rock, Gregg took the other two Trans Am events (with help from Haywood at Watkins Glen) to collect his second straight SCCA title and establish Porsche as the Trans-Am's leading manufacturer. Meanwhile in the Camel GT, Gregg lost at the April Road Atlanta

season opener to Holbert and his partner, Elliot Forbes-Robinson, after Gregg and Haywood had problems with their still factory-supported RSR.

At Laguna Seca several weeks later, Gregg again had difficulties, finishing third in the first half of a twin-feature show and not appearing in the second (RSR drivers Elliot Forbes-Robinson and Milt Minter were the two victors). After that Gregg got on track, winning at Ontario, Mid Ohio (with Holbert), Charlotte, and Lime Rock to clinch the Camel honors for the year.

As for the Carreras, which often took the first five places, their only defeats came at Talladega and Daytona, where they were beaten by the Corvettes driven by Minter and John. In addition to Holbert and Gregg, both Keyser and Haywood emerged as first-place finishers on Porsche's IMSA Carrera hit parade.

While the Carrera RSR's dominant statistics may have sat well in Zuffenhausen, they were less welcomed by IMSA head John Bishop, who wanted no part of a continuing Carrera stampede. A reflection of this attitude could be seen in the Greenwood Corvette, with its wild fender flares and near-total tube-frame body, which appeared first at the Road Atlanta opener. The Corvette's aerodynamic package and its chassis structure marked a significant departure for IMSA in terms of the Camel rules, which previously had adhered to the FIA's Group 4 scriptures.

In late 1974 Bishop announced the rules for a new class of IMSA racer, the All-American GT. Created with the help of Chevrolet's then-racing head, Vince Piggins, and using technology from Greenwood's Corvette, the All-American GP division represented Bishop's attempt to legislate an American look to his championship by making it as easy as possible to defeat the turnkey RSRs.

Interestingly, Gregg's last RSR, one of the lightest of its type ever made, had a set of rear fenders whose lines would be repeated later on the 935 Turbos, a coincidence due in large measure to the part played by the factory in their design. IMSA, even though it had no problems allowing the AAGT contingent such leeway in fender shapes, ordered Gregg to switch the car back to the more conventional flares. That resulted in a lawsuit by Gregg, whose out-of-court settlement remains unpublicized. Still, the rumors have persisted that Gregg gained something from the deal between himself and the sanctioning organization, enough so that in the future IMSA was reluctant to single out a particular model for such harsh treatment.

Put in perspective, the RSR was not just another outstanding example of Porsche's winning engineering. It also represented the first Porsche that the "masses" could purchase and finish in front of the pack with. As such, it holds a deservedly high place in Porsche's motorsport tradition.

In terms of Porsche's factory interest in production cars, there is one further arena to look at. This is the sport of rallying: not the slow-paced, mathematically based, time-speed-distance affairs where computer-generated directions are king, but rather all-out wilderness competition in which cars and drivers are tested to—and sometimes beyond—their limits.

In the summer of 1973, Porsche and Roger Penske collaborated on the creation of what would become the basis for the 1974 Carrera RSR. Technically, these cars were RS models intended for Penske's new IROC series, pitting the world's top drivers against each other in identical vehicles. Noteworthy is the tray-like rear spoiler, which was common to all subsequent Carrera racing coupes, and the revised front bumper/spoiler. *Porsche Werk*

For the Watkins Glen 6-Hour in 1973, Porsche shipped a special long-tail 3-liter Carrera RSR to Roger Penske for Mark Donohue and George Follmer. Despite the car's advanced technology, problems kept it out of the top five. This particular car was later sold in Mexico and was run privately at Le Mans in 1974. *Bill Oursler*

Over the years, Porsche's accumulated record in rallying has been impressive, including four victories in the famed Monte Carlo winter event, a prize which more often than not pits multimillion-dollar factory teams against each other with all the support trimmings in place. The singular feature of Porsche's rally excursions, however, is just the opposite, for, unlike its rivals, Porsche has never committed the huge expenditures of money for rallying most consider essential to success. Instead, Zuffenhausen and Weissach traditionally have adopted an attitude somewhere between benign neglect and highly limited enthusiasm.

In actuality, Porsche has used the reliability of its cars to win rallies almost from the time the company began to publicize itself through its competition endeavors. The first victories came in

1950 in the Swedish and Alpine events and were followed in 1951 by triumphs in the Liege-Rome-Liege and Tulip rallies, as well as class victories in the Monte Carlo and eventually even the European rally title. These, of course, were scored by various versions of the 356.

By 1965 Porsche was an established part of the wilderness racing scene. Still, not even the most seasoned observers were quite prepared for the sight that greeted them when the competitors lined up for the 1965 edition of the Monte Carlo round. There, sandwiched in among the Mini Coopers, Citroens and other sedans, was a much smaller, lower, and sleeker automobile—a Porsche 904 Carrera GTS, a car designed strictly for circuit competition. Well, perhaps not strictly, since the 904 owner's manual contained a great deal of

information concerning its use on public roads, including tips on winter driving. Piloted by Eugen Bohringer and Rolf Wütherich (the man who was the late James Dean's companion on the movie actor's final, fatal run in his 550 Spyder up a California highway in 1955), the 904 came in an amazing second overall, in a performance even more unexpected than its initial appearance. That performance masked an event that would have lasting influence on the rally community—the entry of a factory-sanctioned 911 for Peter Falk and Herbert Linge.

It was not, however, until 1968 that the six-cylinder really blossomed, when Vic Elford and his navigator, David Stone, took their factory 911 to an overall triumph at Monte Carlo. That was the first of three consecutive victories for Porsche, the other two being scored by Björn Waldegaard in 1969 and 1970. The 1968 effort also saw 911 driver Paul Toivonen back Vic Elford up with a second place finish.

While Porsche would not win again at Monte Carlo with a factory team, after its 1970 triumph it did make one other noteworthy effort in this prestigious affair, when it entered a trio of 914/6 GTs in 1971. Unhappily, the extremely snowy conditions that year worked against the midengined roadsters, their best finish being the third place recorded by Waldegaard. But, once more, this "failure," if one can call it that, was part of the enthusiasm from the engineers to pursue the development of new ideas as well as to score good results.

Manfred Jantke, who, during the 1970s and 1980s was responsible for Porsche motorsport

A similar long-tail 3.0 RSR was brought to the Glen for Peter Gregg and Hurley Haywood, who likewise had problems with it during the 6-Hour. Gregg subsequently drove the car in the following day's Can-Am, finishing credibly in the top 10, although the vehicle was totally unsuited to the unlimited technology of the sports racing series.
Bill Oursler

In 1978 Porsche created a special lightweight 911 SC for the East African Safari. Painted in the Day-Glo red trim of its Martini sponsor, the car was impressive looking. However, it failed to achieve its purpose of winning the East African affair, one of the few major rallies never to fall to Zuffenhausen.
Leonard Turner

public relations, once described how Peter Falk and several others, including Jürgen Barth, prepared a two-year-old 911 Carrera on a small budget for Björn Waldegaard to drive in the 1973 East African Safari. As Jantke noted, where other factories had large groups of mechanics, massive stocks of spare parts, and fleets of service vehicles to help their entrants to the finish, Waldegaard's Carrera was backed by himself, Barth, two mechanics, some volunteers, an old 911 ex-rally car, and a bunch of semi-refurbished but still battered, locally purchased Volkswagens.

It is interesting that when Porsche's in-house enthusiasts decided on their back-door Safari effort in 1973 (keeping in mind that Falk himself did a great deal of the development work with a patched-up 911 at Weissach), the car they eventually produced and got accepted by the international authorities wasn't far removed from what a customer interested in a dual purpose streetable track machine might order.

The basis of Waldegaard's 1973 Safari entry was a somewhat simplified 911 Carrera with a standard 2.7-liter engine whose body and suspension components were reinforced and whose front

stub axles were mounted lower on the struts to increase ride height (the rear suspension "bananas" being adjusted to meet the new specs). Also installed were Bilstein gas pressure shocks, a 19-millimeter front and a 24-millimeter rear sway bar, as well as an aluminum roll cage, sump shields, a 100-liter gas tank, a different clutch with stronger springs, an oil cooler for the transaxle, 6x15 forged wheels, and a package of five auxiliary high intensity lights.

Waldegaard led the Safari up through the final 400-mile stage. It was then, during what should have been an easy run to the finish, that the former Monte Carlo winner, while enjoying a 35-minute advantage over second place, was brought to a halt by a broken halfshaft. It took Barth and his crew more than a half-hour to reach their stranded driver and another 40 minutes to replace the offending part, leaving Waldegaard some 30 minutes behind the eventual first-placed Datsun. Still, the Porsche man had one or two things left to demonstrate as he floored his rather tired Carrera, arriving at the finish just 14 minutes back in a display of talent that years later continues to be remembered.

As engraved as Waldegaard's performance is in the history of the sport, its importance is overshadowed by what happened in 1978 in Monte Carlo, where Jean Pierre Nicolas took his privately entered 911 SC to victory over the giant factory Fiat and Ford teams, which spent the last half of the 1970s battling each other for supremacy on the World Championship Rally tour. To put this in context, it would be very much like having the 100th-place college team take on Oklahoma or Nebraska and win in the Orange Bowl. Indeed, the fact that a privateer such as Nicolas could defeat the well-organized factory squads was impressive enough, but the fact that he did it with a car whose origins went back to the early 1960s was truly amazing.

When one looks at the specifications for Nicolas' 1978 Monte Carlo winning 911SC, surprisingly, one finds little difference in the specifications from Waldegaard's car of five years earlier. As listed in the homologation papers for Nicolas' Porsche, the weight given for the 1978 version was 960 kilos (2,117 pounds) and the

In the early 1980s Porsche began work on its awesome turbocharged Group B 959 coupe. As part of that car's development program, Porsche entered a hybrid model, based on the 911SC but using the 959's four-wheel-drive setup, in the long-distance Paris-Dakar Rally. Preparations for the affair attempts were made at the factory racing headquarters in its Weissach test center. These later, full-specification 959s would earn their keep in the difficult early winter African affair by giving Porsche yet another victory. *Porsche Werk*

By 1986 Porsche had taken on the Paris-Dakar event with a finalized version of the 959 Group B rally coupe, claiming the win after a near-perfect run through the desert with René Metge and Dominique Lemoyne. This was the final appearance for the Porsche works team in an event now dominated by truck-like vehicles. *Porsche Werk*

engine displacement was boosted to 2,994 cc (95-millimeter bore, 70.4-millimeter stroke) with a 10.8:1 compression ratio. Also listed was a five-speed transaxle along with a 1,437-millimeter front track and a 1,462-millimeter rear track.

As with any competition vehicle, there were other subtle changes made to the 911SC throughout its career. However, when Jean Luc Therier won the Tour de Corse Rally in 1980, his Porsche maintained the same basic specifications as its predecessors. Perhaps even more telling about the durability and competitiveness of the 911SC, despite its age, is the fact that a year later, in the

1981 San Remo Rally, multitime World Rally Champion Walter Röhrl posted the fastest time on the opening stage in one of these cars—and with factory support, to the surprise of all concerned.

Röhrl's association with Porsche that year came about after his initial employer, Mercedes Benz, decided at the last minute to cancel its 1981 rally program. While continuing to pay Röhrl, Mercedes left him free to drive for other teams. Those "others" turned out to be Mercedes' cross-town Stuttgart rival, Porsche, which used Röhrl's considerable talents to develop its 924 GTS Turbo on the German Rally Championship tour.

the new Audi Quattro coupe, as well as Peugeot's upcoming 205T-16 all-wheel-drive turbo, by creating the 959. Porsche aggressively pursued the motorsports side of the new 959, beginning the car's development program by entering a four-wheel-drive 911SC RS, using 959 components in the 1984 Paris-Dakar endurance rally. A 22-day affair that covered some 9,000 miles of rock-strewn wasteland and trackless dunes, it offered the chance to enter and compete in an unhomologated vehicle, a perfect venue to test the 959 concept. Sponsored by Rothmans, three of the hybrid preprototype 959s actually ran, with the one piloted by Rene Metge and Dominique Lemoyne taking a surprising first overall.

The factory returned to the event in 1985 with a more advanced prototype of the 959, now clothed in that car's new sleeker-shaped bodywork, but still without its 450-horsepower turbocharged engine. Unfortunately, all three of the Rothmans entries broke that year, but that didn't prevent Falk and Bott, from fielding a trio of true 959s in 1986.

This time there was more than enough glory as Metge and Lemoyne again won, with Ickx and his navigator, Claude Brasseur, taking second. Sixth place went to the parts support 959 of Roland Kussmaul and Hendrick Unger, the two repeating the feat of Falk and Linge at Monte Carlo 21 years before.

That wasn't the end of the car's motorsport career, though. As the dust covers were being thrown over the Paris-Dakar coupes, the new 959-based 961 circuit racer was being readied for the 1986 Le Mans long distance classic, where in an unsponsored white paint scheme it won the Group B category, finishing seventh overall. Later that year it was entered at the International Motor Sports Association's fall Daytona finale, but was never a factor, retiring after a series of tire failures on the steep, G-loaded banking this failure was brought about by regulations that significantly "undertired" the powerful coupe. Interestingly, the 961's performance at Daytona led to many writing off the advantages of all-wheel drive in pavement competition, a posture that changed dramatically after Piëch's Audis won the SCCA's Trans-Am championship in 1988.

In 1987, the 961, now backed by Rothmans, again appeared at Le Mans. This time there would be no triumphs, the car catching fire after blowing its engine on Sunday morning. With that, the brief racing career of the 959 was over.

A trio of all-wheel-drive competition Porsches line up at Weissach for a family portrait. On the left is the 959 Paris-Dakar winner, while in the center is the production version, and on the right the Type 961 circuit racer, which claimed its class at Le Mans in 1986. *Porsche Werk*

Röhrl was impressed with the turbo 924, saying it was a good car that would have been really impressive had he had more time with it. Röhrl's talents garnered the 924 its only rally success, as he guided it to a first-place finish in the Hessen round of the German title chase.

In 1984 Porsche rehomologated its aging boxer six-cylinder coupe as the 911SC RS to meet the new Group B "super car" era rules, even though the vehicle remained essentially the same as it had been previously. It was during this time, however, that Porsche decided to get seriously into the Group B business and challenge

Production Turbos

8

I t was, depending on how you looked at it, either a logical extension of what had been, or a grand experiment reaching toward the future and what should be. Either way, Porsche's 1974 Turbo RSR represented the high point for the line of racing 911s that stretched back to 1966, as well as the bridge to the 935s that would carry the company's name through the mid-1980s.

During the Piëch era, little work was done on the 911 to develop it for competition, other than the abortive 911R. That changed in 1972, when Ernst Fuhrmann took over as chairman of Porsche's management board. The factory, having left the World Makes scene after the authorities legislated the 917s out, began to explore the possibilities of creating a new contending version of its long-standing coupe. Engineer Norbert

---

The Group 5 factory Porsche 935/77 was a major departure in rules interpretation from what the FIA had intended when it created the "silhouette" prototype formula. Not only did the factory Porsche feature a sloped nose intended to create significant amounts of front downforce, it also included a raised rear roof added on to the normal structure to improve airflow to the rear wing and generate greater downforce there as well. *Bill Oursler*

Porsche's first step toward the 935 came in 1974 with the 2.1-liter turbocharged Carrera RSR Coupe. Run strictly as a prototype by the factory, with Martini sponsorship, it achieved a number of excellent placings, including a second at Le Mans. The turbo RSR featured an extremely large rear wing, and a slightly raised rear roof to further improve its aerodynamic effectiveness. The wide rear tires and huge rear wing of the 1974 factory Martini Turbo Carrera RSR are easily seen in this photo taken at the Monterey Historic Event honoring Porsche in 1998. Less evident is the restructured roof. Reshaping the 911's roof line would be Porsche's engineer Norbert Singer's plan for the factory's 935/77 and 935/78 models. *Leonard Turner*

Singer was given the assignment. The result was the Carrera RSR model, introduced in 1973 at Daytona.

After the 1973 season was consigned to the record books, and with the Arab-Israeli War causing, in part, the decision of the SCCA to effectively bar the 917 Turbos from the Can-Am for the coming year, there was the question of what the factory should do for 1974. Certainly there was no pressure for Porsche to worry about either on the international Group 4 production car scene or any of the national championships the RSR ran in. This is because the slightly revised 1974 customer model was even more potent than its predecessor, which had had relatively little trouble dominating in its intended arena. Moreover, since the company's Can-Am involvement was now a matter of history, the resources allocated there could easily be reassigned to another arena. Lastly, there was the clear possibility that in 1975, FIA would revise its prototype regulations, scrapping the custom-constructed sports racers and replacing them with silhouette production-based entries whose roots could easily be traced to factory assembly lines.

The plans of the FIA did not proceed exactly as had been hoped. For one thing, the new prototype formula was not initiated until 1976 and after it was, the ties between factory and on-track design were loosened so much that by the time the FIA's new Group C classification reintroduced the sports racers in 1982, there was little common ground between what could be purchased in the show-room and what could cross the finish line first.

Regardless, the need to create, test, and develop a production contender for the upcoming formula was the obvious reason for the inauguration of the 1974 Turbo RSR program. There were some who felt initially that the car should indeed be a "silhouette" machine employing a Porsche sports-racing tube frame with a 911-type body shell hung over it. (This was, of course, what happened during the 935 era, when the 1978 *Moby Dick* long-tail was brought forth by Singer and his engineers.) Dr. Fuhrmann vetoed the idea, insisting that the new 1974 boosted RSR maintain a strong link with what was being shipped to the company's dealers. It was the first shot in a battle between Fuhrmann and the racing department that would see other confrontations down the road.

Still, since the Turbo RSR was going to run as a prototype, there was little need for Singer and his group to follow the constraints imposed by the production classification rules. Having been forced to accept the basic 911 body shell as their starting point, the Weissach team wasted no time in extensively modifying it. At the rear, much of the 911's standard sheet metal engine support structure was cut away, replaced by a tubular aluminum subframe that would also serve as a place from which to hang the motor and much of its turbocharger system. The fuel tank was moved from its normal front-mounted location and put within the interior of the passenger compartment where the right rear jump seat normally was, this arrangement providing a better overall weight balance between full and light fuel conditions. Likewise, there was no spare tire, this not being a requirement under the prototype regulations. By making these changes, not only was it possible to lighten the front, but also to modify it for better brake cooling.

As for the suspension, any reliance on torsion bars was dropped in favor of competition coilover shock/spring units. The standard MacPherson strut arrangement was retained at the front. Welded struts and semi-rear trailing arms of steel and aluminum replaced the standard items at both ends of the car. Additionally, the geometry was modified to reduce squat under acceleration and dive under braking, while the front spindles were raised on the strut to reduce ride height, as had been done with the original nonboosted RSR prototype in late 1972.

The brakes were the same ventilated, cross-drilled, four-puck units fitted to the less adventuresome RSR models. The centerlock alloy wheels,

standard RSR equipment, were used front and rear, the latter's width being increased to 17 inches.

Looking again at the body, Singer and company installed an aluminum roll cage designed to accept most of the stresses the shell would face in its career, allowing the engineers to substitute fiberglass for steel when it came to the deck and trunk lids, doors, fenders, and what remained of the bumpers. (In fact, at the rear there was really none, the space occupied by the normal center section being used for the turbo and wastegate system.) At the front, what might have been

There were a number of improvements and changes made to the 2.1-liter boosted flat-six that powered the turbo RSR of 1974. One of the final configurations was this flat-fan example, which took most of its air from scoops in the blanked-off rear quarter side windows. Later versions of the engine would not only power the 935, but also the 936 Group 6 sports racing prototype spyder, which would win Le Mans on three occasions. The Number 22 Turbo RSR Coupe of Manfred Schurti and Herbert Müller demonstrated the potential of Porsche's prototype Carrera at Le Mans in 1974 by finishing second overall. Only the supposedly much more sophisticated Matra V-12 sports racer was able to beat it. In 1979, the successor to the boosted Carrera, the 935, would win the race, the first time a production-based car had done that since the early 1950s. *Porsche Werk*

The original 935 didn't look that much different from its street-legal 930 progenitor. However, by the time it began to race, things had changed, as Norbert Singer had discarded the standard fenders, modifying their shape so that they sloped down at the same angle as the front hood, placing the headlights in the front bumper. Although the FIA wasn't pleased, it was all legal under the rules.
Porsche Werk

called a bumper previously was now a fully reshaped airdam, whose top contour followed the slope of the front hood line.

Not only did these changes improve the weight of the Turbo RSR (which was about 1,655 pounds empty when it rolled onto the track), but also the aerodynamics. To further help in this latter area, Singer's crew endowed their creation with a huge, rear wing that again brought them into conflict with Dr. Fuhrmann. Despite the positive results of the initial test sessions, Fuhrmann was insistent that something be done about the wing, which he said made the car look like a "monoplane." Telling his engineers that Porsche was in the business of selling automobiles and not vehicles capable of flight, he ordered that the situation be rectified before the car was shown publicly.

Thus entered stylist Tony Lapine and his people, taking the Turbo RSR to the Stuttgart wind tunnel, where they blended the wing into the bodywork by extending two arches back from the sides of the roof to meet the wing. More importantly, perhaps, Lapine also raised the rear roofline slightly and incorporated a flush-fitting rear window to improve

the airflow to the wing, increasing its effectiveness considerably. (Singer would use a loophole in the subsequent silhouette scriptures to do the same things with the 1977 factory 935 and the later 1978 *Moby Dick*, with such benefits that the idea was copied by virtually all 935 builders thereafter.)

Despite these efforts, there was continued unhappiness in the executive quarters at Porsche over the presence of the wing, which was further disguised through a clever paint scheme when the Turbo RSR was clothed in Martini's corporate colors. This cleverness consisted of using black in the wing area to diminish its visual importance against the silver, red and blue paint scheme.

Even if the body and suspension modifications pointed toward the future of 911 racing development, they still had to take a backseat to what was going on in the engine compartment, where the technology of the Can-Am was being mated to the tradition of Porsche production-car innovation for the first time. Ironically, when Porsche began its turbocharging journey in 1971, it did so not with the 917's flat 12-cylinder engine, but rather with the Type 901 boxer six of the 911.

That marriage, if it could be called that, was only for the purpose of testing the general principles of turbocharging. Yet the similarities between the two engines made the transfer of information useful between them, a fact that was to assume some more importance in the Turbo RSR project.

Initially, the single turbo RSR system used one half of the Bosch fuel injection twin-log manifold setup found on the unfettered Can-Am 917s. Subsequently, this was replaced by a single plenum chamber, which was simpler and less fragile and which, with few modifications, was retained throughout the 1974 season.

As for the engine itself, unlike in the Can-Am, the authorities mandated a formula that multiplied actual for turbos by a factor of 1.4 to give the "official" capacity size. Since the limit for the prototype division remained at 3 liters for 1974, that meant the actual maximum displacement could not exceed 2,143 cc.

In the end, Porsche's engineers came up with a 2,142-cc unit using a standard 2-liter production crank mated to Nikasil-coated cylinders with an 83-millimeter bore. The cylinder heads were from the old 906 with slightly enlarged valves (intake 47 millimeters, exhaust 42 millimeters). The valves themselves, however, were sodium-filled for better cooling. Polished titanium rods were employed with new flat top pistons that brought the compression ratio down to 6.5:1. To complete the package, the engineers fitted the breakerless capacitive discharge ignition system from the standard RSR.

The real key to success, though, came from a different direction. When Porsche was exploring the possibility of doing the Turbo RSR, it spent a great deal of time calculating how much horsepower it would need to compete on a relatively equal footing with its all-out, sports-racing rivals. Those calculations showed that on average Porsche's custom-constructed opposition could count on about 480 horsepower, while the 2,142-cc turbo six most likely wouldn't put out much beyond 430 horsepower.

Under normal circumstances that should have ended the program. But the engineers had a new solution: better cooling to overcome the horsepower hurdle. Today intercoolers (nothing more than radiators, in actuality) are commonplace. Back in 1974, no one had really thought of them as an answer to increasing turbo performance, and yet, in retrospect, they seem the obvious choice.

Briefly stated, turbocharging involves heat. Since cooler air (and a cooler air/fuel mixture) is

The original 935 poses for its formal portrait at Weissach. As conceived by the FIA, the Group 5 "Silhouette" production-based prototype formula instituted for 1976 was intended to infuse new life into sports car racing by creating stronger identification ties between the car and the fans. By the time the Group 5 silhouette era ended in the early 1980s, the cars, particularly the 935, barely resembled their assembly-line counterparts. *Porsche Werk*

By the end of the 1976 season, the factory Martini 935 had changed considerably. Not only was the nose sloped, but the rear fenders had been much modified to carry the air-to-water turbocharger intercoolers demanded by the FIA after the first race of the year. With the exception of a "running board" between the front and rear fenders, this was the basic configuration in which the Porsche factory sold the 935 to its customers for the next three years. *Porsche Werk*

The Watkins Glen 6-Hour in 1976 was a mixed affair. Here the Jacky Ickx/Jochen Mass 935 leads the IMSA All-American GT Chevrolet Monza of Michael Keyser from the North American-based Camel series. The Monza was the first of the tube-frame road racers, built specifically to combat Porsche's entries in the IMSA title chase. Ickx and Mass would finish second at the Glen after midrace brake problems. However, a sister car would take the victory, helping the factory to secure its claim of the FIA Makes Championship. *Porsche Werk*

denser than hot air, thus providing "more bang for the buck." By cooling the fuel/air mixture, more power is available, and thus, the intercooler becomes necessary. In fact, cooling was a problem for the engine itself, and after the initial tests, it was decided to enlarge the oil cooler. Later in the season, prior to Le Mans, the engineers swapped the vertical fan for a horizontal fan version that further reduced engine temperatures.

In all, there were three engines used: the so-called Phase I powerplant, with a log manifold and a vertical fan; the Phase II model, still with a vertical fan but with a central plenum chamber; and the final edition, with the horizontal fan and single plenum chamber. At the beginning, Porsche was seeing somewhere around 440-plus horsepower from the early versions. By the end of 1974, 500 horsepower was the norm (this being accompanied by 406 ft-lb of torque).

One area, however, that would cause problems throughout the year would be the Type 915

For 1977, 935 project leader Norbert Singer dreamed up something new, the 935/77. Not only did it feature revised tenders, but also, a raised rear roof that covered the rear portion of its original counterpart. This use of another loophole in the Group 5 regulations permitted Singer to greatly improve the airflow to the rear wing, thus increasing its effectiveness. Before he was done, Singer would take the Group 5 silhouette concept into territory never envisaged by the FIA with his famed 935/78 *Moby Dick* of the following year, which featured a shape only somewhat connected to a 911. *Porsche Werk*

Although originally intended as a "factory only" entry, in 1980, Porsche allowed its customers to copy the 935/77 design for themselves, and even built new cars for Porsche privateers. Among these latter 935/77 recipients was American Bruce Leven, who used his to win the 1981 edition of the famous 12 Hours of Sebring. This 935/77 belongs to Porsche and resides today in its Zuffenhausen Museum. *Porsche Werk*

From the rear, the 935/77 presents its unique shape with its raised rear wing and fenders that are more indented at the rear when compared to the original 935 of 1976. Not so evident in the photograph is the fact that project leader Norbert Singer has raised the rear roof, covering the original with a fiberglass extension that substantially improved the car's aerodynamics. In varying forms, this innovation would be employed on every subsequent 935 model built, with the exception of the two batches of customer racers constructed in 1978 and 1979. *Porsche Werk*

five-speed transaxle, which would experience a number of internal failures at inopportune moments. On the other hand, the single-plate, 225-millimeter-diameter clutch was for the most part up to its task, as were the halfshafts borrowed from the 917. For the majority of tracks a limited-slip differential was used, although a completely locked rear was substituted on occasion.

The first public appearance for the Martini Turbo RSR came during the Le Mans test session weekend heat races, where Porsche entered two cars, one for Gijs van Lennep and Herbert Müller and the other for Helmuth Koinigg and Manfred Schurti. Both broke, Koinigg and Schurti departing in the first heat with a rocker arm failure, and van Lennep and Müller retiring in the second with the only broken clutch of the year.

For the first two Makes rounds at Monza and Spa, Porsche came with a single car for van Lennep and Müller, collecting a fifth and a third. At the Nürburgring both RSR Turbos were present, finishing sixth and seventh after some crash-related body problems. For Imola, the van Lennep/Müller duo was given the Phase III engine, while Koinigg and Schurti made do with a Phase II unit. Both were classified as nonfinishers, the "first team" entry's engine showing its newness with turbo difficulties and the second string's older model getting stuck in fourth gear. Still, both were running at the finish.

The next event was Le Mans. Here Porsche engineers thought they had their best chance, and they took special care in their preparations, even going so far as to replace the normal magnesium engine crankcases with aluminum substitutes for durability. Van Lennep and Müller once more had

From the side, the 935 presented a unique silhouette. In its only North American appearance, the factory entry easily won the 1977 Watkins Glen 6-Hour with Jacky Ickx aboard. In later years customer versions would gain victories at Daytona and Sebring. However, they would do so against tough opposition. In 1977, the 935/77 ruled supreme, gaining Porsche its second straight Manufacturers crown. *Bill Oursler*

the Phase III engine, while Koinigg and Schurti again were powered by the Phase II unit. Both cars had slightly revised cooling duct arrangements, the air now being taken from the quarter windows, which were blanked off, instead of the sides of the rear engine cover.

Porsche was hoping for just a bit of luck to pull a win off, but none came its way. After six hours, the Koinigg/Schurti car blew its engine in spectacular fashion before coming to a flaming halt. Fortunately there were no injuries and the blaze was quickly extinguished. Bad omens were there, however. They came again much later after van Lennep and Müller had worked their way into second. This time the troubled transaxle let them down, the pair losing several gears including fifth. (As it was, the winning Matra had to have its own Porsche-designed transaxle completely rebuilt in one of the greater ironies of the event.) Despite their problems, the Porsche drivers held on to finish in the runner-up slot.

The van Lennep/Müller duo then went on to pick up a seventh in Austria, a fifth at Brands Hatch (with only second gear functioning), a seventh at Paul Ricard, and another strong second

behind the Matra team at Watkins Glen. In France, Koinigg and Schurti ran the second car, but were disqualified for a push start, ending the year on a less than upbeat note.

After the FIA pushed back the date for the introduction of the Silhouette Group 5 World Makes formula until 1976, there was some speculation that Porsche might again enter the RSR Turbos, but having learned what they wanted and facing the reality of the costs of racing, the company kept the unique cars parked in Zuffenhausen. Even so, replicas of the engines appeared in several aging 908 prototypes with a mixed result.

Only once more did a Turbo RSR actually run in public. That came at Daytona in 1977 when Ted Field and Danny Ongais ran one example, minus its Martini paintwork, for Vasek Polak, who had purchased it from the factory. Unhappily, the two Interscope men were nonfinishers, retiring early with mechanical problems.

Even though the history of the RSR Turbos was short, it represented a then-high watermark for the development of the original 911 racing model line, employing a number of previously used techniques

opposite: The original design for Norbert Singer's 935/78, better known as the *Moby Dick*, featured fully covered doors and a low-mounted rear wing. Later these were modified to include a large NACA duct, as seen here. However, having been manipulated so often by Singer, the FIA finally balked and ordered the doors uncovered. Although later Singer and Porsche did include a small front fairing over the doors, the low wing had to be discarded in favor of a higher mounted example that increased drag. *Porsche Werk*

that were blended with future engineering concepts to produce a car which, while it may not have achieved outright victory on the track, was a thoroughbred progenitor for the turbos that would follow.

When the FIA finally did give the green light to its silhouette prototype formula to begin in 1976, Singer and Porsche were more than ready. Not all new turbos had grown from the boosted RSR project: the prototype Group 5 935, and its far more restricted Group 4 customer-oriented "production" counterpart, the 934—both models being based for approval purposes on the newly introduced 911/930 street turbo.

While the weight restrictions imposed on the Group 4 category virtually forced Porsche to keep much of the street interior and bumpers of the 930 for the 934 coupe, such was not the case with the 935, of which the factory ran two examples for the 1976 season. For the 935, Singer and his people fully stripped the basic body of the 930, reinforcing it with a full-alloy roll cage. To achieve the better torsional rigidity at the front, an aluminum crossbrace structure was added between the original front inner fender panels, effectively linking the two front shock towers together and covering the top of the 42.2-gallon fuel cell.

As with the Turbo RSR, the torsion-bar springing, while remaining on the car, was present only to satisfy the rulemakers. The job of providing suspension mobility was instead entrusted to the same basic coilover spring/shock absorber unit as were seen on the earlier turbo coupe. Bilstein gas pressure shocks were used, along with progressive-rate titanium springs.

For the most part, the rest of the normal 911 suspension geometry was retained, the exception being at the front, where it was modified to improve the 935's antidive characteristics, and to eliminate some of the less-than-desirable extreme camber and castor changes associated with the MacPherson front strut design. Sway bars were fitted to both front and rear, the latter being driver-adjustable.

The brakes were similar to those of the 917, consisting of ventilated discs (43 millimeters in diameter at the front and 38 millimeters in the rear) and four-piston calipers. Except for Le Mans, the discs were cross-drilled. (Porsche engineers were afraid of cracking because of the heat extremes produced by the unique Sarthe circuit.) Additionally, brake balance was adjustable front-to-rear.

Both BBS multipiece and Porsche cast rims were used. At the front these were 16 inches in diameter and 10.5 inches wide. At the rear the width increased to 15 inches, the diameter rising to a gigantic 19 inches. This was done primarily to improve brake cooling, a decision that caused Dunlop to produce some extremely low-profile rubber so that the wheel/tire combination would clear the rear fender area.

Even though the weight policy for Group 5 was far less restrictive than Group 4, it was still a factor in deciding what size engine to use. This was crucial for the 935, since the displacement would be directly linked to the car's minimum acceptable poundage on the FIA's official scales. With the FIA multiplying the actual displacement of turbocharged powerplants by a factor of 1.5, Porsche eventually chose a theoretical 4-liter limit for the boosted six it intended to mate up with the 935's five-speed transaxle. This gave a real-world displacement of 2.8 liters and a weight of 2,139 pounds. With a bore of 92 millimeters and a stroke of 70.4 millimeters, the actual displacement came out to be 2,808 cc. Titanium connecting rods, a flat fan, dual ignition, and a Bosch injection unit were used along with a single KKK turbocharger. As with the 1974 Turbo RSR, compression was set low at 6.5:1. Depending on the boost used, the horsepower figures ranged from about 600 horsepower to nearly 700 horsepower.

Surprisingly, these figures were tied to the 935's controversial body shape. This retained much of its inner structure, but lost most of its external sheet metal. Indeed, aside from the roof, most of the exterior was covered by fiberglass. The officials had little problem with the material used by Porsche; what bothered them in particular was the form in which it was molded.

Providing sufficient rear downforce would prove over the years to be far easier than finding the right amount for the front. While the front hood of the 911 sloped down toward the bumper in a fashion that supported the achievement of this goal in downforce numbers, the standard fenders, with their headlights, did not. Singer, however, read the regulations carefully and came up with an unusual solution: put the headlights in the bumper and slope the fenders at the same angle as the hood to provide the extra downforce needed.

This definitely was not what the FIA had intended. However, under the regulations, which permitted unrestricted shapes for the fender flares (and which failed to state what was a flare and what was a fender), Singer found the freedom to move the silhouette formula in a direction not

wanted by the authorities. In the coming years, he would do this again, eventually converting the shape of Group 5 vehicles into something that bore little relationship to the assembly line.

At the first event of 1976 in Mugello, the FIA's inspectors found themselves in a quandary when they saw what Singer had done. They couldn't, as much as they might have wanted to, demand a return to the standard front nose shape without leaving themselves open to questions and second guessing. Instead, they chose another path, one that involved the engine cover.

Porsche had revised the engine compartment tail section of the 935 at least once during its development to conform to the rulemakers' wishes. Now, the two-tiered bewinged tail attracted new and unwanted attention. The problem this time wasn't the aerodynamics; rather, it was what was under the fiberglass, which also served as the exterior for the engine compartment cover itself. At its heart, the issue centered around the location of the turbo's intercoolers.

The most efficient intercooler was air-to-air, and it was this variety that was being fitted under the 935's tail. In one of those convoluted exercises in logic that have made the FIA so famous, it was decided that because the air-to-air intercooler would not fit beneath the deck lid of the standard 930 on which the 935 was based, it was illegal.

The fact that the FIA had more than enough time to come to this conclusion before the season

began was of little importance. As far as the inspectors were concerned, they had repaid Singer for his front fenders in full measure, and they were happy. As a result, Porsche was forced into a hurry-up development program that saw the air-to-air intercooler arrangement replaced by a pair of air-to-water intercoolers that were now located at the forward ends of a revised set of rear fenders.

Not only was the new system less efficient in that it could not keep the incoming air mixture as cool and compressed at high boost levels over long periods of time, it also had a number of bugs that had to be worked out even as the cars were being raced. While Mugello, where the air-to-air units were used, went into Porsche's win column, it wasn't until Watkins Glen, in mid-July, that an air-to-water-intercooled 935 was again first overall. In spite of this, Porsche did, with the help of a third victory at Dijon, take the inaugural Group 5 title.

Although the 1976 935s were strictly factory items, Porsche did provide kits that would allow privateer 934 owners to upgrade their cars to Group 5 specs. Although these weren't the full equal of the factory Martini entries, they were potent, and several privateers, including the Kremer brothers, took advantage of the pieces to convert their coupes.

Until this point, the 935 story is relatively straightforward. From 1977, things became more complicated. Interwoven in the fabric of this change were politics and public acceptance. Looked at from an overall viewpoint, the era of

the 935 was an almost complete box office failure in international competition, where the public was accustomed to factory-supported sports racing cars, vehicles largely describable as two-place Formula One machines with fenders. For the most part, European audiences, whose numbers determined success or failure for the silhouette cars, saw the 935s and their counterparts as a retrograde move. On the other hand, North American spectators on the IMSA Camel GT tour saw the turbocharged Porsches as a step up from the older, non-turbo Carrera RSRs and their boosted 934 successors.

Added to this was the commitment of IMSA and its promoters to using the silhouette Porsches as the means of making the Camel GT the North American continent's premier road course series. Even here politics were in evidence. The worries of IMSA's John Bishop about Porsche's technical achievement with the 935 led him to initially want to keep it out of his series. Only after Josef Hoppen, Porsche's North American competition boss, got Camel's management and promoters to apply pressure to Bishop, did the IMSA boss revise

his stance and allow the 935 in for the 1978 season. In fact, the cars that came to the Camel GT showed quite a bit of development over the initial factory versions of two years earlier. After the 1976 season, Porsche had produced a run of single turbo "customer" 935s, mainly for the European market that were virtually identical to the factory prototypes. Indeed, about the only difference was visual, this coming about with the addition of "running boards" between the front and rear fenders. What came to America were twin-turbo machines with improved aerodynamics.

While this was going on, Singer was taking the next step. Following the completion of the 1976 season, he, along with other manufacturers' representatives, met in Paris with the FIA to revise the interpretation of the Group 5 regulations for 1977. The participants decided to allow the raising of floors to the tops of the rocker panels (this in order to permit the easy routing of the massive turbo exhausts for the front-engine Ford and BMW camps, should those companies decide to go to turbocharging), and to reduce the basic car body structure to that which was contained between

The 935/78 *Moby Dick* in its final configuration as a factory entry at Le Mans with partially enclosed doors. The car featured tubular front and rear extensions attached to a tubular center roll cage structure to form what was, in effect a full tube-frame vehicle. As permitted by the rules, the body floor was raised by several inches, essentially lowering the car in overall height by the same amount. A suspected oil leak at Le Mans kept *Moby Dick* from being a contender for the win there in 1978. *Porsche Werk*

In its Day-Glo red Martini livery, the 935/78 *Moby Dick* was a memorable sight. However, in terms of its statistical performance, the car never lived up to its potential, failing to add any substantial triumphs to Porsche's record of success. However, replicas built for customers in 1982 did achieve some glory. One, in the hands of Britishers John Fitzpatrick and David Hobbs, finished fourth overall and first in the IMSA GTX division at Le Mans in 1982. This example was allowed to run with the fully covered doors intended, but not permitted by the FIA, for its factory progenitor. *Porsche Werk*

the forward and rear bulkheads defining the passenger compartment. Beyond this, the FIA allowed the engine compartment bulkhead to be moved into the passenger compartment by several inches to permit the plumbing associated with the turbo system to be more readily installed.

Eventually, Singer would use these concessions to build the famed *Moby Dick* tube-frame 935/78. In the immediate months following the Paris get-together, though, Singer was occupied with the 1977 version of the 935. While this included fenders redesigned for better aerodynamics, its major visual difference was the raising of the rear roof to improve the effectiveness of the substantially revised rear wing structure by smoothing the air flow, as had been done on the Turbo RSR.

All this was possible because according to the regulations, any rear aerodynamic device was acceptable as long as it was contained within the profile of the car when viewed head-on. What Singer did was to add a second roof and rear window over the original (which according to the regulations had to be maintained) to achieve the profile he wanted. In the engine bay, the all-air-cooled six got a new turbo system with a second turbocharger, this being the engine that was used by Porsche when it built the second run of customer 935s for the 1978 season.

In Europe, the 1977 Group 5 scene had become a Porsche 935 parade, the only difference being that the customers had to play a supporting role to the Weissach 935/77 of Singer's engineers. When Porsche decided to limit its 935/78 *Moby Dick* to just a few events in 1978, the customers assumed a much more important part in furthering Porsche's honor on the FIA's World Manufacturers Group 5 tour.

If the Porsche 935/77 again was not what international authorities had in mind when they decided to switch the World Makes Championship from sports racing prototypes to vehicles whose origins were strictly production-based, its successor, the 935/78 *Moby Dick*, really raised their ire.

From an American viewpoint the 935/78 was not all that unusual, but for the European perspective it was a radical departure from the norm. What made 935/78 unique was the fact that Singer built it as a tube-frame "special." Previously, no matter how modified they were, Group 5 entries retained a large measure of their original body structure. Such was not the case with the *Moby Dick*.

Having done away with the front and the rear of the chassis, Singer now discarded the floor, substituting a fiberglass structure that, as permitted by the rules, was level with the top of the door sills. Effectively, this dropped the whole car by some 3 inches toward the ground. What Singer had at this point was a pair of front and rear subframes and an unreinforced central section. The bodywork for this included the roof, the windshield posts (A-pillars in automotive parlance), the front cowl and dash, as well as the door frames, rear quarter windows.

To increase the stiffness of the center section, Singer used a third tubular roll cage structure, firmly attached to what remained of the original body. When brought together with the front and rear tubular subframes, Singer had what amounted to a European version of an American NASCAR

In 1986 Porsche produced the circuit racing version of its 959 Group B rally car, the Type 961. Like the 959, it featured a water-cooled, turbocharged, flat six-cylinder engine and all-wheel drive. Run at Le Mans in 1986, it won its class with relative ease. However, in its other two race appearances, at the fall 1986 IMSA Camel GT Finale and at Le Mans the following summer, it failed to finish, suffering tire problems in America and a blown engine at the Sarthe. *Porsche Werk*

The Little 935: *Baby*

In 1977 Porsche's plans for the 935 took a different twist, when Zuffenhausen decided to enter the under-2-liter category then being contested in Germany by Ford and BMW. Somewhat dismayed that no manufacturers seemed to want to challenge the 935 in Group 5, Porsche decided to go where the competition was. The result was the car known as *Baby*.

Basically a lightened 935 with a modified version of the company's then-current factory 935/77 bodywork, *Baby*'s principal feature was its 1.5-liter downsized powerplant. Built in a hurry, *Baby* ran but two races. The first was at the Norisring on June 30, where an overheated cockpit left Jacky Ickx to struggle to a sixth-place finish. The second time out, at Hockenheim, with several improvements including a pair of 19-inch-diameter rear wheels, Ickx had no trouble in crushing the opposition. Following that appearance, the car was retired to the Porsche Museum, but not before it made a stop at Kremer's along the way.

Indeed, there is much intrigue surrounding *Baby*'s stay in Cologne with the two brothers. Reportedly, the Kremers offered to take the car back to Porsche from Hockenheim as a favor to the harassed Weissach engineers. Interestingly, the journey took some time to complete, during which the Kremers were said to have explored *Baby*'s aerodynamic secrets quite thoroughly. In the end, the Kremers' highly successful K3 was said to have owed much of its sophistication to *Baby*'s Cologne visit.

Porsche designed and built a special 1.5-liter 935 for racing in Germany during 1977. The car, known as *Baby*, made just two appearances in the hands of Jacky Ickx, winning one and losing the other. Outwardly *Baby* resembled its bigger brother, the 935/77. However, underneath it pioneered the use of tubular front and rear frame structures that would be later incorporated in the ultimate 935, the 935/78. *Porsche Werk*

racer. An interesting side note is the fact that Porsche decided to make the 935/78 right-hand drive, basing it on a 911SC rather than the 930 Turbo. The body was much sleeker than before, featuring a nose whose upper shape was more curved than in the past, and an extended set of rear fenders, which gave the car its distinctive shape. As with the 935/77, a second, slightly raised rear roof was added to improve the airflow to the rear wing.

Unfortunately, the aerodynamics, including the wing, had to be modified substantially from what Singer had intended after yet another political hassle with the FIA. As designed originally, the doors of the *Moby Dick* car were covered completely by an extra set of skin panels that blended together the front and rear fenders. Built into the revised door was a large NACA duct that fed air to the rear fender radiators. The basis for the Porsche engineer's decision to do this was the fact that the regulations did not specify how far forward one could extend the rear-mounted aerodynamic aids. The new doors, which substantially improved the airflow and reduced the aerodynamic drag, permitted Singer to use a low-mounted rear wing (placed in much the same position as the special ones used later on the Le Mans 956/962 tails) that took advantage of the cleaned up airflow to do its job, while also helping to improve the drag.

At first, the FIA reluctantly agreed but later changed its mind, decreeing that the door could not be covered over. Singer and his group went to work again, coming up with a partial covering for the front of the door area that continued the front fender line. While probably no more legal than the first, it was accepted by the officials who uncharacteristically tried to make amends for their indecision. At the same time, the low-mounted wing was scrapped for a higher placed and narrower substitute, and the radiator ducts in the forward section of the rear fenders were revamped to compensate for the changes. Regardless of the compromises, 935/78 represented the slickest production-based shape yet seen in Group 5.

For all of his chassis and bodywork innovation, Singer kept virtually unchanged the suspension geometry from the previous 935/77. This meant that the coilover-type front MacPherson struts stayed, while at the rear, the coilover shock/spring combination remained. New wishbones were used at the front to increase the track from 1,502 millimeters to 1,602 millimeters, while also reducing static camber. At the rear, the track was widened from 1,560 millimeters to 1,575 millimeters. In the process, the production steel trailing arms from the 930 were replaced by specially fabricated aluminum ones. The pick-up points also were raised to help prevent rear end squat under acceleration. Anti-sway bars were fitted front and rear as in the past, the front being driver adjustable.

Retained were the 11x16-inch front and 15x19-inch rear rims. Changes, however, were made to the brakes. The diameter of the original 917-based ventilated discs was increased from 12 to 13 inches, while the thickness went from 32 millimeters to 35 millimeters. Additionally, a new one-piece, four-piston aluminum caliper replaced the former three-piece unit. Interestingly, the practice of cross-drilling the discs that had been used everywhere but Le Mans (except for the 1971 winner) was now employed on the 935/78 without any problems.

If the structure of *Moby Dick* was a departure from prior practices, no less so was its drivetrain. Porsche had won the 1977 Le Mans 24-Hours with an all-air-cooled 936 spyder sports racer prototype, but just barely, as its boxer six suffered a burnt piston in the final stages. The engineers, worried that the operating temperatures were getting too high for reliability, decided to go with a water-cooled head version in 1978, one that included a four-valve layout. Designed in various bore/stroke combinations, this 911-derived unit was intended not only for the 935/78 but, in 2.1-liter form, for the 936 as well. These two units were to serve as trial horses for the 2.65-liter version Porsche hoped to eventually use in its then-upcoming

For 1993, Norbert Singer and his engineers created a unique "one-off" 911 Turbo that would effectively serve as the prototype for the customer-oriented 911 GT2 turbocharged coupes that would appear in 1995. First seen in Brumos colors at the Sebring 12-Hour that year, where it finished seventh, the car was also run under factory direction at Le Mans, where it retired after a minor accident in the hands of Walter Roehrl. *Porsche Werk*

Indianapolis 500 program. How well they achieved their objective can be seen in the fact that while the Indy program was canceled for political reasons, the water-cooled head engine lived on. Using various Motronic induction systems, it powered the 956s and 962s, winning Le Mans some eight times (including the 1981 victory in a 936) and was the inspiration for the 959 and all GT1 powerplants as well. For *Moby Dick*, Singer employed the 3.2-liter version, this having a 95.7-millimeter bore and 74.4-millimeter stroke for an actual displacement of 3,211 cc. Additionally, the compression ratio was put at 7.0:1. The intake valves were 35 millimeters in diameter and were set at an angle of 14 degrees, while the exhaust valves were 30.5 millimeters in diameter and had a 16-degree angle.

One interesting fact about the 3.2-liter flat six was that while there were common boxes to house the dual cams, it came with six individual heads, one for each cylinder. The reason for this arrangement was Weissach's feeling that the weakest part of the turbo motor was in the area of the head gaskets. By going to individual heads, the engineers were able to weld them directly to the cylinders, thus eliminating any potential gasket problems. Ironically, one of the other purposes of going to the four-valve layout with its consequently smaller valves was that this reduction in diameter would allow the valves to be fitted through the completed head/cylinder unit.

When finally installed in *Moby Dick*, the six produced a healthy 740 horsepower at 8,200 rpm, using 1.55 bars of boost. To transmit this power, the four-speed Type 930 gearbox with its locked rear end was again used. Wanting to reduce the angle at which the halfshafts operated, the engineers turned the transaxle upside down, something Porsche also did in the run of 1979 customer 935s it constructed. Retained too was the Fichtel and Sachs single-plate racing clutch.

In terms of performance, the 935/78 *Moby Dick* was awesome, with a top speed on the Mulsanne straight at Le Mans of 227 miles per hour, about the same as its 936 cousin. This was a considerable improvement over its 935 predecessors, the fastest of which was clocked at 219 miles per hour on the Mulsanne.

For all of its performance potential, the record of *Moby Dick* was not that impressive. While it won the Silverstone six-hour enduro, it failed to finish at Vanelunga because of a broken injection pump belt, and also at the Norisring where it was retired due to problems with the brake balance bar. At Le Mans, where it was driven by Rolf Stommelen and Manfred Schurti, it finished only eighth. That result might have been better had not the engineers discovered what they thought was a serious oil leak and ordered the two drivers to take it easy to the finish. Later it was discovered that the oil leak was a minor one, and that the engine could have been run much harder. Whether or not that would have allowed *Moby Dick* a chance at victory will, however, remain a matter of speculation.

Le Mans might have been the end of the *Moby Dick* saga, except for the fact that a number of Porsche's 935 customers began to clamor for duplicates. Eventually, the factory supplied Reinhold Jöst with the plans for the 935/78. Jöst then built two examples, JR-001 in 1981 without the door covering (later sold to Dr. Gianpiero Moretti) and JR-002 in 1982 with the original factory-designed double-skin doors that went to John Fitzpatrick.

Driven by Fitzpatrick and David Hobbs, JR-002 started its career with a victory in the IMSA GTX category at Le Mans in 1982, coming home fourth overall despite losing a cylinder during the latter stages of the affair. JR-002 had a relatively short life, being destroyed the following April at Riverside in an accident that killed Stommelen.

As for Moretti's JR-001, it has survived after being driven with indifferent success under the Momo banner on the IMSA tour during the early 1980s. Moretti sold it to a collector when he moved into IMSA's GTP classification and recently it has been put on the market again.

Perhaps even more important than the replicas were the cars that *Moby Dick* inspired. These included the Kremer K3 and K4, and the American-built Andial car, which won Daytona in 1983 for Preston Henn in the hands of Bob Wollek, Claude Ballot-Lena, and A. J. Foyt. Also inspired by the 935/78 was Bob Akin's monocoque L-1 935; its successor, the Dave Klym-designed-and-built tube-frame 935/84 that was the last of the 935 breed; and the John Paul, Jr., tube-frame 935, which helped the young Paul win the 1982 IMSA Camel GT driver's championship.

In 1993 a new 911 Turbo ran under the direction of the factory at Sebring and Le Mans. While it didn't win either event, it provided the data that would lead to the creation of the 911 GT2 turbo coupe, which was sold to Porsche's customers starting in 1995, and which dominated the international GT2 category for a number of seasons thereafter. *Bill Oursler*

Return to Open Wheel

9

T hey say timing is everything. This was the case with Porsche's first involvement with the Indy Car scene in the late 1970s. Unfortunately for Zuffenhausen, the timing was wrong, ultimately dooming the project. Even so, its effect on Porsche's long-term competition future was, if not profound, at least significant.

The man behind Porsche's aborted Indy program was Josef Hoppen, who had migrated to the United States in 1958 to work at a local dealership in Daytona Beach. He began his American racing by campaigning a series of Porsche Spyders in SCCA events. He had also found work with Volkswagen of America. Shortly after the introduction of the VW-based Formula Vee category, VoA decided to have Hoppen help oversee the new open-wheelers. In 1968, VoA made Hoppen its permanent racing chief,

---

The Vels-Parnelli Porsche Indy Car sits next to the original Porsche open wheeler, the 1.5-liter all-wheel-drive Formula One Cisitalia of 1947. Although of radically different design, the two cars would share one notion, that of a boosted induction system. The Cisitalia's expected output was something over 300 horsepower, about half that of the six-cylinder 2.6-liter 935-type powerplant. *Leonard Turner*

Porsche's first Indy Car was a Vels-Parnelli chassis, which had its Cosworth V-8 replaced by the water-cooled-head Porsche 935 turbocharged flat-six. For its initial testing during the late summer and early fall of 1979, not even the car's traditional black color paint scheme from the Interscope team of Ted Fields was changed. Fields and Interscope were to be partners with Porsche in the Indy project. *Porsche Werk*

establishing him as the manager of its Special Vehicles Department, under which all its motorsport efforts, including Porsche's, would be coordinated.

During the 1970s Hoppen established strong ties to the U.S. Auto Club, the Indy Car sanctioning body at the time, through Volkswagen of America's Formula Super Vee program, USAC running one of the two FSV title chases then in existence. For Hoppen, who had a good working knowledge of the Indy situation, the logical step for Porsche was to move its racing emphasis there.

"At the time," recalled Hoppen, "the U.S. market was one of the most important for Porsche. With the end of the Can-Am, Porsche's main focus was on GT racing, both in IMSA and the SCCA. I felt, however, that we needed to participate in an arena with the maximum amount of exposure possible. Indy cars, with the Indianapolis 500, fit that description perfectly."

The rational of Hoppen's position was obvious. With an on-site crowd of more than 400,000,

as well as a radio and television audience measuring in the hundreds of millions worldwide, the Indy 500 was (and still is) the largest single one-day sporting event anywhere. Yet, even though the potential publicity harvest was great, many within Porsche's management weren't convinced.

This was especially true when it came to Dr. Porsche, who, while having bowed out of the everyday management of the company, still remained very close in its operational programs. The experience of the factory's previous 1960s Formula One project was still vivid for Dr. Porsche. Yet, the logic of going to Indy couldn't be denied, particularly since a happy set of circumstances had substantially reduced the costs of such a program.

At the heart of all of this was a young American named Ted Field. Wealthy in his own right, Field had a good business sense and the contacts to go with his feel for commercial matters. Field was also heavily involved in racing.

Surprisingly, the turbocharged 935 boxer six, with its water-cooled head, fit neatly into the Vels-Parnelli chassis, which required little or no modification to accept it. This engine, which had originally been seen in the Porsche 935/78 and the Porsche 936/78 spyder at Le Mans that year, would go on to power the Group C and IMSA GTP 956/962 prototypes of the 1980s. *Porsche Werk*

By 1977, his Interscope team, with driver Danny Ongais, was a major force in IMSA with its Porsche 934 Turbos. In addition, Interscope, Field, and Ongais were quickly branching out to become featured players in Indy Cars as well. Moreover, Field himself was racing Super Vees, a program that brought him in close contact with Hoppen. Their relationship was further strengthened by the fact that one of Field's closest motorsport advisors was California Porsche dealer Vasek Polak—a friend and ally of Hoppen's, who, like him, saw the full sales potential of Indy for Porsche.

Because of Polak's position as one of the stars in Porsche's sales universe, he was listened to in Zuffenhausen. It wasn't long before Polak was touting the joys of Indy Car racing to the company's upper management structure. More important perhaps than his advocacy was the fact that Polak could bring Field and the Interscope team to the table. What this meant was not only did Porsche receive the benefit of Field's own financial strengths and stability, but also the inclusion

of Field's sponsor, Panasonic, as a monetary partner in the project.

Ironically, Porsche's victory at the 1977 24 Hours of Le Mans also figured into the equation. In spite of that triumph, the winning factory 936 Spyder had been forced to limp across the finish line on five cylinders, the stress of running nearly flat out against the Renaults having caused a piston to burn through during the final stages. That led Porsche's Weissach engineering staff to look at a water-cooled head version of the 936's faithful turbocharged boxer six for the 1978 running at the Sarthe. Several variants were developed. The smaller of the two used at Le Mans that June. The 2.1-liter unit was used in the 936, while the larger was the motivational inspiration for the company's 935/78. Both engines featured water-cooled, four-valve per cylinder, double-overhead-cam heads and twin turbochargers. It was from these that Porsche would develop the Type 935/75 2.65-liter single-turbo version that could be used at Indy. In fact, with a team and

Porsche has displayed its 935-powered Parnelli Indy Car at several historic events in the years since the program's abrupt cancellation during the spring of 1980. Political problems over the amount of boost pressure the Porsche would be permitted to use at Indianapolis caused the factory to quit the Indy Car scene. It would later return with a V-8 engine and a chassis of its own design. *Leonard Turner*

sponsor in place, and the ease of converting an existing powerplant to Indy Car specifications, the lobbying by Polak and Hoppen, along with others, was beginning to have its effect.

Throughout the winter of 1978–1979, the discussions about Indy became ever increasingly focused. Finally, by the late summer of 1979 an agreement had been reached for Porsche to enter Indy in 1980 with Interscope as its team of choice and Panasonic supplying sponsorship. At the time Interscope was campaigning a Parnelli chassis powered by a Ford DFX turbocharged V-8 Cosworths. It was decided for any number of reasons that the Parnellis would be used for testing, several being fitted with the Type 935/75 engines.

In fact, while the press conferences in Stuttgart, New York, and Los Angeles were held late in the year, considerable testing had been done with the test mules during the interim before the official unveilings. One problem encountered was that of keeping oil on the bearings. Eventually it would be solved. There were, however, bigger difficulties facing the project, which had nothing to with its mechanics.

Those woes were of an outside nature, involving the future course of Indy Car racing itself. Prior to the mid-1970s it was possible for a number of the smaller teams engaged in USAC's top division to do well on not only what was known then as the "Championship Trail" (the title given to the Indy season-long title chase season), but also at the annual Memorial Day 500 classic as well.

For the most part the powerplant of choice was the ancient but reliable four-cylinder Offenhausers that had been around the Indy Car arena for more than three decades. It was cheap and got the job done. However in 1976, things changed. That year the 2.6-liter turbocharged version of Ford's 3-liter Formula One Cosworth V-8 was introduced. By 1978 the engine had won Indy. Not only that, but it was clear that anyone not having a Cosworth probably wasn't going to make very much money in the sport.

The trouble was that the owners of the little teams couldn't afford Cosworths. Neither could they attract the sponsorship necessary to allow them to purchase the expensive units. That money went to the big teams, such as Roger Penske's, Jim Hall's, Dan Gurney's, or the folks at McLaren.

The little guys were frozen out. Indy Car racing was heading toward full-time professionalism and only a few were able to keep paying the ever-increasing fees that would permit them to continue

When Porsche publicly introduced the Indy Car in December 1979, it featured a white paint scheme with the Interscope logos of the Ted Field organization. Lacking were the logos of expected sponsor Panasonic. Unfortunately the termination of the program in the spring of 1980 left not only Panasonic but Porsche and Ted Fields spinning in the wind. Outside, it was difficult to distinguish the Porsche-powered Parnelli chassis from its Cosworth engine counterpart. In performance, at 56 inches of boost, the Porsche was every bit the Cosworth's equal. Unhappily, it was never shown in real competition. *Porsche Werk*

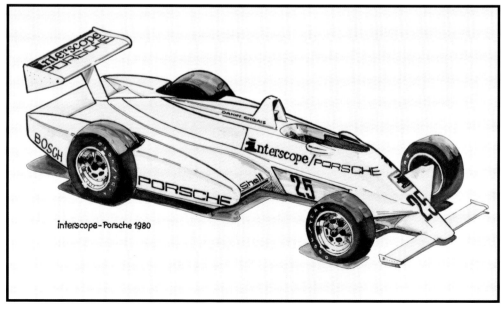

interscope-Porsche 1980

An artist's rendering of what should have been the official Interscope-constructed Porsche chassis. Ironically, while it never ran with Porsche power, it was built and raced by Interscope. Driver Danny Ongais was severely injured in it in a crash at the 1980 Indy 500. *Porsche Werk*

In the early 1980s, at the invitation of McLaren's Ron Dennis, Porsche became involved in the design and construction of a 1.5-liter V-6 Formula One engine, which first appeared under the TAG banner in a McLaren chassis during the latter part of the 1983 season. The Porsche TAG turbo V-6, which was the mainstay of the McLaren Formula One program between 1984 and 1987, not only was responsible for McLaren winning several constructors titles, but also for Niki Lauda's last World Driving crown and Frenchman Alain Prost's first. *Leonard Turner*

playing. It was, in short, a classic case of the "haves" vs. the "have nots." Unfortunately for the "haves," USAC was a democracy. The "have nots" with their greater numbers could vote to change the rules for Indy Car racing as they saw fit.

With the investments of the more well-financed teams in jeopardy, Penske and oil company man Pat Patrick (a long-time Indy entrant) got together with a number of their colleagues to form a new owners' group in the summer of 1978. This was Championship Auto Racing Teams, Inc., better known as CART.

Shortly thereafter the Indy scene not so quietly came apart. Veiled threats and much posturing on both sides was evident as the fall of 1978 approached. Finally, with autumn in full swing, USAC decided to hold a meeting at its Speedway, Indiana, headquarters. At that gathering the USAC stalwarts made it clear to the CART representatives, then still within the USAC organization, that things would be done their way and if the CART teams didn't like it, that was tough. The result was that the CART camp voted to start its own series for 1979, thus setting off what was to become the CART-USAC war, a conflict that would soon engulf Porsche's Indy plans.

As all this was taking place, Hoppen was meeting with USAC president Dick King, the two of them agreeing that the boost pressure limit for Porsche's flat six should be set at 54 inches, halfway between 60-plus given the Offies, and the 48 permitted the Cosworth DFXs. Unfortunately, none of this was put down on paper—it was just a gentlemen's agreement, and that was a problem, since USAC had its own worries, chief among which was its less-than-stable position on the Indy scene. Although it wasn't in danger of being kicked out as the sanctioning organization for the 500, elsewhere its schedule was less firm. In fact, about the best thing USAC had going for it was A. J. Foyt, who, after initially joining CART, had switched back to USAC's side.

Foyt was the only "star" USAC had, and he wasn't pleased with the boost arrangement for Zuffenhausen. Shortly after New Year's in 1980 he began to lobby for a change in Porsche's boost pressure figures, suggesting he hadn't made up his mind about where he was going to run in the upcoming season. A hurried trip to Weissach for USAC technical maven Jack Beckley and Foyt's crew chief of the time produced few changes in Foyt's posture.

While Interscope and Porsche continued to test, the politics continued to ferment. By late

March, things were reaching a crisis point. Finally, USAC put out a technical bulletin saying that the boost limit for Porsche would be no more than that given to the Cosworths—48 inches. With less than a month remaining before the start of practice for the 500, Porsche's response was quick. In its own, terse one-page press release, the company announced it was canceling its Indy program, citing the fact that it hadn't tested at the lower boost pressures and that it had an inadequate amount of time in which to do so. Like that, it was over.

Outside of Porsche's engineers, Ongais and the Interscope team, no one had ever seen the Porsche on the track. Now, no one would ever have the chance to do so. Yet, even as the cars were being put under dust covers, the technology developed was simmering back at Weissach. In 1981 Porsche 936s would return to dominate Le Mans, using the engines developed for Indy. Later, those same powerplants would be developed further to become the basis for those in the new Group C 956. Yet, Porsche wasn't through with open-wheeled competition.

During the more than 15 years since Porsche's departure from Formula One at the end of 1962, things had changed, the 1.5-liter cars giving way to the 3-liter machines, and skinny tires to the fat, low-profile rubber so familiar today. Other than Ferrari, the Grand Prix tour belonged to the independents, largely British, and nearly all were powered by the Ford Cosworth double-overhead-cam V-8.

As he had been during Porsche's 1960s venture, the man at the head of the field was Colin Chapman, who, with the ground-effects Lotus 79 that took Mario Andretti to the 1978 World Championship title, had again moved the technological goalposts. Put simply, Chapman, through the use of carefully shaped underbody tunnels and sliding skirts attached to the outer edges of the sidepods, was able to evacuate air from underneath his car more quickly than it flowed over the top of it. This was the heart and soul of ground effects, and it was truly a "something for nothing" proposition in that the suction created and subsequent

In 1987 Porsche returned to the Indy Car scene with its own chassis-engine combination. The eight-cylinder turbocharged Porsche powerplant, based in large measure on the company V-6 TAG Formula One turbo, was constructed in-house, as was the Type 2708 chassis. It is seen here testing prior to its public debut in the late summer 1987 at Weissach. The 2708 proved uncompetitive. However, the engine enjoyed a career that spanned the length of the Porsche Indy program, which ended with the conclusion of the 1990 season. *Porsche Werk*

Porsche introduced the Type 2708 and its turbocharged V-8 at the 1987 CART Laguna SCA event. The driver for the occasion was Al Unser, Sr., who retired early. Looking on at the right of the photograph prior to the start was Porsche engineer Norbert Singer, who was responsible for the design of the 2708. Oversized and overweight, the car proved a disappointment to Zuffenhausen and project head American Al Holbert. *Leonard Turner*

increase in tire grip came with no drag penalty. While there were definite drawbacks, about the only people who didn't like ground effects were the FIA. In part that dislike came not so much from the higher cornering speeds generated as it did from the fact that "ground effects" were the creation of the British contingent led by Formula One Constructors Association (FOCA) head Bernie Ecclestone, the man battling then FIA president Jean Marie Balestre for control of the sport.

Balestre's reasoning was simple: if Ecclestone and his English pals wanted it, the FIA did not. Thus, for several years the war between the two camps raged until at the end of 1982 the FIA and FOCA agreed to "flat bottomed," nonground-effects cars. To gain back the downforce and its consequent grip in the corners, the Formula One engineers returned to the notion of large, complicated wings. While effective, they produced a

tremendous amount of drag. That might not have been such a problem if it had not been for the folks at Renault.

During the early part of the 1970s, the French manufacturer had developed a neat 2-liter V-6 that it used to swamp the opposition in the smaller sports racing prototype category. In 1975, with a slightly enlarged version fitted with a turbocharger, Renault went after the large prototype crown. Although Renault won the honor that year, its subsequent attempts to recapture the title as well as the honors at Le Mans were frustrated by Porsche's 936 until 1978, when Renault finally gained the 24-hour victory it so desperately desired.

That success allowed the French company to begin full concentration on Formula One, a project that had been brewing since 1976, when it reduced the V-6 turbo's displacement to a Formula

One-legal 1.5 liters and stuffed it in its first in-house-designed chassis for testing purposes. By the time the FOCA-FIA battle was at full swing, the Renault turbo was coming into its own. More importantly, others, such as Ferrari and BMW, had noted the extra power the boosted unit pumped out in comparison with the Ford Cosworths. This became even more important with the banning of ground effects, since now the horsepower edge of the turbos really came into play.

One who wanted to climb onto the exhaust-gas turbocharging wagon was Britisher Ron Dennis. The owner of the Project Four operation, Dennis had fielded a number of successful F2 and F3 entries, as well as a ProCar BMW M-1 for Niki Lauda under the Marlboro banner. At the beginning of the 1980s, Dennis acquired a stake in McLaren from Bruce McLaren's widow and her partners, Teddy Mayer and Tyler Alexander. By 1982, Dennis had bought the remaining stock in the company to gain full control.

Coming with Dennis to McLaren's headquarters in Woking, Surrey, was the brilliant designer John Barnard, the man who had created the Chaparral 2K Lotus 79 look-alike Indy Car, with which Jim Hall's Pennzoil team won the Indy 500. Barnard, who felt he hadn't been given enough credit for the 2K, was anxious to rectify that situation at McLaren, going to work on the first McLaren MP4 F1 single seater. This car was designed to get the most out of the Cosworth. To Dennis, though, that engine was well past its prime. While he could only suspect that the FIA would find a way to get rid of ground effects, he fully subscribed to the belief that the turbocharged 1.5-liter powerplant was the long-term way to go in F1. To that end, he began to shop around for someone to build such a motor. His search took him to Honda, Toyota, and General Motors, as well as Cosworth, all without results. (Although the Cosworth camp did express some interest, it couldn't give Dennis what he wanted in the time frame he needed.)

The Porsche V-8 Indy engine had its origins in the TAG Formula One V-6 turbo program. Unlike its earlier Indy adventure, Porsche chose the same engine configuration as its rivals, eliminating the earlier controversies of boost pressures. *Porsche Werk*

For 1988, Porsche decided to abandon the 2708 in favor of a new March chassis, hiring driver Teo Fabi in the process. The talented Fabi and the Porsche Quaker State team were hampered by compatibility problems between the Zuffenhausen turbocharged V-8 and the British-built tub. Although no victories were scored by the end of the year, there was promise of better things to come. *Porsche Werk*

In August 1981, Dennis turned reluctantly to Porsche, figuring that Zuffenhausen, because of its previous single-seat experiences, especially in light of its aborted flat six Indy project, wouldn't be interested. Instead, Dennis found a company willing to explore the possibilities of such a project. Faced with what both believed to be a three-year development program, the two parties came to a preliminary, six-month agreement that would see Porsche carry out the initial paper design work, while Dennis sought funding that would allow the effort to move forward to the metal stages. Interestingly, under the arrangement, the ownership of the drawings, should the project have ended at that point, belonged to Dennis and not to Zuffenhausen, a protection the Britisher insisted on so that the technology might not slip out to his F1 rivals.

Happily, Dennis found a backer in Mansour Ojjeh and his Techniques d'Avant-Garde Company, a conglomerate with interests in everything from aircraft to art galleries. Under the agreement, TAG set up a new subsidiary, TAG Turbo Engines (TTE), which actually sold the powerplants to McLaren. It was also initially intended, although never realized, for TTE to sell customer units as well.

The man who headed things for Porsche was turbocharging veteran Hans Mezger. He started with a clean slate in producing the TTE P01, creating an 80-degree alloy V-6 with aluminum heads and block and Nikasil-coated aluminum cylinder liners. This arrangement allowed the maximum width for the still-permitted ground effects tunnels. With a bore of 82 millimeters and a stroke of 47.3 millimeters, the displacement of this oversquare

design came out to 1,499 cc. Internally, the TTE P01 featured a steel crankshaft running on four main bearings with titanium rods and Mahle lightweight alloy pistons. Belt-driven double overhead cams and four-valve (intake 30.5 millimeters, exhaust 27.5 millimeters) cylinder heads were featured, along with a Bosch single-plug, double-processor Motronic injection system. The initial compression ratio was set at 7.0:1, later raised to 7.5:1. Twin KKK turbochargers with water intercoolers were fitted.

Officially, the rev limit came at 12,000 rpm, the horsepower figures listed by the factory at 750, and later moved up to 800 horsepower. (There is more than a little suspicion that in actuality the numbers were far closer to 1,000 horsepower, at least for short bursts.) Two water and two fuel pumps were used, while the engine mounting points were made similar to those for the Cosworth DFV.

Dennis, wanting the smallest package possible, demanded and got from Mezger and his team a unit that would essentially fit within the confines of a two-foot square cube, the TTE P01's length coming in at 24 inches, while measuring 24.6 inches in height and 24.4 inches in width. Total weight was 148 kilograms (326 pounds), while boost was set at a maximum of 3.2 bars.

In all, some 56 examples of the engine were said to have been produced, 24 being employed at any one time in the race and test program, with a further eight held back for development work. According to insiders, each engine took 155 man-hours to rebuild. One noteworthy aspect of the program was the fact that Bosch used it to develop and perfect the Motronic units for Group C racing, whose fuel limitations were becoming increasingly more stingy as the years went along. (In fact, Porsche is said to have kept one 956 Group C coupe, chassis 006, for in-house testing of the TAG V-6.)

The first TTE P01 went on the dyno in December 1982. The first car fitted with it, the MP4/1E, appeared in the hands of Lauda at Zandvoort for the Dutch Grand Prix in August 1983. Barnard, who had worked closely with Mezger, was not particularly happy with the chassis, feeling that it had been compromised too much. In fact, it was the previous year's ground effects machine, revamped to the new non-ground-effects formula, then revamped again to take the Porsche TAG unit in place of the Cosworth. For Barnard, mixing an old DFV technology chassis with the new motor was not what he wanted.

Nevertheless, the car proved to be totally competitive, if fragile, there being a number of DNFs

Although Fabi ran the March Quaker-State Porsche well, he didn't run long, dropping out early in the event. It would be the first of a number of frustrations for the Italian, who had put his name on the map earlier in the decade when he had won the pole position for the 500. Fabi, unfortunately, would never achieve that success again while part of the Porsche team. *Leonard Turner*

posted by both Niki Lauda and John Watson as the teething problems were sorted out. Even so, the potential was clear. The Marlboro-backed McLaren camp got a further boost before the start of the 1984 season when Alain Prost joined the team in place of Watson. While some thought the Northern Irish driver had not been treated well by Dennis in the process, it was clear that with Prost partnering Lauda, McLaren had one of the best driver line-ups in the business.

Further, it was to have the best car. Barnard's new MP4/2 chassis was exactly what the doctor ordered for the TAG Porsche V-6. Though Bosch had to work out preseason testing woes with the Motronics, by the time Brazil rolled around, they were fixed. Indeed, they were more than fixed, as between them, the McLaren twins won no fewer than 12 Grands Prix: Prost taking the South American season-opener, as well as San Marino, Monaco, Germany, Holland, Portugal, and the Grand Prix of Europe at the Nürburgring. South Africa, France, Britain, Austria, and Italy wound up in Lauda's column.

Portugal was the ultimate cliffhanger, Lauda needing to finish second if Prost won in order to

garner his third world crown. The race for the Austrian started out badly, with Prost taking off in the lead, followed by the Lotus 95T of Nigel Mansell. For 52 laps Lauda remained in third, until Mansell departed with mechanical woes. The next 18 laps saw the McLarens run one-two, finishing that way as Prost captured the race, and Lauda the title, by a mere half point, one of the closest season outcomes in Formula One history. Lauda, who would only win the Austrian Grand Prix the following season, retired at the end of 1985 to tend to his ever-growing airline, Lauda Air, while Prost went on to claim his first two World Championships (1985 and 1986). Interestingly, Ayrton Senna, who would leave his own mark on McLaren and the F1 scene, was third in that Portugal thriller.

In all, while others would catch and eventually surpass the McLaren TAG Porsche combination, between 1984 and 1987 it would rack up a victory string second to none. Perhaps more importantly, it would be the last small specialty automotive manufacturer to do so.

As it concluded its F1 adventure, Porsche again became involved with Indianapolis-type racing.

And, as it was the first time, the situation was driven more by America than Germany. Unlike the previous episode, however, there was no involvement with Volkswagen of America. Rather, in this instance the man bchind thc push to go to Indy was Al Holbert, who after Porsche's 1984 marketing split with VoA, had been named to head Porsche's motorsports efforts in the United States.

Like his predecessor Hoppen, Holbert found himself drawn to the American single-seat racing scene. For Holbert, though, that pull was more personal than business, this being reflected in his association with CART and Indy as a driver. During 1985 and 1986, Holbert lobbied hard for an Indy effort with Porsche's management, eventually getting the factory to commit to a program after bringing Quaker State Oil to the table as a sponsor.

Porsche's second bite of the Indy apple would be quite different from the first, both from a philosophical and a mechanical viewpoint. Unlike Hoppen's arrangement with Interscope, Porsche would own the team. Moreover, while Weissach would consult Holbert, in the end the factory would determine the choice of personnel working on the project from the design and engineering stages right through to the operational side.

Unlike what had transpired in 1979–1980, Porsche would create a new powerplant for its second Indy adventure, this one being a 2.6-liter, double-overhead-cam, motronic, single-turbocharged unit whose origins were rooted in the TAG Formula One Turbo V-6. Designated the Type 2780, it featured an 88.2-millimeter bore and 54.2-millimeter stroke, as well as Nikasil-coated cylinders. As with that Grand Prix unit, Mezger was again the man in charge of bringing it to life. The responsibility for the chassis was given to Singer, who was anxious to move away from the sports racing prototype arena into the open wheel scene. The engine, even though Mezger would struggle with it at times over the next few years, eventually would become both reliable and, even more important, one of the most powerful in CART. By 1990, the final season of the factory's involvement, Mezger's offspring not only could stay with the best of its rivals, it could outpull them.

So why, if Porsche came to the front ranks of CART and Indianapolis in terms of its powerplant—considered the heart of any such program—did it ultimately fail in the American open wheel universe? The answer is found in a combination of circumstances, and, as had happened back in the 1960s when it overreached in Formula One. That lack was immediately apparent when

Porsche unveiled Singer's new Type 2708 chassis in the summer of 1987, prior to its debut at Laguna Seca that fall.

The good news for Porsche was that at least this time the parameters weren't clouded by the CART-USAC conflict. The bad news was that with CART having triumphed over its sanctioning body rival during the first half of the 1980s, the Indy Car participants had spent the intervening years honing their skills and equipment. In terms of the then-current Indy playing field, the 2708 was an overly bulky package that in no way was ever going to be truly competitive without such extensive revisions as to make it a whole new car. For a first try it was to be applauded. However, given that Porsche's commercial success and reputation were based on its ability to win, it was little short of a disaster.

Driven by Al Unser, Sr., at Laguna Seca, it retired early, while at Miami, its second and last

The 1991 Porsche Formula One V-12 was an impressive looking creation. Unhappily, Porsche engineers, suffering from a lack of development funds, were unable to cure its ongoing oil pressure difficulties. As a result, Porsche's association with the Footwork Arrows team ended prematurely before the season was concluded. *Porsche Werk*

The calm before the storm. The crew gathers around the Foster's Quaker State March Porsche prior to the start of the 1990 Indianapolis 500. This was to have been the highlight of the Porsche Indy Car program. However, problems arose from a lack of testing, due to construction problems with the British-built chassis. Porsche was far less successful at Indianapolis, and for the rest of the 1990 season, than Zuffenhausen had hoped. At the end of the year, drivers Teo Fabi and John Andretti found themselves out of a job, as the factory discontinued its Indy efforts, in favor of Formula One. *Leonard Turner*

appearance, it was abandoned by Unser and driven, if ever so briefly, by Holbert himself, who failed to qualify it. With the 2708 having demonstrated its incurable faults, the issue for Porsche and Holbert came down to how should they deal with 1988. Throughout the winter the internal debate continued, before it was finally decided to throw a dust cover over the 2708 and purchase a March 88C chassis. The problem for Porsche was that the outboard location of its engine's oil and water lines was not necessarily compatible with the configuration of the March 88C tub.

Although the engineers were eventually able to mate their powerplant to the British-made chassis, it was a struggle that was never completely resolved. This led to a largely disappointing season, even though Holbert and the factory had secured the services of the outstanding Teo Fabi, then considered one of the best drivers on the CART PPG tour. The best he could do with the Quaker State March Porsche was a fourth at Nazareth in the fall.

Further adding to the woes was the question of who was really in charge. At the beginning, Holbert, despite his "consultant's status," believed he would oversee the program operationally, withPorsche supporting him with its technical expertise, much in the same way as it had in the 917 era with John Wyer's Gulf team. Porsche, on the other hand, maintained its hands-on approach, sending Helmuth Flegl to America as its active representative. For all of Flegl's brilliance and reputation, especially that gained during Porsche's Can-Am years, he was not familiar with the Indy scene. And, to be successful at Indy, a driver and his engineers must act in full concert with each other—something clearly lacking in the Quaker State organization.

This situation might have been resolved had not it been for Holbert's tragic death in a private plane crash near Columbus, Ohio, in October 1988. Without Holbert's presence, there was virtually no American voice for a program that was run almost completely by the Germans. Fortunately, there was some help coming in the form of Derek Walker, the Britisher who had struck out on his own after working so successfully for many years with Roger Penske. But, even with Walker, and even with an extra year to iron out the bonding problems between the March chassis and its Porsche powerplant, 1989 was only moderately—at least from Porsche's viewpoint—better than the previous season. At Indianapolis, where Fabi had finished 28th in 1988 after going out early, he could make no improvement with Porsche's 89C successor, finishing a disappointing 30th in the Memorial Day classic.

However, despite this, it wasn't a totally rainy CART parade for Porsche, with Fabi collecting five fourth-place finishes, two seconds, and a third, all of which was topped off by his victory late that summer at Mid Ohio. Collectively, it was a consistent performance that saw him wind up fourth in the season standings. While 1989 might not have been exactly what Porsche had wanted from its Indy program, it did appear to form a solid basis for 1990 when, under Walker, it would add John Andretti, Mario's nephew to the team, in a second car.

Unfortunately, history again repeated itself. As had happened in Formula One, when the promise of 1960 led to hopes for success in 1961, the factory's aspirations were not to be realized in 1990. Sponsorship problems, which eventually saw Fosters Beer become the prime monetary partner, contributed. However, the real difficulty came when CART refused to approve the composite chassis around which the team's March 90P was to have been built. This led to a hurried substitution of an aluminum honeycomb structure, which in turn left Porsche without much time to test. And, as if this weren't enough, the revised 90P entered the CART fray with an advanced and complicated gearbox, as well as a new, forwardly located turbo, both of which needed exactly what wasn't available—private time on the track. As might be expected, the year was one to forget, with the two cars failing once more at Indy. In the end, the best placing by either driver was Andretti's fifth at Vancouver. With a return to Formula One as part of the Footwork

Arrows team in the wings, Porsche had had enough, and pulled out at the end of the season.

And, even though no one knew it, Porsche's return to F1 would be no better as the company's normally aspirated V-12 proved to be almost totally uncompetitive in 1991. This led Arrows to sever ties with Weissach before the conclusion of the year. In the case of Indy and CART, one can speculate that Porsche could have done well had it gone about things a little differently and accepted input from the veterans of the sport more than it did. As for Formula One, there the problem lay in the fact that things had changed dramatically in Porsche's five-year absence. When it left in 1987, it was still possible, if barely, for a small manufacturer such as Porsche to compete on an equal level. The hundreds of millions spent afterward by giants like Honda, Ferrari, Ford, Renault, and eventually Mercedes left those whose resources were limited with no chance.

Zuffenhausen could not go home again. If it wanted to bask in the center stage spotlight, it would now have to do so in its old arena: sports cars, where its tradition of excellence had been bred. The open wheel adventures were gone.

Porsche's last venture in open-wheel competition came as an engine supplier to the Formula One Footwork Arrows team in 1991. The association proved to be brief, as the Porsche-supplied 3.5-liter V-12 suffered from a number of problems, forcing Arrows to look elsewhere for its powerplant needs. *Porsche Werk*

Prototypes to the Forefront

10

The origins for Porsche's "modern era" turbocharged family of prototypes go back to the mid-1970s and what must be considered one of Porsche's more spectacular "ad hoc" creations: the 936. To understand the 936, it is necessary to know that it truly owes its existence to the politics of international motorsport. In the mid-1970s, after several abrupt rules changes, the FIA decided on a new path as a cure for the slump into which this segment of the sport had sunk. This new direction decreed that the headlining World Title Makes prototypes would be based on what came from the factories of auto manufacturers rather than from their experimental departments.

The Porsche 936 underwent considerable aerodynamic development during its career as a factory racer. Originally raced on the World Sports Car tour, it was limited to racing only at Le Mans from 1977. This is 936-022 as it appeared right after its Sarthe victory in 1977. *Porsche Werk*

Porsche 936 turbocharged Spyder as it appeared at its first race at the Nürburgring in April 1976. The 936, which was to enjoy a hugely successful career that included three Le Mans victories, was very much an "ad hoc" vehicle. It was designed as a hedge against a possible cancellation by the FIA of Porsche's "silhouette" prototype Group 5 formula, in favor of the more traditional sports racing spyders. The 936 borrowed heavily from the parts bins for the earlier 908 and 917 models. *Porsche Werk*

The problem for Porsche and its managing director, Ernst Fuhrmann, was that such decisions often were retracted or substantially modified before they were actually put in place. While the new production-based Group 5 category did in fact become a reality in 1976, it did so a year later than had been originally announced. This further reduced the confidence level at Porsche in the FIA's ability to stick to a course of action.

After conferring with men such as Helmuth Bott, Peter Falk, and Norbert Singer in the summer of 1975, Fuhrmann came to the conclusion that Porsche needed to have a fall-back position in case FIA decided to feature the sports racing prototypes instead of the silhouettes for the 1976 season. Further bolstering this attitude in Fuhrmann's mind was the fact that even if things did go according to its initial production-oriented plan, FIA also seemed set to stage a separate World Sports Car championship title chase in 1976, so any effort in this direction would not be wasted.

In reviewing their potential sports racing opposition, Fuhrmann and the Weissach engineering staff could see only one real rival, Renault and its A-442 V-6 turbo, which had backing from the French government. Added to these considerations was the fact that Le Mans officials had declared that their race would run in 1976 to its own formula, which included the sports prototypes as well as the Group 5 silhouette vehicles.

With the first event of the 1976 FIA sports racing season less than eight months away, the task of designing and producing a new car might have been impossible for anyone but Porsche, whose vast experience and previous involvement in this type of competition had left it with shelves full of spare parts from its earlier programs. In reality, therefore, Fuhrmann's hedge against the vicissitudes of the FIA required little more than the design of a new frame along with a figurative shopping basket stroll through Weissach's motorsport warehouse.

From the 908/03 came the uprights, wheels, and steering rack, while the 917 provided the brakes, hubs, springs, shocks, antiroll bars, and the five-speed transaxle (intended for but never actually used in the long-distance coupes). Meanwhile, Wolfgang Berger's design team likewise pirated the 2.1-liter, single-turbo flat six from the 1974 Turbo RSR, which at 1.4 bars put out a conservative 520 horsepower—more than enough for the needs of the 936. Meanwhile, the all-new tube-frame chassis closely resembled those of its 908/03 and 917 predecessors. It was clothed in a fiberglass shell that was a visual reminder of the 917/30 Mark Donohue Can-Am roadster.

By February 1976, Porsche had the first 936, chassis 001, ready for testing at Paul Ricard, where the black-painted machine left the engineers with wide smiles on their faces. Those expressions,

For Le Mans in 1976, 936-002 had acquired a high airbox. With Jacky Ickx and Gijs van Lennep aboard, it ran a perfect race to score Porsche's first 24-hour triumph since 1971. The 936 suppliers went on to win at the Sarthe the following year and again in 1981. They also finished second in 1978 and 1980. *Porsche Werk*

however, were somewhat less in evidence when the team appeared for the April 4 Nürburgring season opener. Although FIA had finally put its new sports racing prototype scriptures into effect, apparently no one told Renault that there were new regulations for the embryonic series. When the French rolled their two-seat, open cockpit machines out of their transporter, they were in the same configuration as they had been the previous season with wider-than-permitted wheels and a higher-than-allowed rear wing. To be fair, this was a trick that also had been tried in the past by Porsche to its own benefit.

After some discussion, the Renaults were allowed to run with the provision that the rim widths be reduced at the next race. As for the wing position, the officials decided to allow the rest of the competition to raise theirs to the level of the French, something Porsche quickly accomplished, although again doing so with a renewed lack of confidence in the ability of FIA to stand firm when faced with a difficult decision. All the prerace posturing turned out to have little effect on the final results, as the Renaults crashed together in the first corner and retired while 936-001 sat forlorn on the course with a broken throttle cable. Fortunately for Porsche, Reinhold Jost's much-modified turbo 908/03 came home ahead of the rest of the opposition to salvage some honor for Weissach.

That blot, however, was to be the last on the 936's record for the year. After the Nürburgring, Weissach debuted chassis 002, leaving 001 for testing and back-up duties. Using its 936 fleet, Porsche took the remainder of the available victories in the World Sports Car championship. Additionally,

Jacky Ickx, the regularly assigned driver of 002, brought his Porsche home to an easy first-place finish at Le Mans, partnered on this occasion by Gijs van Lennep. (Normally, Ickx teamed with either Jochen Mass or the late Rolf Stommelen.) The two led all the way in what was a trouble-free run. The same, however, could not be said for 001, which at the Sarthe was entered for Joest and Jürgen Barth. Their day went south when the car retired with a transmission failure after running slightly more than 16 hours. Overall, it was a historic triumph for Porsche, the 2,963.9 miles being covered by Ickx and van Lennep at an average of 123.49 miles per hour, marking the first turbo victory in the history of the 24-hour enduro.

With the conclusion of the 1976 campaign, Porsche rethought its position for 1977. Having won both the Group 5 World Manufacturers crown and the World Sports Car championship, Porsche decided to cut back for 1977, pursuing a second Manufacturers Championship with a revised version of the 935 while limiting the appearance of the two 936s to Le Mans. Because

Because of the piston problems it suffered with the 936 in the 1977 Le Mans race, the Porsche factory installed water-cooled engines in its 936 fleet for the 1978 Sarthe event. This resulted in reprofiled bodies that featured side-mounted radiators and revised rear wings. Despite the modifications, Renault beat the Porsches after they encountered transmission and other difficulties
Porsche Werk

they now had but a single purpose, Porsche adapted the 936s to the special conditions of the 24-hour affair, centered around the need for top speed on the nearly four-mile long Mulsanne straight. Mechanically, 001 and 002 had their tracks reduced by 2.2 inches from 62.2 to 60 inches, while receiving new 32-millimeter ventilated disc brakes at each corner. The engines remained the same 2.1-liter two-valve units of the previous year but were now fitted with the twin KKK turbos for better throttle response and reduced turbo lag. The body shape underwent extensive wind tunnel testing, emerging with a much more rounded form, along with an extended tail section and a new front splitter. How well the engineers did their job could be seen not only in the 216-mile per hour speed recorded by the 936s on the Mulsanne, but more importantly, in a second consecutive Porsche victory.

This time, however, that first place was not so easily achieved. For Le Mans, 002 was again entrusted to Ickx, with former Le Mans winner Henri Pescarolo as his teammate, Barth and Hurley Haywood drawing 001. The first hurdle placed in front of Porsche's aspirations came just before 7 P.M., when 002 retired with a broken connecting rod (a failure some felt was caused by Pescarolo's over-revving the engine). Ickx was quickly moved over to 001, which was struggling among the midfield contestants following a fuel injection pump problem four hours after the start. With little to lose, Ickx stepped into 001 while it was shown in 41st place. From there on, he and his new cohorts pushed their way up through the standings while the Renault Turbos, back to avenge their wounded pride from their 1976 Sarthe defeat, dropped out with a series of burned pistons. By midmorning Ickx, Barth, and Haywood were secure at the head of the field, aiming for what now appeared to be an easy triumph.

Then, late Sunday, the American brought 001 in with its own burned piston. For more than an hour the crippled 936 remained on pit row before

In 1980, the factory took an uncompleted 936 and built it into a full car for Reinhold Joest. Although it was always carried on the factory's books as 936-004, politics led the factory to require Joest to call it a 908-80. Regardless of its moniker, it was attended by factory personnel in 1980 at Le Mans, where it finished second with Jacky Ickx and Joest driving. It might have won had it not suffered some transmission woes during the affair. The last appearance for the 936 came at Le Mans in 1981, where the newest factory chassis, 003, won with Jacky Ickx and Derek Bell. It was a preview run for the upcoming 956 Group C Coupe, which would make its debut the following season. Both cars used the same basic engine, although the one in the 956 was equipped with electronic fuel injection. In addition, Porsche replaced the 936's tube-frame chassis with a monocoque tub, the first for a Zuffenhausen competition car. *Porsche Werk*

Barth took it out to gingerly complete the final required lap to conclude the event. Thus, despite its problems, 001 won, covering a total of 2,902 miles at an average speed of 120.95 miles per hour, a respectable showing considering everything.

The difficulties encountered at Le Mans, however, led Weissach to the conclusion that the totally air-cooled turbo was at its limit. It decided therefore to develop for 1978 a new flat six that incorporated water-cooled, four-valve heads.

Because extra radiators were required by the new heads, some revisions were necessary to the body and chassis. Porsche modified 001 to carry those radiators just ahead of the rear wheels, cutting two long NACA ducts into each side of the body. As for 002, it kept its all air-cooled configuration. Porsche also built a new water-cooled chassis, 003.

At Le Mans this latest 936 had Ickx, Mass, and Pescarolo as its drivers, while 001 was piloted by Barth and Bob Wollek, Haywood and his mentor, Peter Gregg, being entered in 002. Facing the Porsches was a Renault team determined not to lose again. In pursuit of its goal Renault had done a great deal of testing, including some high-speed work at the Ohio Transportation Research Center's eight-mile track.

In spite of Renault's massive preparations, Porsche almost pulled off a third straight first-place finish at the Sarthe. Again Ickx was involved. After fuel injection problems and ignition difficulties began to hamper 003's progress, he was moved over to the higher-placed 001, where he, Wollek, and Barth soon looked to be winners. However, a late race 41-minute stop to repair their transaxle let the Renault A-442 of Jean-Pierre Jassaud and Didier Pironi claim the victory. Nevertheless, the troubled 936 motored home in second place, just ahead of Haywood and Gregg. As for 003, it was counted as a DNF following an early morning accident when Mass put it up against a guard rail, damaging the rear end too badly to continue.

After Le Mans, Porsche relegated the well-traveled 002 to show car and display duties. As for 001 and 003, their eventual fate was less certain. Indeed, not until the month before the 1979 Le Mans race did Porsche finally decide to enter the two cars in France. The result was a total disappointment, with Wollek and Haywood, who had the best chance, dropping out in 001 after 19 hours when their engine broke. Disqualified two hours previously was 003, when Ickx and his teammate, Brian Redman, received outside help in changing an alternator belt. Any chance they might have had to challenge for first place had evaporated many hours before following a devastating flat suffered by Redman that destroyed much of 003's rear bodywork and suspension. About the only thing brightening the outcome was the fact that the Whittington brothers, Don and Bill, along with Klaus Ludwig, took their private Kremer 935 K3 to the head of the Le Mans field at the final flag.

Following their unsuccessful Le Mans appearance, 001 and 003 joined 002 in Porsche's museum, gathering dust until Porsche's new president, Peter Schutz, ordered them brought out of retirement for the 1981 edition of the 24-hour event. Schutz

and Bott wanted to use the 936 as a trial horse for the new 956 Group C coupe they had decided to build for the upcoming 1982 World Endurance Championship. While the 956 would have a ground-effects body and a monocoque chassis, it would be powered by a version of the 2.65-liter, four-valve, water-cooled head Indy turbo six. It seemed appropriate to drop this engine into 001 and 003 (which required no modifications to accept it) to see how well it performed under race conditions.

With Ickx and Bell installed in 003, the youngest factory 936 had an uneventful time as it swamped its opposition, leading the entire distance without any serious difficulty while covering a total of 2,998.07 miles at an average speed of 124.92 miles per hour. The longest pit stop for 003 was just under four minutes, a rare achievement in endurance competition and an ironic throwback to the 936's first Le Mans appearance in 1976. Balanced against 003's success was the performance of 001, which fared far less well, starting off with a broken spark plug and finishing up with clutch difficulties that put its drivers, Haywood and Vern Schuppan, in 12th at the checkered flag.

Surprisingly, despite its more powerful engine, the final version of the factory 936 wasn't that much quicker than the 1977-winning 001 in a straight line, being clocked at the Mulsanne at 218

In 1981, the factory returned to Le Mans with 936-001 and 936-003, both using the turbocharged six-cylinder engine with the water-cooled head, originally intended for Zuffenhausen's aborted Indy program. Piloted by Jacky Ickx and Derek Bell, 003 led all the way in a flawless run that was a near duplicate of the 936's first Sarthe win in 1976. This was to be the model's last time at Le Mans, the factory being represented in the 24-Hour classic the following June by the new 956 Group C coupe, which also used the boosted Indy engine, but with a motronic injection system for improved fuel economy.
Porsche Werk

miles per hour, just 2 miles per hour better than the two-valve, air-cooled boxer six. Part of the reason for that lack of improvement may well have been the handling of the 936, which according to Barth, was less than perfect. "It was," said he, "a car to which you had to pay attention if you didn't want it to get away from you."

Regardless of any potential faults, there were many outside the factory who wanted a 936, one of whom was Joest. In the winter of 1979 he talked Bott into letting him purchase chassis 004, a car that had not yet been completed at that time. Bott agreed, but because of pressures from other customers, Joest kept the arrangement a secret, and the car initially appeared as a "908/80."

With Joest and Ickx in the cockpit, the "underground" 936-004 almost collected the honors at Le Mans in 1980, leading for much of the way

above: The biggest difference between the venerable 936 and the new Group C 956, was the latter's monocoque chassis, the first ever produced by Zuffenhausen. While the chassis ended at the engine bulkhead, the powerplant itself wasn't used as a full-stressed design component, being supported in part by a tubular structure that bolted to the monocoque. With Porsche's director of customer racing at the controls, the prototype 956, chassis 001, took its shakedown laps at Porsche's Weissach test track in March 1982. The car made its debut a month later at Silverstone in Rothman's colors, with Jacky Ickx and Derek Bell as its drivers. Note the car's short-tail configuration, used throughout its career virtually unchanged. For Le Mans, a long-tail deck lid was substituted to reduce the car's drag and improve its top speed on the 3.5-mile-long Mulsanne straight. *Porsche Werk*

left: Winning at Le Mans in 1982, for the second straight year, were Jacky Ickx and Derek Bell in their factory Rothman's long-tail 956. That Sarthe edition was a Zuffenhausen benefit, with the three factory Group C Coupes sweeping the top three positions, and a private 935 taking the IMSA GTX division with a fourth overall. *Porsche Werk*

before transmission problems forced it to settle for second. Later in 1981, Joest and Mass won the Kyalami long-distance season closer with it, after which Wollek took it to the German championship title in 1982.

That same year, the Kremer brothers introduced their own 936 for Stommelen in the German series, where he scored one victory and two seconds. Beyond this, the Joest team entered another homegrown Group C version of the 936 on occasions in the 1982 FIA World Endurance Championship, but achieved very little with it.

One Zuffenhausen design that almost everyone agrees has achieved landmark status is the 956/962 prototype coupe, which was still capable of winning races 12 years after its 1982 debut. Like so many other Porsche competition-oriented products, this teardrop-shaped coupe was steeped in political intrigue throughout its racing life.

Still, unlike other long-lived significant racing Porsches, the physical changes to the 956/962 over the course of its long life were minimal, consisting largely of variations in bodywork and powerplant choices. Indeed, the only thing separating the 956 from its 962 sibling was the latter's increase in wheelbase. This was an alteration demanded first by International Motor Sport Association president John Bishop and subsequently adopted by the FIA on the grounds of safety, which involved moving the front axle line ahead of the driver's seat. Interestingly, Bishop's demands that Porsche modify its 956 appear to have had as much to do with the IMSA founder's efforts to keep the Porsche prototype from competing in his Camel GT championship as it did with concern for the driver's welfare. Here, however, we are getting ahead of our story.

Until the era of the 934 and 935 Turbos, Porsche had viewed its presence in motorsport as a cost-effective means to promote itself, its engineering talents, and its automobiles. Moreover, customer cars were a standing tradition going back to the 550s of the 1960s, and while factory machines excess to its needs were sold off to private teams, the money earned primarily went to reduce the costs of Zuffenhausen's participation. With the 935 and its less-modified brother, the 934, Porsche found a new source for profits. Put simply, the gentleman drivers populating IMSA ranks, as well as their well-heeled counterparts elsewhere in the world, were enthralled with the car because of its initial reliability as well as the plentiful supply of its replacement parts. The privateers didn't have to concern themselves with

developing their equipment. That had been done for them. All they had to do was perform basic maintenance and set up work, and they too could run at the head of the field.

Once having snagged this lucrative gentleman driver privateer market, Porsche was reluctant to let it go when it came to the replacement for the 934/935, the new Group C 956. Clearly, Porsche had the car for the new international regulations, and just as clearly Bishop wasn't going to go along with them. The result was a split in philosophy that in one form or another plagued the sport for the better part of the next two decades.

Still, what was it about these scriptures and the Porsche race car they spawned that created such fierce reactions? The answer lay not so much in the area of the chassis as it did in the engine compartment, a fact that brings us back to 1976 and the *raison d'être* for the 936: Fuhrmann's worries about the commitment of the FIA.

Between 1976 and 1978 Le Mans benefited from the war between Zuffenhausen and Renault, which saw the 936s take two victories to the one for its French rivals. But while the Porsches would continue to race for the next three editions of the Sarthe classic following the French manufacturer's withdrawal, there was a paucity of FIA sports racing prototypes from the other manufacturers. This caused concern among the ranks of Le Mans officials. They solved the problem by developing their own set of rules, which they dubbed the "Group C" category. In many respects the new prototype division was not far removed from what had gone before except that it catered exclusively to coupe bodies. When the FIA began to look at replacing its production Group 5 prototypes, it decided to utilize the Le Mans structure as the foundation for its new Makes formula (which would undergo several name changes over the course of time, but which initially was called the World Endurance Championship).

If the FIA found salvation in a proven set of chassis and bodywork rules, it took the opposite tack when it came to the engines. Here the authorities decided to control the situation with an approach based on fuel economy. One could run any type or size powerplant one wanted, but strict limits on the maximum amount of fuel used during a particular event would be enforced. Given the Arab-caused fuel crises of the 1970s, it wasn't a bad approach. However, it was one that favored electronically controlled fuel injection systems of the type that Bosch had been supplying Porsche. One could argue that in some measure lobbying

In 1984 Porsche produced the longer-wheelbase version of the 956, the 962. This was to meet the demands of IMSA President John Bishop, who wanted to move the driver's feet behind the front axle line. For IMSA, the 962 was equipped with the all-air-cooled engine from the 935. Later, when the FIA demanded the use of the long-wheelbase variant, it acquired the water-cooled drivetrain of the 955 to produce the 962C. This version was later allowed to run in the IMSA series as well. *Porsche Werk*

by Zuffenhausen might have helped to mold the character of Group C in a manner favorable to Porsche. However, no matter what the reason, it was clear that Porsche was going to have a big advantage, and that was something Bishop wasn't about to tolerate.

During the course of 1980 and 1981, as FIA representatives sought to get him to change his mind, Bishop decided to part ways with the international community and Le Mans, putting together his own Camel GT prototype category. While similar to group C, the Camel GT incorporated numerous differences intended largely to keep the European interlopers, especially Porsche, out of Bishop's North American title chase. Bishop, believing that his spectators, regardless of who might or might not win, would not accept a fuel economy-driven program, opted instead for a set of scriptures based on power to weight rational. If Group C was to favor Porsche, GTP did the same for the American-motivated pushrod V-8s that Bishop saw as the backbone of his world.

The love-hate relationship between the IMSA president and Porsche extended back to the earliest days of his organization in 1969 and 1970, when he turned to Porsche's U.S. racing boss, Josef Hoppen, for help. Only too ready to find an alternative to the Sports Car Club of America, then hassling Porsche about the 911's domination of its

class in the Trans-Am, Hoppen agreed, supplying cars and teams for IMSA's fledgling championship in 1971. It was support that came at a price, however, as Porsche soon dominated Bishop's universe. From the Carrera RSRs to the 934s and 935s, if one didn't own a Porsche, then one probably had no real hope of winning. In fact, so frustrated was Bishop that he created the tube-framed All American GT division just to provide a variety of competition. His concept worked for a couple of seasons, but was drowned in a seemingly endless parade of 934s and 935s.

Thus, when presented with the opportunity to alter the balance with the introduction of the new prototype regulations, Bishop moved to end Porsche's stranglehold. In addition to his engine requirements, Bishop also mandated that the driver's feet stay behind the car's front axle line, something not the case with the original 956. Bishop, while not necessarily knowing the specifics, knew enough of the broad general outline of the 956 design by the fall of 1981 to write it out of the Camel GT tour. In fact, the parameters for the factory's Group C coupe weren't that hard to understand.

Like the 936 before it, the 956 made use of a number of previously proven components, these coming for the most part from the 936. Chief among them was the spyder's turbocharged flat six. Now fitted with a Bosch Motronic system to promote the needed fuel economy while still providing the maximum in performance, the 2.6-liter was the heart of the new 956. Mated to it was a new five-speed gearbox used in the 1981 Le Mans affair where it performed well in Porsche's first-ever turbocharged 944. The 956's front suspension was quite conventional, featuring double wishbones on each side supported by Bilstein coilover spring/shocks and an antisway bar. At the back, the 956 employed an inboard mounted rocker arm suspension, also featuring Bilstein coilovers with conventional lower wishbones. ATE ventilated discs were fitted while the 16-inch-diameter Speedline alloy rims were 12 inches wide at the front and 15 inches wide at the rear.

If all this was an evolution of what had been done before, what was completely new was the chassis, which was Porsche's first monocoque. Moreover, it used its flat six-cylinder engine as a stressed member, hanging the rear suspension off it. Further, the 956 was a "ground effects" vehicle with a tunneled undertray that forced the relocation of the engine's twin turbochargers to the outboard pods just behind the driver's compartment. Interestingly, in its long-tail form, the teardrop body was quite similar to that of the open-topped 936. In its more frequently seen short-tail configuration, where its rear wing was

mounted high on a pair of larger-sized sidepods, this was far less evident.

When bolted together, the 956 had a 2,650-millimeter (103-inch) wheelbase, which was increased for the 962 to 2,770 millimeters (108 inches) by moving the front suspension pick-up points forward. The initial front and rear track figures for the 956 were 1,648 millimeters (64 inches) and 1,548 millimeters (60 inches) respectively, while those for its 962 sibling were 1,634 and again 1,548 millimeters. Likewise, at the 956's introduction, its weight was set at 840 kilograms (1,852 pounds), while the 962 tipped the scales at 850 kilograms (1,873 pounds). Over the coming years these poundage figures would change, generally increasing as officials tried to keep the Porsche from totally dominating its environment.

And dominate is exactly what the Rothmans factory-run 956 did in its early career, although at first it found itself at a disadvantage against a pair of open-topped Lancia prototypes grandfathered into the 1982 title chase to help enlarge the fields during what the FIA considered a transition season. Even so, when the year was over, the title belonged to Porsche. Not only that, but there was a one-through-three sweep for the factory 956 team at Le Mans, led by Jacky Ickx and Derek Bell. For 1983, the 956 was released to Porsche's customers, the factory continuing its own Rothmans-backed 956

The final version of the 962 appeared as a flat-bottomed GT car in 1994. Supposedly the brainchild of privateer Jochen Dauer, who wanted to sell it as a street legal machine, it was shepherded throughout by factory engineer Norbert Singer. The payoff came at Le Mans that summer, where the car was victorious. *Porsche Werk*

program as well. Again, the Porsche, led by the factory entries, eclipsed its opposition with the 956, not only taking its second straight FIA championship crown, but nine out of the top 10 spots at Le Mans.

As remarkable as the 956's achievements were, the factory still felt it had missed the mark by being excluded from America with its wealthy pool of potential buyers. Thus, in the summer of 1983, Porsche's Jürgen Barth was sent to negotiate with Bishop over when and how the 956 might gain access to the Camel GT. Given its domination in FIA competition, there was little incentive for the IMSA president to move away from his initial decision on the fate of the Porsche prototype. In his series, there were a number of equally matched headliners, including pushrod Detroit-engined prototypes from Lola and March, as well as the Group 44 team's V-12 XJR-5 Jaguars, not to mention several "home-built" 935s that could well hold their own in the new world of GTP racing.

What Bishop had relied on was the fact that Porsche would not have the resources to change the 956 to meet the basic specifications laid down for his version of the sports racing vehicle. And at least in the beginning, that seemed a wise course, as Porsche stayed away. However, having gained experience with its new car, Porsche was ready to adapt it for IMSA, a fact Barth made clear to Bishop during their meeting.

Thus was born the 962. With its longer wheelbase came a single turbo 2.8-liter all-air-cooled version of the 935's venerable flat six (demanded by Bishop as a further price of admission). This was,

like its twin turbo 956 sibling, fitted with a Motronic injection system. The first 962s featured bodywork that included a shorter and steeper sloping front nose and a tail midway in configuration between the low drag Le Mans fiberglass and the high downforce shape used elsewhere.

This was the configuration in which 962-001 made its chassis debut as a factory entry at the Daytona 24-hour enduro in 1984 with Mario and Michael Andretti as its drivers. Although they would retire because of mechanical woes, they set the stage for the customer cars that were to follow. By spring, Bruce Leven's Bayside team, Bob Akin's Coca-Cola sponsored example, and Al Holbert's Lowenbrau entry were all engaged on the Camel tour. While the first two remained much as they had been delivered, Holbert's began to undergo revision within two months of its inaugural race. The most important alteration was the substitution of the 3.2-liter, mechanically injected 935 flat six used in Holbert's 1983 title-winning March 83G for its original 2.8-liter boxer engine. Later Holbert would discard the medium tail for the high-winged variant used by 956s in Europe.

Indeed, other than the distinction of wheelbase length, the lines between the 956 and 962 became increasingly blurred over the years. For example, John Fitzpatrick's Skoal-sponsored 962 entry at Le Mans in 1984 swapped everything aft of its cockpit for a complete 956 bodywork and drivetrain transplant. (Later the car, restored as a full 962, was sold to BF Goodrich to race in IMSA.) Eventually, the FIA, in the interest of increased safety, ordered that the longer-wheelbase 962 replace its predecessor, this beginning with the

1987 season. The factory made the switch three years prior to that, suffering early handling problems brought on by the change in models. Nevertheless, whether in international or North American competition, the 956/962 was the king of its universe.

On the western shores of the Atlantic, Holbert was the man, his team winning three straight IMSA crowns, two with Holbert and the other with Chip Robinson. In the rest of the world, from Europe to Asia, it was more of the same, the Porsche winning both international and local championships at will with the factory Rothmans team still out front of its customers for the most part. Indeed, the 956 collected no fewer than four consecutive Le Mans triumphs—two courtesy of the Reinhold Joest team—between 1982 and 1985. Then it was the turn of the 962, which added another two straight in 1986 and 1987. Of note is the fact that Holbert shared not only in those latter two triumphs but also in the factory's dramatic 1983 victory, where the winner's engine blew on the final lap.

But even as there was sunshine for Porsche to enjoy, the horizon began to fill with clouds. The first of these came in the form of the Tom Walkinshaw Jaguars, which debuted in 1986 under the XJR-8 label. By the next year, the Jags not only had equal performance when compared to their Zuffenhausen rivals, but they had pushed the envelope a step further. About the only disappointment that year for the British organization was their loss to the factory Porsches at the Sarthe. By 1988 they were in command, taking Le Mans as well as the FIA honors.

By this point, the factory-supported Sauber Mercedes were also in the middle of the fight, the factory adopted team winning Mercedes' second Le Mans affair (the first was in 1952) with a trio of V-8-powered C-9s in 1989. And, as if that weren't enough, Walkinshaw had taken his Jaguars to IMSA, where they won their debut appearance at Daytona over BFG's 962 in 1988. In part, the increasingly untenable position of the Porsche was due to its age. It was a much larger package than its newer-designed opposition and was not nearly as aerodynamically effective. The other reason why the 962 faded can be attributed to the rulemakers, particularly those working for Bishop, who decided again to promote variety by crippling the 962 with weight and small air inlet restrictors. Thus, the Nissan and then the Toyota teams jumped to the forefront on the Camel tour, leaving the 962s hog-tied in their wake. Despite this, there was life left in the old girl.

Like most long-lived Porsche racers, the 962, as it became the sole focus of the factory's and its customers' motorsport aspirations, underwent a great deal of detail development—new stronger monocoques with thicker bulkheads, revised suspension

geometry, and different brakes all kept it at least within sight of the front, and on occasion better than that. In fact, the 962 continued winning in IMSA through 1993, claiming the 1989 and 1991 Daytona 24-hour affairs in the process. A home-built Kremer brothers spyder would add to that total in 1995 when it beat a fleet of Ferrari 333SPs.

Perhaps, though, the most fitting tribute to the 962's engineering came at Le Mans in 1994, when a flat-bottomed version, running on narrow-rim tires under the theoretical control of Jochen Dauer, won the race outright—12 years after its first Sarthe appearance. Interestingly, political intrigue surrounded the 956/962 to the end, the Dauer 962 qualifying for Le Mans under a rules loophole that allowed it to be entered as a GT division vehicle. Ironically, it was that success which led to Porsche's next Le Mans winner: the factory-leased Joest spyder of 1996–1997.

Here, begins the tale with Walkinshaw. As noted, in the late 1980s, Tom Walkinshaw Racing (TWR) was riding along on the crest of a very high wave. The Scottish driver-turned team owner had built on his earlier associations with Jaguar to become the brand's racing maven in the middle of the decade. It was quite a change for Jaguar to rely on an outside, contracted design structure, but one foreseen nearly 10 years previously. During its heyday in the 1950s, when it won Le Mans five times between 1951 and 1957, Jaguar, like Ferrari and Porsche, was strictly an in-house operation. Even in the early 1960s, when American Briggs Cunning-ham represented the company, what was seen on the track was a product of Jaguar engineering.

In the 1970s, when Jaguar returned to racing in the United States with Bob Tullius' Group 44,

things began to change. While Group 44 (and Huffaker Engineering) used the XKE V-12 as a base for their B Production SCCA national championship models, much of the needed modification to make them effective was the result of teams' efforts. When the XJS sedan entered the professional North America road racing wars with Group 44, that was even truer, the Group eventually constructing its own tube-framed XJS, which owed little beyond its drivetrain and overall shape to Jaguar. Likewise, when Walkinshaw's own XJS models were dominating the European Touring Car scene, they too bore the fruits of design labor that had few roots at Jaguar.

By the start of the 1980s, Jaguar in North America decided to take the next step. This came in the form of Group 44's Lee Dykstra-created XJR-5, first seen in 1982. The only thing connecting the XJR-5 to Jaguar, other than the nameplate, was its basic V-12 engine block and heads. And it was with the XJR-5 that "Jaguar" returned to Le Mans in 1984.

While the Tullius team was performing with modest success at the Sarthe, Walkinshaw and his people were taking careful notes. In late 1985 Tullius shipped one of the XJR-5s to the Jaguar museum in Great Britain. Somehow the car wound up with Walkinshaw, who tested it before turning it back over to its permanent Jaguar keepers. By the summer, Walkinshaw had his own prototype, the aforementioned XJR-8, good for both international Group C competition as well as the American GTP arena.

The Walkinshaw machine, which like the Tullius entry utilized little more than the V-12 Jag block and heads (and, of course, the Jag name), would remain in front-line service through 1990, winning Le Mans twice and Daytona once under a

variety of designations, these included the XJR-9 and XJR-12. Toward the end, the venerable TWR design, while still competitive in long-distance events, lost much of its steam in shorter affairs. This led to the XJR-16, a much neater, smaller turbocharged V-8 package created by TWR that owed nothing to the Jaguar brand other than its official designation. As advanced as the XJR-16 was, however, there were political winds beginning to blow that would soon make it obsolete.

Formula One's Bernie Ecclestone, backed by his friend and now FIA president Max Mosley, decided that the Group C prototype arena should eschew its diet of production-based engines and follow the Grand Prix tour into the world of high-revving, high-tech, and certainly high-cost non-boosted 3.5-liter powerplants. There were several consequences as a result. One was that not only did the cars themselves grow smaller, they also grew more nimble and their straightline performance improved. Most of all, though, they showed themselves to be far too expensive to maintain the formula, the FIA Makes Championship shutting down before the 1990s reached the midpoint of the decade. Still, in 1990 it became obvious to Walkinshaw and Tony Dowe, then a key executive cog at TWR, that something was needed to replace the XJR-16.

"It began in 1990," remembered Dowe. "What Tom wanted was nothing less than a two-seat Formula One car of advanced design that would remain competitive for a number of years into the future. To accomplish that aim, Tom hired a team of Benetton F1 engineers and spent the necessary large amounts of money to achieve his objective." Although Dowe didn't say it, how close Walkinshaw's team came to meeting the goal could be seen in the fact that the car in its Porsche guise conquered Le Mans for a second time seven years after it left the drawing table. That, however, was in the future.

When this flexible creation was first introduced in coupe form, it presented a minimalist silhouette with a tiny, narrow cockpit area and slim flanks. At the rear there was a "biplane" wing, while at the front could be found a chisel nose between the fenders. Underneath, in the engine compartment, rested a secret advantage. In fact, the unit really wasn't secret at all, being nothing more than the 3.5-liter Cosworth Formula One V-8, whose roots could be traced back to 1967 and the Lotus 49. What made the Cosworth (naturally badged as a Jaguar) so effective was its induction system.

"What we did," recalled Dowe, "was to mate the engine to a Bosch Motronic unit. That not only cured some of its problems, it turned the engine into a very good performer."

While on the outside the Dauer 962 didn't appear much different than its predecessors, underneath it was totally flat bottomed, without the ground effects tunnels that so characterized the original design. The change, which did nothing to improve the car's handling, was the price Porsche had to pay for exploiting the rules loophole that permitted the coupe to run at Le Mans. *Leonard Turner*

Other factory cars

Although historians might wish it so, history is not always neat—loose odds and ends always seeming to be in need of sorting out. The recounting of Porsche's factory efforts in motorsport is not immune from this syndrome. While Zuffenhuasen's competition programs can be, for the most part, easily defined, there are the odd projects here and there that don't quite fit into the sandbox.

Chief among these are the 356 GTL and 2000 GS production-based models of the early 1960s, originally intended to keep Porsche's privateers on a winning track, but which were later employed by the factory itself as a stopgap measure to preserve its reputation in sports car racing, during an era when its primary focus was in Formula One.

The 356 GTL, better known as the Carrera Abarth, and the 2000 GS, a 356 whose body resembled those of the RS61 coupes, came into existence because of a loophole in the FIA rules, which defined a production car on the basis of its chassis and running gear, rather than its coachwork. As long as the platform and the mechanicals remained the same, the FIA didn't care what the shape that clothed them was. This was very much in the European tradition, in which the wealthy would purchase cars from major manufacturers without bodies, and then have master craftsmen subsequently create them to their own individual tastes. For those involved in racing, this largess was a godsend. Among others helped by it were the Cobra folks, who transformed their unaerodynamic roadsters into the sleek coupes that captured a manufacturer's crown for Ford in 1965.

Another using those regulations to its advantage was Porsche, which was concerned about how to stay ahead of the opposition with the introduction of its 356B street coupe in 1959. After some debate, it was decided to continue the limited production of a lightweight four-cam Type 547-engined 356 competition-oriented Carrera model using the new platform as a base.

To ensure its continued success, Porsche's management insisted that the car be fitted with a purpose-designed competition aluminum alloy body. The contract for this went to Zagato, the specialized Italian coachwork firm whose creations also adorned various racing Fiat and Simca vehicles. Because these latter were rivals of Porsche, Zuffenhausen didn't want to publicize any potential association with Zagato. Thus, it again brought in as its representative Carlo Abarth, who had last acted as an agent for the factory in the Cisitalia project so many years before.

Abarth would be the official contractor, subcontracting the work to Zagato, an arrangement that satisfied Porsche perfectly—even though the resulting Carrera Abarths looked much like their Fiat and Simca counterparts. Despite initial shortcomings in design execution and quality control, the 356 GTLs proved to be immediate winners, dominating from the start. Indeed, as a factory entry at Le Mans, it won the GT category three years in a row, from 1960 through 1962. In fact, the 356 GTL was the only car to represent the factory at the Sarthe on that latter occasion.

Slightly less successful were the Butzi Porsche-bodied 2000 GSs of 1963, the last 356s raced by the company, Although rather distinctive looking, they were far better aerodynamically than even the Carrera Abarths. Perhaps more importantly, they served, in terms of their shape, as trial horses for the 904s, which would be introduced in 1964—cars considered among the finest of Butzi Porsche's work. Their factory career was brief, however, and while they finished fairly well at such places as Sebring and the Nurburgring, they failed at Le Mans, thus departing the stage to mixed reviews.

Seven years later, Porsche introduced into competition the six-cylinder Porsche 914/6GT—the racing version of its "everyman" mid-engine, entry-level roadster. Entered at Le Mans in 1970 under the Sonauto banner, it finished an amazing sixth overall and first in the GT division. Later, factory-supported

Porsche turned to its old friend, Carlos Abarth, in 1959 when it decided to rebody its 356A Carrera competition coupe with a sleeker shell. The actual contract was with the Italian coach firm Zagato. However, because Zagato also did bodies for some of Porsche's rivals, including Fiat and Simca, it used Abarth as the go-between. The result was the Carrera Abarth Coupe, which not only was used by Porsche's customers to uphold Zuffenhausen's reputation in the early 1960s, but by the factory itself, particularly at Le Mans, where it was always a class winner. *Porsche Werk*

Hidden away these days in Porsche's basement is the only factory 944 Turbo Coupe ever built by the factory for racing. The unique car, based on Zuffenhausen's 924 turbo prototypes of 1980, made only one appearance, at Le Mans in 1981, where Jürgen Barth and Walter Roehrl drove it to seventh overall. The Porsche, classed as a prototype because of its experimental engine, ran without any problems, spending the least time in the pits of any car in the race. *Bill Oursler*

examples dominated the Martharon de la Route at the Nürburgring. Porsche also tried out its midengined flier in the 1971 Monte Carlo Rally with far less successful results, the lack of traction in ice and snow leading to its defeat. After that, the 914/6GT's career was left to the privateers. One example, in the hands of Peter Gregg and Hurley Haywood, would go on to win the inaugural IMSA GT Championship.

In 1980, the factory entered three 924 Carrera GTP Turbo Coupes, the spiritual successor to the 914/6GT at Le Mans. Running as prototypes, all three finished, the one driven by Jurgen Barth and Manfred Schurtl taking sixth overall and third in the prototype category. The following year, a 924 GTO fitted with a 944 turbocharged four-cylinder was entered at the Sarthe for Barth and Walter Roehrl, the car running without problems to again finish third in the prototype division. Another of the 924s, using its original powerplant, but now listed as a production-approved 924 GTR, was fourth in its class after suffering gearbox woes.

As with the 914 before it, the 924 Turbo would go on to enjoy a highly successful career, particularly on the IMSA GT tour, in private hands after the factory was finished with it. Indeed, when Al Holbert took over as head of Porsche's North American motorsports program, he used the 924-944 as a basis for his 944 GTR turbo production car program, that effort failing to achieve its full potential in light of his untimely death in October 1988.

Even with its far better powerplant, there were still problems with the car itself. "There were some aerodynamic things that we didn't get quite right in the beginning," confessed Dowe. "However, the really serious problem was with the gearbox, which forced us to run the linkage down the center of the car. Since most everyone else used a linkage that sat to the right of the driver, this caused a number of headaches. Fortunately, the poor opposition we faced in the FIA series didn't expose the car's shortcomings too much. In fact, if I remember correctly, we wound up using it to win the manufacturers' title in 1991."

The next season was a little different, as the XJR-14 was brought to the United States and entered in the Camel GT series. There, in the hands of Davy Jones, during one of the championship's most competitive years, it was fast, but its potential was never truly realized, mainly because of its inherent flaws. That was it for Jaguar's management anyway, as the now Ford-owned company moved on to other projects, like producing cars that the public wanted to purchase.

With Jaguar having disappeared, Walkinshaw turned to Mazda, which decided the XJR-14 would do just fine. Unhappily, however, it would have to do so without the trusty Cosworth V-8, which was replaced by a Judd V-10. "That forced us," said Dowe, "to rework the rear bulkhead of the driver's compartment a bit, but not much else. Still, performance-wise, I thought it might have been better to stick with the original V-8 arrangement, but that wasn't what they wanted."

Even so, the car, now officially a Mazda, was competitive, if not successful, against its major FIA competition, including Peugeot (which was in the

After McLaren won the 1995 Le Mans race, Zuffenhausen sent Norbert Singer back to his drawing board to create a car that could beat the supercar. The result was the Porsche 911 GT1 Turbo, half production 911 and half prototype 962. Although fastest at the Sarthe for the three years from 1996 to 1998, the Singer-conceived turbo didn't achieve its ultimate goal of an overall victory until June 1998. Porsche didn't lose out entirely during the intervening two years, the British-built and Porsche-powered TWR open-topped prototype winning both times under the direction of Reinhold Joest's team. *Porsche Werk*

process of winning the second of two-in-a-row victories at Le Mans) during the 1993 season. With the cancellation of the FIA Makes tour in 1994, one might have expected the XJR-14 to have ended its career as part of either a public or private collection. That, though, wasn't to be.

Again Dowe: "In 1994 I was sent to the Ligier Formula One team for awhile. When I came back that summer to TWR's U.S. headquarters in Indiana, Tom made it clear to me that I had to find a project to keep the operation going, or he would shut things down. We had done some preliminary work on transforming the coupe with its ground effects tunnels into a flat-bottomed, open-topped World Sports Car already. However, we needed a partner to make it a reality."

That turned out to be Porsche, still high after its 1994 victory at Le Mans that June with Dauer's aging 962. At that race, representatives from the International Motor Sports Association talked to Porsche about participating in its series. While IMSA stood fast about its rule barring turbos in the World Sports Car category, it did say it would permit such cars to run in their own separate Le Mans category (boosted engines were legal for the Sarthe) at Daytona and Sebring in 1995.

Dowe, aware that something was up at Porsche, called Alwin Springer, head of the factory's North American racing efforts, in August, suggesting a deal. "There was a great amount of sentiment," remembered Springer, "for doing something in the wake of our victory at Le Mans. I, myself, wanted to take advantage of that enthusiasm, and this seemed the right way to go."

With no time to design and develop its own chassis, the proven TWR design seemed a good substitute in which to place the well-sorted Porsche flat six turbo. Quickly things became more serious. Funding from the United States and Germany was discussed. Porsche's then worldwide racing boss, Max Welti, then paid a visit to Indiana, and finally in the early fall of 1994 a joint venture agreement was put in place.

By this time, Springer had already sent Dowe a mock-up engine to be test fitted into the car, which was just a bit premature, according to the TWR man. "We really wanted this to happen, so we ourselves did some of our own mocking up, making it appear in the photographs we sent to Porsche and Alwin that we were somewhat further along than we actually were. Still, by the time Porsche's engine men arrived at our place we were ready for them."

Perhaps, but then again, perhaps not. One major obstacle was the transmission, which TWR had hurriedly redesigned in a tense few weeks to improve its performance and ease of operation. Another was the car's aerodynamics, which had been seriously compromised by cutting off its roof and swapping its ground effects underside for a flat bottom. In spite of this, Dowe and Springer thought they had a winner, which was a good thing since Porsche's aim was not just to claim Daytona and Sebring, but to win again at Le Mans.

"There were some problems, of course," said Dowe. "Basically the engine guys were enthusiastic. After all, they were putting their powerplant in what they saw as a modern, up-to-date chassis. For the chassis folks, it was a different story. They didn't particularly like the car. Possibly because of the not-invented-here syndrome, or maybe because it really didn't handle that well initially."

Indeed, at the new Porsche's first test, the handling was not what anyone wanted, with the drivers, including Bob Wollek and Mario Andretti, saying it was nearly undriveable. That was just before Christmas. After the holidays and much additional work, the Porsche spyder reappeared at the early January IMSA Daytona test session with chassis expert Norbert Singer in attendance. Although not perfect, the new-born German contender was better, enough so at least to be almost on par with the Ferrari 333SP World Sports Cars that were then the lead dogs in the series. Unfortunately, Ferrari, which desperately wanted a victory at Daytona, complained to IMSA about the TWR Porsche, with the result that the sanctioning body, which had within its grasp the renewal of the legendary Ferrari versus Porsche contests of the golden 917/512 era, backtracked on its assurances to Springer and Zuffenhausen.

Not only were the turbo restrictors made smaller in terms of the holes the engine breathed through, but weight was added as well, making the car totally uncompetitive (about eight seconds off the Ferrari pace) for the overall victory. IMSA justified its actions on the basis that they believed the Porsche camp was sandbagging. Not only that, but they said they didn't want a nonseries regular coming in and "cherry-picking" one of its key events.

The reaction from Porsche was swift. Even as a highly modified Kremer 962 spyder was achieving an ironic win in the 24-hours over a tattered Ferrari fleet, Porsche was buying out TWR and shipping the cars and spares back to Germany "We sent them most everything we had, including the two cars, all the spares and even some of the body molds," reported Dowe, who noted that in addition to the hardware, TWR also sold the design

rights to the car as well, this meaning that the drawings went too.

For more than a year, the cars remained unused. Then in 1996 it was decided they would play a back-up role to Porsche's attempt for yet another Le Mans triumph with the new 911 GT1. This was a "just-in-case" proposition. As such, they were dusted off and "leased" to Reinhold Joest, whose drivers found them still somewhat uncomfortable. Again, Singer, the man behind the GT1, was called in, and by race day the TWR Porsche spyders were in fine form—so fine, in fact, that despite one's retirement, the other led the 911 GT1s home for the win.

In 1997 Joest returned with a single TWR Porsche chassis, supposedly presented to him because of his efforts the year before. This time the car performed as an unintended back-up for Porsche, taking over and going on to claim a second straight victory at the Sarthe after both 911 GT1 Evos dropped out. In 1998, there were two TWR Porsches on hand, this time fully equipped with GT1 drivetrains and now officially counted as part of the Porsche team, although still managed by Joest. Perhaps it was the air, or the gods, but it wasn't the time for the TWR Porsches, both failing to finish as Allan McNish brought the 911 GT1 98 LM its first Le Mans victory.

That triumph in itself was the result of a convoluted set of circumstances created when the FIA abandoned its prototype Makes tour, the ensuing chaos leaving men such as Porsche's customer team boss Jürgen Barth facing what amounted to ruination. As Barth put it, "My job was to sell Porsche race cars. However, with the cancellation of the FIA's championship, that had become a most difficult task, since there really was no place for our customers to run what they had bought from us." Thus was born the BPR Global Endurance Challenge, a "self-help" series put together by Barth and his pals, Patrick Peter and Stéphane Ratel in 1994.

The idea was to make the BPR a strictly privateer affair, using modified street vehicles such as Porsche's 911 GT2 Turbo, a car whose foundation was rooted in the 993 variant of the company's more than three-decade-old bread-and-butter 911 coupe. Not overly expensive in terms of competition car prices of the time and requiring relatively little maintenance, the 911 GT2 was seen as a headliner that, along with its leading rivals, such as the French Venturi and Ferrari F-40, would provide the kind of stability that would not only attract entrants but also bring fans back to the sport.

Ironically the success of the BPR was confirmed by FIA's decision to take the series over for itself after the 1996 season, renaming it the FIA World GT Championship for the following year. However, what the sanctioning body got was something far different from what the BPR had started out to be. Instead of a road-going set on steroids, the FIA found itself hosting thinly disguised prototypes, whose credentials as street legal vehicles were at best a vast stretch of one's imagination.

This escalation was, at first, innocent, starting when McLaren was asked to convert its BMW V-12-powered three-seat F1 GT supercar coupe into a racer for Le Mans and the BPR. The midengined machine, with the driver placed between the two passengers, had many of the same features found in the Group C/GTP prototypes, including double wishbone suspension and multi-piston, ventilated

In lieu of building its own World Sports Car spyder, Porsche purchased the rights to the Tom Walkinshaw Racing example in late 1994. Originally conceived as a Groupe C Jaguar prototype, ground effects coupe, the car had also been run as a Mazda before being turned over to Porsche, which installed its own turbocharged, water-cooled boxer six in its engine bay. Leased to the Reinhold Joest team as a backup to the new factory GT1's, the WSC open-topped machine claimed the top prize at Le Mans in 1996 and again in 1997.
Leonard Turner

disc brakes. What separated the million-dollar McLaren from its competition progenitors was that its performance attributes were clothed by the civilized amenities the company thought purchasers of the high-priced F1 would find most attractive. But suddenly, McLaren found a new set of customers, ones that appreciated the fact that the F1 would make an outstanding competition entry and were clamoring to become owners of the Anglo-German creation.

Suitably stripped of its luxuries and sporting race-capable suspension, brakes, and drivetrain, the competition F1 GTR swamped the opposition in its inaugural 1995 season, including an overall victory at Le Mans, where it became one of the few entries ever to win the famed 24-Hour the first time out. The success of the McLaren wasn't lost on Zuffenhausen, which decided to take on the challenge of designing and developing a GT contender strong enough to send the McLaren crowd away scratching their collective heads.

The man chosen to head the project was Singer, who would face some unique limitations in transforming management's edict into winning reality. For one, it was decreed that the new "GT" prototype would at least have to look something like the standard 911. Another constraint was the use of the 993's floor pan, cowl, and inner front sheet metal, this permitting Porsche to forego the costly impact tests needed to make its new spear carrier street legal.

If Singer had to contend with restrictions, he could also count on back door loopholes to make his task easier. In truth, perhaps never in the history of motorsport has there been an individual more adept at exploiting regulatory opportunities than Singer. This fact was clearly evidenced by

Porsche's triumph at the Sarthe in 1994 with Jochen Dauer's "GT" 962.

When he began the 962 GT project in the late summer of 1993, what intrigued Singer about the following June's French classic was the fact that unlike the BPR, which required multiple street-legal units to be constructed before any proposed GT entry could receive approval to compete, Le Mans required that only one such vehicle be produced in order to gain homologation approval. Having used the rules to produce a winner in 1994, Singer began work on repeating that for 1996, a mission that would result in the 911 GT1. While resembling the 911, unlike that venerable coupe, the new car would have its powerplant placed ahead of its transmission in the classic mid-engined tradition of prototype racers adopted almost universally since the mid-1960s.

Using what amounted to the lower front two-thirds of the 993's chassis, Singer and his crew constructed a load-bearing tubular frame and roll cage structure to which the 3.2-liter water-cooled, twin-turbo boxer six (with a bore of 95 millimeters and stroke of 74.4 millimeters) and a six-speed transaxle were attached. This drivetrain produced a listed 600 horsepower and 480 ft-lbs of torque.

As for the suspension, double wishbones were employed at both ends in conjunction with a pushrod coilover arrangement not unlike that of the 956/962 series in basic philosophy. The carbon fiber disc brake units had eight-piston calipers at the front and four-piston ones out back. The wheelbase for the GT1 was set at 2,500 millimeters (97.5 inches) with a front track of 1,502 millimeters (58.5 inches) and a rear track of 1,588 millimeters (61 inches), the car weighing in at 1,050 kilograms (2,315 pounds). Single-piece BBS racing rims, 11.5x18 at the front and 13x18 at the rear, were specified, these being shod with Michelin Pilot radials.

The new 911 GT1 was clothed in a carbon fiber shell that left no doubt as to its 911 origins. (Interestingly, the engineers drew the roof lines so that a standard 911 Speedster windshield could be used, rather than having to employ a more costly one built from scratch.) In all, the 911 GT1 was a very slick piece, whose existence was rooted in the same Le Mans scriptures that had fostered and then nurtured the Dauer 962. Having completed the one road-going example required by the Automobile Club de l'Ouest (ACO), the Le Mans sanctioning body, Porsche's racing operation then began constructing three competition GT1s, a test car and the two team entries that would make their official debut at Le Mans in June 1996.

After a spring in which the first racing chassis, 001, was thoroughly wrung out, the other two chassis, 002 and 003, were prepared for the Sarthe. The attention of the factory and the fans quickly focused on the 911 GT1s. The glare of that spotlight soon proved troublesome for Karl Wendlinger, who on the first night of qualifying destroyed the front of chassis 003. This forced Porsche to charter an early morning flight from Stuttgart to Le Mans to transport the parts and the extra factory personnel needed to make the GTI whole once more.

During the race itself, both GT1s suffered minor problems: not enough to drop them out of the top three, but enough that they had to settle for the spots behind the winning TWR-Porsche spyder. Still, there were rewards for the midengined coupe, as the second-placed 002 of Hans Stuck, Thierry Boutsen, and Bob Wollek claimed first in the GT division, while 003 with Wendlinger, Yannick Dalmas, and Scott Goodyear was third overall and second in class.

At this point, one might have expected Porsche to park the cars, since they weren't eligible for the BPR tour until the following spring. Instead, what happened next was a decision that would come to haunt Porsche. A loophole in the BPR regulations defined an approved GT model not as one already built in series, but one with confirmed orders for future examples. Porsche decided to run a limited BPR schedule with its midengined entries, starting at Brands Hatch in September. The factory had received enough orders by that date to get the 911 GT1 into the championship.

Brands Hatch proved to be a Porsche walkover, with Stuck and Boutsen taking 002 to a relatively uncontested victory, following that up with an equally impressive win at Spa the next week. One man upset about the presence of the 911 GT1 at the Belgian round was British sports car racer and McLaren advocate Ray Bellm. "It seemed," he complained, "that the 911 GT1 drivers had time to watch the start of the F1 race on TV, go shopping at the Stavelot supermarket and still finish a lap ahead. It made us look rather silly."

To cap off the year, both 002 and 003 were entered for the Zhuhai finale in China, where Ralf Kelleners and Emmanuel Collard brought home the victory, Stuck and Boutsen finishing fourth. All in all, it was a good season but one without closure in light of the GT1's finish at Le Mans behind the TWR-Porsche entered by Joest.

While Porsche was building 1996-model 911 GT1 customer cars for its privateers during the winter of 1996–1997, Singer and company were busy improving the design to create a more potent version for 1997. Among the changes made were several to the coupe's aerodynamics, as well as its suspension geometry. Those to the aerodynamics were to increase downforce while those to the suspension geometry were to improve the GT1's mechanical grip and handling balance. Both would be needed because Porsche, which had decided to run a full schedule in the FIA's GT title chase, that had now supplanted the BPR, would have to face off against the new Mercedes CLK coupes. These lightweight, mid-engined fliers had been crafted from the same philosophical mold

The TWR-built Porsche World Sports Car spyder tested at Daytona in January 1995 in preparation for that year's IMSA 24-Hour season opener. Despite the fact that its laps were no better than its Ferrari 333AP rivals, the U.S.-based sanctioning organization caved in to pressure from the Italian camp by adding weight to the car and forcing it to use smaller turbo inlet restrictors. As a result, Porsche pulled the car from the race, and the spyder did not reappear until June 1996 at Le Mans, where it won. *Porsche Werk*

For 1998, Porsche produced a new version of the 911 GT1 Turbo, this one featuring an all-composite carbon fiber chassis. While the car failed to beat its Mercedes rivals on the FIA World GT tour, it did humble its cross-town Stuttgart rivals and its Toyota opposition at Le Mans with a stunning outright victory. *Porsche Werk*

that had produced the GT1. And, like its Porsche rival, Mercedes had not yet made enough of them to get them homologated for FIA action. Indeed, it appeared that Mercedes had not even built the first street legal example before applying for FIA approval.

Following the same dispensation made by the BPR the previous year, the FIA accepted the CLK, based on its future sales commitments, a decision which led to Porsche being humbled by Mercedes in the 1997 FIA series. Not once was the 911 GT1 able to beat the CLK. At least Mercedes decided against putting its cars to a 24-hour test and skipped Le Mans, giving the 911 GT1 its chance to shine in Porsche's ultimate arena.

And shine is what the two Porsches did, leading the revised Joest TWR-Porsche spyder handily as dawn rose over Le Mans on Sunday morning. While many might criticize the tactics, the two 911 GT1s had been permitted to race each other from the start as they steadily pulled away from the field. Although some might have opted to preserve the cars, Porsche did not, the consequences of which began to become apparent when Wollek had a halfshaft fail at breakfast time, putting the car he shared with Stuck and Boutsen out.

That left Kelleners, Collard, and Dalmas with a substantial margin over the Joest spyder. Then, as the noon hour approached, Kelleners pulled off course with his GT1 engulfed in flames. Although Kelleners was not injured (thanks to a hasty exit from the car), chassis 004 was done for the day, leaving the open-topped Joest entry to win for a second straight time.

Thanks to the opportunities to be had in America, there was redemption for the GT1 in 1998. Porsche turned loose two of its 1997 factory GT1s, 006 going to the Jochen Rohr team as a one-time effort for Daytona; and the other, 005, to Champion Racing, in whose employ it would remain for the next two seasons. Although the Champion example retired at Daytona, the Rohr team with Allan McNish, Danny Sullivan and Dirk Müller came home second overall and first in the GTS category. For Rohr it was a final jewel in a crown he initially put together with his 1996-spec privateer GT1. Using that coupe, he had claimed the 1997 production car championship on the Professional Sports Car Racing's tour.

With 006 shipped back to Germany, Champion's 005 went to the PSCR 1998 opener at Sebring, where it nearly won the famed 12-hour with Boutsen, Wollek, and Andy Pilgrim aboard. Unfortunately, a refueling infraction dropped them to third after being assessed a lengthy penalty. Even so, with a victory at Watkins Glen and a consistent finishing record, Champion was able to secure the driver's title and manufacturer's class honors for Boutsen and Porsche respectively in the rival United States Road Racing Championship series. Not only that, but the team went on to garner the GTS victory at Road Atlanta's Petit Le Mans affair—a preview of the American Le Mans Series which was to open at Sebring in March of 1999. With no other options, Champion would soldier on with its now aged 911 GT1 throughout the inaugural ALMS campaign, finishing consistently, but out of the money and the spotlight. What Champion needed was a newer car, and that wasn't to be had, although six such coupes (one street and five race versions) existed at Weissach.

These cars, designated GT1-98LMs, carried on the GTI tradition, but in truth they were virtually new, featuring full carbon fiber chassis. The creation of the new GT1 variant was in response to the CLKs, which would appear in improved form for a full schedule of 1998 events, this including Le Mans. The new GTI was longer, wider and lower than its predecessors. Most important, it was also 100 kilograms (220.5 pounds) lighter. As a bonus it was also stiffer, which improved its handling characteristics even more than the 1997 spec coupe.

Unfortunately, the GT1 proved to be a disappointment, again losing to the Mercedes camp by a wide margin on the FIA World Championship circuit. At least, it would have been over were it

not for Le Mans. There, after the Mercedes and BMW efforts crumbled early, the Singer creations battled furiously with a determined Toyota team, outlasting the Japanese as McNish, Stéphane Ortelli, and Laurent Aiello led a one-two Porsche sweep with Wollek, Uwe Alzen, and Jorg Müller finishing second.

What made the triumph even more special was the fact that it came on the eve of Porsche's 50th anniversary. Still, later in the season, worry would be mixed into celebration when Dalmas, driving with Alzen and McNish, flipped his GT1 at Road Atlanta while leading the Petit Le Mans show. The accident appeared to be caused by Dalmas' hitting turbulence from the wake of a car he was passing, this upsetting the Porsche's aerodynamics and sending it cartwheeling through the air.

Happily, Dalmas survived shaken but intact. Even so, it is worth noting that the two regular factory team cars were subsequently taken to Hockenheim for extensive testing, following which Porsche announced it would withdraw from

the sport as an official factory entrant. Further, unlike previous years, Porsche refused to release any of the carbon fiber GT1s to its customers.

So why this abrupt ending to a career of which most others would have been proud? Even though the factory has remained silent on the issue, there are clues to be found in the disaster a year later that constituted the Mercedes effort at Le Mans in 1999. There, no less than three of the latest CLK coupes somersaulted their way into the black side of the history books, again happily without any serious injuries. What many believe happened is that Mercedes, finding the CLKs too slow, sacrificed some downforce for speed, thus resulting in a lessening of the design's stability.

Whether or not that is the case and whether or not a similar trade-off would have had to be made to make the 1998 GT1s competitive for 1999 are questions still shrouded in mystery. Speculation aside, the 911 GT1 series can stand proudly on its record of achievement at a time when that was made more difficult to achieve through the turmoil that plagued the sport on a worldwide basis.

The 1998 GT1 finally achieved the goals the factory set for it when it won at Le Mans that year. In fact, the GT1 did better than that by coming home in the first two positions, thereby humbling its Mercedes and Toyota rivals the the process. *Porsche Werk*

191

index